The Fortunes of the Courtier

THE
PENN
STATE
SERIES
IN THE
HISTORY
OF THE
BOOK

James L. W. West III, General Editor

The series publishes books that employ a mixture of approaches: historical, archival, biographical, critical, sociological, and economic. Projected topics include professional authorship and the literary marketplace, the history of reading and book distribution, book-trade studies and publishing-house histories, and examinations of copyright and literary property.

Peter Burke, The Fortunes of the *Courtier*: The European Reception of Castiglione's *Cortegiano*

James M. Hutchisson, The Rise of Sinclair Lewis, 1920–1930

The Fortunes of the Courtier

The European Reception of Castiglione's *Cortegiano*

PETER BURKE

The Pennsylvania State University Press
University Park, Pennsylvania

Published in 1996 in the United States of America and Canada by The
Pennsylvania State University Press, University Park, PA 16802

First published in 1995 in the United Kingdom by Polity Press in association with
Blackwell Publishers Ltd.

Library of Congress Cataloging-in-Publication Data

Burke, Peter.
    The fortunes of the Courtier : the European reception of
Castiglione's Cortegiano / Peter Burke.
        p.   cm. — (Penn State series in the history of the book)
    Includes bibliographical references and index.
    ISBN 0-271-01516-0 (cloth)
    ISBN 0-271-01517-9 (paper)
    1. Castiglione, Baldassarre, conte, 1478–1529. Libro del
cortegiano.   2. Courts and courtiers.   3. Courtesy.   I. Title.   II. Series.
BJ1604.C33B87   1995
170'.44—dc20   95–17617
                                                                                                              CIP

Typeset in 11 on 13 pt Sabon
by Best-set Typesetter Ltd., Hong Kong
Printed in Great Britain

This book is printed on acid-free paper.

It is the policy of The Pennsylvania State University Press to use acid-free paper for
the first printing of all clothbound books. Publications on uncoated stock satisfy
minimum requirements of American National Standard for Information Sciences
— Permanence of Paper for Printed Library Materials, ANSI Z39.48–1992.

Contents

Contents

List of Plates

Preface and Acknowledgements

———————

Since I first read it in the late 1950s, Castiglione's *Cortegiano*, or *Courtier*, has been one of my favourite books. I read it then, as an Oxford student taking a Special Subject on the Italian Renaissance, in a historicist manner as a text which represented that movement. It is doubtless for that reason that the dialogue has been so often reprinted and translated in the last century or so, in Italy from the 1880s and in the English-speaking world from 1900, where it has appeared in the form of an Everyman, a Doubleday Anchor Book and a Penguin Classic.

During the Renaissance itself, on the other hand, the book was read for very different reasons. It was treated as a guide to contemporary conduct, not to the values of a past age. If modern readers tend to annotate the passages on graceful behaviour or the 'universal man', sixteenth-century readers often marked the jokes or the instructions on riding. The distance between the two kinds of reading has come to appear more and more fascinating. To understand, if not to close, the gap between the historicist and the pragmatic readings is my intention here, an intention complicated by the fact that the *Courtier* has long been interpreted in a variety of ways. It has been criticized as too cynical by innocents and as too innocent by cynics. It has been viewed as both idealistic and pragmatic, serious and frivolous. Whereas the text itself has been studied very carefully in recent years – indeed, it has almost been buried under a mass of commentaries – its readers have so far received much less attention. In this essay, on the other hand, they will occupy the foreground.

I have written primarily for people who already know and love the *Courtier* and would like to know more about its context, but I have done my best to make it intelligible to readers for whom Castiglione is little more than a name, in the hope that they will be attracted to his book. Since the text has been published in so many editions, it will be cited not by pages but by book and chapter (following the numbering of chapters in the 1884 edition, which has now become canonical). The Greek and Latin classics will be cited in a similar way. Unless otherwise stated, translations into English are my own, and spelling has been modernized in quotations, except for the name of Count Baldassare himself, which occurs in so many picturesque variations in the period. The portraits of Castiglione have been included not only as decorations but also as a visual parallel to the reception of the text.

In writing a study such as this, which sets out to explore the reactions and responses to a single book by readers scattered over a considerable part of the globe, the author has naturally accumulated many debts, which it would be extremely discourteous not to acknowledge. Derek Brewer scrutinized chapter 2 with the keen eye of a specialist in medieval literature, while Virginia Cox made constructive criticisms of the chapters on Italy. For advice, references, off-prints, books and other assistance I am indebted to Jim Amelang; Catherine Bates; Donna Bohanan; Maria Lúcia Pallares-Burke; Richard Bushman; Daniele Fiorentino; Teodoro Hampe; Frieda Heijkoop; Manfred Hinz; Harald Ilsøe; Marc Jacobs; Kurt Johannesson; Bent Juel-Jensen; Gábor Klaniczay; the late Tibor Klaniczay; Dilwyn Knox; Thomas Krogh; Jirí Kropácek; J. M. Laspéras; Elizabeth Leedham-Green; Antoni Mączak; Brian McGuinness; Carmela Nocera; Stephen Orgel; Herman Roodenburg; Elena Santiago; David R. Smith; John Stevens; György E. Szönyi; Dora Thornton; Dalibor Vesely; John Woodhouse; and the librarians of five Cambridge colleges – Emmanuel, Jesus, King's, St Catharine's and Trinity. My hearty thanks to them all.

I am also grateful to the Getty Center at Los Angeles for having offered me the opportunity to write the book there, even though I was unable to accept the offer. I should have loved to have been able to discuss this essay with Sir John Hale, who encouraged my entry into the field of Renaissance studies, and about whom one of my students once remarked that she understood the *Courtier* better by watching him light a cigarette than by any number of lectures.

This essay grew out of a talk delivered in various forms in Budapest, Cambridge, Canberra, Clermont-Ferrand, Constance, Edinburgh, Gothenburg, London, New Haven, Oslo, Oxford, Paris, Princeton, Warwick and Wolfenbüttel. It is appropriate that a study of dialogue should have developed in the course of dialogue, and that a book about responses to Castiglione should itself owe a great deal to the constructive responses of these diverse audiences. It is dedicated to the person who most influences my own behaviour, my wife Maria Lúcia.

Abbreviations

BL   British Library

BLO   Bodleian Library, Oxford

BNM   Biblioteca Nacional, Madrid

BNP   Bibliothèque Nationale, Paris

DBI   *Dizionario biografico degli Italiani*, 43 vols, in progress, Rome, 1960–

DNB   *Dictionary of National Biography*, ed. Leslie Stephen and Sidney Lee, 63 vols, London, 1885–1900

OED   *Oxford English Dictionary*, second edn, 20 vols, Oxford, 1989

TCC   Trinity College, Cambridge

UL   University Library, Cambridge

I

Tradition and Reception

————————◆————————

In the dedication to the translation of the book which he
published in 1724, Robert Samber wrote that 'The *Courtier*
was too great to be confined within the narrow limits of
Italy . . . nor was it sufficient that he was read, loved and admired
by the most celebrated courts in the Universe, unless, in order to
become more familiar to them, they might dress him in the habit
proper to each country.' In similar fashion the political theorist
Sir Ernest Barker once remarked that 'it would be a fascinating
study to examine comparatively the different national tinctures'
to Castiglione's ideal.[1]

This essay is an attempt to respond to these challenges. Its
primary aim is to reconstruct the local and personal meanings
of an international movement, thus putting bibliographical and
sociological minutiae to use in answering broad general questions.
I shall be emphasizing the elements in Castiglione's text which
appealed to readers most widely or for the longest time, notably
the discussion of grace and *sprezzatura*, while attempting to avoid
reducing the many-sidedness of the dialogue, in the manner of
some of its sixteenth-century editors, to a few simple propositions.

The period on which the book concentrates is essentially the
first century after the *Courtier* was published in 1528, although
the concluding chapters will discuss references to the text in later

---

1 Barker (1948), 143. It is not clear whether he was aware of earlier studies in
this field; Toldo (1900); Schrinner (1939); Krebs (1940–2).

periods. The area with which I am concerned is essentially Europe, despite occasional references to readers further afield, from India to the Americas. My strategy has been to concentrate on readers outside Italy, because the greater the cultural distance from the author's milieu, the more clearly the process of active reception is revealed. Although this was not the original intention, I have found myself paying particular attention to Castiglione's reception in England, and hope that the close examination of a single culture, more or less from within, will compensate for the dangers inherent in any broad international survey.

The breadth is necessary because I hope to make a small contribution to the understanding of the 'Europeanization of Europe', in other words the gradual integration of European culture over the centuries.[2] I shall therefore try to look beyond the *Courtier*, using the text as a case-study to explore three broader topics: the reception of the Renaissance outside Italy, the history of the book, and the history of value-systems.

The Reception of the Renaissance

From the time of Jacob Burckhardt's *Civilization of the Renaissance in Italy* (1860), if not before, historians have been studying this period as a time of changing attitudes to the self and to others. Burckhardt characterized the new trend as 'the development of the individual', noting both the rivalry and the self-consciousness of the artists and writers of the period, as revealed, for example, in their self-portraits and autobiographies.

More recently, the emphasis has changed. In the wake of studies such as Erving Goffman's on what he called 'the presentation of self in everyday life', leading figures of the Renaissance such as the emperor Maximilian and Thomas More have been studied from the point of view of their self-presentation, 'self-fashioning' or *Selbststilisierung*.[3] These studies of major figures provoke the question whether or not their lead was widely followed at the time. Castiglione's dialogue looks very much like a guide to self-

2 Bartlett (1993), 269–91.
3 Burckhardt (1860); Goffman (1956); Burger (1963); Greenblatt (1980).

fashioning, so it may be of interest to examine responses to it in the Renaissance, not only in Italy but also abroad.

This point about responses has wider implications. Traditional accounts of the diffusion of the Renaissance have often presented it as a triumphal progress through Europe in which one country after another succumbed to the spell of Leonardo, Raphael, Michelangelo, Pico della Mirandola, Ariosto, Machiavelli and other leading artists, writers and thinkers.[4]

There are two basic weaknesses in accounts of this type. The first is the assumption that Italians alone were active and creative at this time, while other Europeans were passive, mere recipients of 'influence', an originally astrological term which has often been employed rather uncritically by intellectual historians.[5] The interest shown by some fifteenth-century Italians in paintings from the Netherlands shows that they at least noticed the originality of foreign artists.

The second weakness in the conventional story of the diffusion of the Renaissance is to identify what was 'received' with what was 'given'. Although the term 'tradition' originally meant 'handing down', it is difficult to deny that changes often occur in the course of transmitting concepts, practices and values. Traditions are constantly transformed, reinterpreted or reconstructed – whether this reconstruction is conscious or unconscious – to fit their new spatial or temporal environments. The classical tradition, for example, was reconstructed in this way in the Middle Ages. Homeric heroes such as Achilles were transformed into knights, the poet Vergil was turned into a necromancer, Jupiter (on occasion) into a scholar, Mercury into a bishop, and so on.[6]

If we shift our focus from traditions to individuals, we will often find them practising a form of *bricolage*, in other words selecting from the culture surrounding them whatever they find attractive, relevant or useful, and assimilating it (consciously or unconsciously) to what they already possess. Some individuals are more attracted by the exotic than others, but all domesticate their discoveries by a process of reinterpretation and recontextualization.

4 Burke (1987).
5 Mornet (1910), 449–50; cf. Skinner (1969), 45–7.
6 Warburg (1932); Seznec (1940).

In other words, readers, listeners and viewers are active appropri-
ators and adapters rather than passive receivers.[7]

It should be added that the appropriation they practise is not
random but has a logic of its own. This logic of appropriation is
often shared by a social group, which may therefore be described
as an 'interpretive community', or on occasion as a 'textual community' in which a book is used as a guide to the group's thought
and action.[8] Such notions of community can be misleading, but all
the same it is difficult to do without them. They are dangerous
insofar as they lead us to forget or minimize individual differences
of opinion, but they remain indispensable in reminding us of what
is shared.

This constant process of reinterpretation and recontextualization in one sense erodes tradition, but in another sense maintains it by ensuring that it continues to meet the needs of different
groups. If for some reason this process of gradual reinterpretation
is impeded, a pressure for more radical change or 'reform' may
build up. The cultural movement we call the 'Reformation', for
instance, is a dramatic instance of a radical reinterpretation of a
Christian tradition.

It follows from the argument presented in the previous paragraphs – an argument which to support adequately would require
a book much longer than this one – that the conventional distinction between 'invention' and 'diffusion' should be viewed as a
difference in degree rather than a difference in kind. Invention
itself is best seen as a process of creative adaptation – the printing
press an adaptation of the wine press, the novel as an adaptation
of the epic, and so on.

In the case of the Renaissance, it may therefore be useful to
abandon the idea of a simple 'influence' or 'spread' of new ideas
and images from Florence outwards, and to ask instead what the
'uses' of Italy may have been for writers, scholars and artists in
other parts of Europe, what was the logic of their appropriations,
and why and how far new Italian forms or ideas were assimilated
into everyday life and into indigenous traditions, from Gothic
architecture to scholastic philosophy. To answer all these ques-

7 De Certeau (1980); Chartier (1987).
8 Fish (1980), 14–15, 171–2, etc.; Stock (1983), 88–240.

tions it is necessary to study the ways in which the recipients interpreted what they saw, heard or read. We have to pay attention to their perceptual 'schemata'.[9] We have to concern ourselves with what literary theorists have come to call their 'horizons of expectation'.[10]

In short, cultural historians have something to gain by assimilating the still somewhat exotic notion of 'reception', using it to modify the traditional idea of tradition. In fact, the word, if not the notion, should not sound too unfamiliar to students of the Renaissance, since the term *Rezeption* first came into use to describe the spread of humanism and Roman law in fifteenth- and sixteenth-century Europe. In any case, the Renaissance debate on the nature of literary imitation (below, pp. 81–2) was concerned with one of the central issues in reception theory, that of the compatibility between tradition and innovation.

The study of the reception of texts raises some large problems. An ordinary working historian would be ill-advised to take sides in current controversies in the field of literary theory, and especially to pronounce on the ultimately metaphysical question whether the true or essential meaning of a text resides in the mind of the creator, in the work itself (which gradually reveals its meaning in the course of time) or in the responses of its readers.[11] All the same, there can be little doubt of the relevance of reception theory (concerned as it is with a temporal process), to the work of cultural historians in general and in particular to historians of the book.

The History of the Book

As a self-conscious approach to cultural history, the history of the book was developed in France in the 1960s, although, as often happens, the approach existed long before it was baptized. Two examples from the year 1910 should remind us that the present generation of historians was far from the first to be interested in this subject. Daniel Mornet made a quantitative study of the

9 Warburg (1932); Gombrich (1960).
10 Gadamer (1960); Jauss (1974).
11 Jauss (1974); Fish (1980).

contents of 500 French libraries between 1750 and 1780, while
Caroline Ruutz-Rees focused attention on the marginal annotations of a single Elizabethan reader, Gabriel Harvey, a name
which will recur in these pages.[12]

Students of Machiavelli in particular have long been concerned
with the variety of responses to his work inside and outside Italy,
in England, France, Spain and elsewhere. They have paid particular attention to hostile responses to his notorious *Prince*, the
banning and burning of the book, for example, and the denunci-
ation of its author as a villain and an 'atheist'. In some sixteenth-
century contexts, so it turns out, Machiavelli was denounced not
(or not only) for his own sake but as a symbol of Italian influence
on England, France or Poland, or as an indirect way of attacking
the ruler – Catherine de' Medici, for example. Yet the condemnation of the author did not prevent more orthodox political
theorists from adopting some of Machiavelli's ideas, which they
were careful to attribute to an ancient writer, Tacitus, rather than
a modern one.[13] Some foreign responses to the *Courtier* followed
the same model, as we shall see.

As these examples suggest, there are a number of possible
approaches to the history of the book, varieties of cultural history
which have attracted many scholars in the last decade or so.[14] One
of these approaches concentrates on editions, their geography and
chronology and the modifications made to the original text by
editors and publishers. Another focuses on translations, adaptations and imitations of the original text. A third approach in-
volves the examination of particular copies for underlinings and
marginalia which reveal the responses of individual readers.[15]
With the rise of the history of reception, it was recently remarked,
marginalia have become central.[16] Finally, there is the study of
library catalogues, auction catalogues, inventories and lists of
subscribers in order to discover what kinds of people were interested in a particular book. All four methods will be utilized at

12 Mornet (1910); Ruutz-Rees (1910).
13 Toffanin (1921); Meinecke (1924); Bleznick (1958); Malarczyk (1962); Raab
(1964); Procacci (1965); Thuau (1966).
14 Darnton (1986); McKenzie (1986); Chartier (1987).
15 Leonard (1949); Brunner (1956); Chevalier (1976); Jardine and Grafton
(1990).
16 Jackson (1992–3).

some point in this essay. They all help to bridge the gap between the great books of the past and the 'mentalities' – the habits of thought or unspoken assumptions – of their period.

I have tried to take the last approach a little further than usual by means of a prosopography or collective biography of 328 presumed readers of the *Courtier* in the sixteenth and seventeenth centuries, readers who are listed in appendix 2. Since reference will be made to this list on more than one occasion, the problems raised by this approach must be discussed, however briefly.

As is usually the case in the history of reading, the sources – inventories of libraries, for example – have more to tell us about owners than about readers. It cannot be assumed that every owner of a given book had actually read it. Eight names in the list are those of booksellers. To make matters worse, the best-documented libraries are generally the larger ones, and as some readers will know all too well, the larger the library, the lower the probability that the owner is familiar with all its contents. The Danish professor Peder Scavenius, for instance, who will be discussed in chapter 8, owned not only a first edition of the *Courtier* but about 6,000 other books. The Colbert family, notably the famous Jean-Baptiste Colbert, Louis XIV's minister, and his son the marquis de Seignelay, owned more than 18,000 books, thus reducing the significance of the copy of the *Courtier* in Italian to be found among them.

Some of the owners to be discussed below will have inherited their libraries rather than built them up for themselves. James VI and I may have been as interested in the *Courtier* as his mother Mary Queen of Scots, but I doubt whether very much should be made of the fact that Castiglione was present in the library of the English lawyer Sir Edward Coke, given that most of his Italian books had come from the collection of the courtier Sir Christopher Hatton. The same goes for a seventeenth-century priest from Besançon, Jean-Baptiste Boisot, who had acquired the library of Cardinal Granvelle.[17]

Despite these problems, it is possible to reach a few conclusions. One of the most interesting points to emerge from this research, which will be discussed in detail in chapter 8, is the importance of

17 Mornet (1910), 452; Hassall (1950); Jolly (1988–92), vol. II, 469.

networks of readers, friends and acquaintances who pass the text on to one another. In other words, although in the long term print helped to diminish the role of face-to-face groups in the diffusion of information, such groups still influenced – as they surely continue to influence – the choice of books to be read and even, perhaps, the way in which their messages are perceived and interpreted. Two examples make this point particularly clear. Discussions of the perfect courtier inspired by the book are recorded by the Lombard writer Matteo Bandello and by the Englishman Thomas Nashe. We have moved from Castiglione's representation of a discussion to the discussion of a representation (itself in turn represented in print).[18] These examples, together with the networks of readers discussed in chapter 8, remind us that a system of oral communication underlay the circulation of printed texts.

Before we study the after-life of the *Courtier*, however, it will be useful to examine the courtier before the *Courtier*, since the book emerged from, as well as helping to form, what is often called a 'discourse', a larger as well as a vaguer unit than the propositions or ideas on which intellectual historians used to concentrate their attention.[19] A discourse may be described as an ensemble of ideas or propositions, more than a random grouping but less than a logical system. The particular discourse, or series of discourses, which will be studied in the following section was concerned with behaviour in society.

The History of Systems of Values

Historians of culture have often emphasized the importance of the study of 'ideals of life', as the Dutch historian Johan Huizinga called them, or 'cultural patterns', 'systems of values', or the 'social imaginary', to use the more recent formulations of Georges Duby and other French scholars.[20] It should be noted that 'values' is a broader term than 'morals'. It is not confined to rules which are supposed to be morally binding but extends to social rules or matters of taste.

18 Bandello (1554), book II, no. 57; Nashe (1589), dedication.
19 Foucault (1969, 1971).
20 Huizinga (1915); Duby (1968, 1972, 1978).

The *Courtier* is one of a series of famous descriptions or codifications of such values to be found in the works of western writers from ancient Greece onwards. As such, it figures, though perhaps not as prominently as it should, in the famous account of the 'civilizing process' by the sociologist Norbert Elias, who devoted two substantial volumes to describing and explaining the rise of self-control in the West.[21] Like other conduct-books, Castiglione's dialogue can be studied as a kind of litmus paper which reveals past ideals of life, on condition that attention is paid to the manner in which readers interpreted and responded to the texts.

To trace the history of European ideals of life in the space of no more than a few pages, it will be necessary to focus on keywords, whether they are best viewed as what a literary scholar once described as 'fashion words' (*Modeworte*) or as what the historian Reinhard Koselleck calls 'fundamental concepts' (*Grundbegriffe*).[22] Such words are generally difficult if not impossible to translate, and this may be no accident. As a leading contemporary novelist with personal experience of two cultures advises his readers, 'To unlock a society, look at its untranslatable words.'[23]

In ancient Greece, one of these untranslatable words was *areté*, more or less 'excellence'. The *areté* of a horse was to run swiftly, while that of a man was to be brave, to be respected, to love honour. The man with most *areté* was *aristos*, from which derives 'aristocracy', literally 'the rule of the best', in practice the rule of a hereditary nobility. This ideal of excellence was exemplified by Achilles and the other heroes of Homer's *Iliad*, and the poem was in turn treated as exemplary. Homer was considered the educator of Greece, and the *Iliad* was studied in schools in ancient Greece and Rome precisely for the sake of the values it was believed to inculcate in the young.[24] When Ottaviano Fregoso, a speaker in the *Courtier*, claims that Homer described Achilles as an exemplary hero (4.47), he was standing in a long tradition.

21 Elias (1939).
22 Williams (1976); Weise (1936); Koselleck (1972); Brunner et al. (1972–90).
23 Rushdie (1983), 140.
24 Jaeger (1933–45), vol. I, 5, 9, 11, 35; Marrou (1948), 162–3; Bonner (1977), 212–13.

Hundreds of years later, in the fourth century BC, the philosopher Aristotle stated his ideals in his *Ethics*, or rather the ideals
of his time, since he claimed to keep close to generally received
opinions on these matters.[25] The kinship between the ideal of
magnanimity (*megalopsychia*) described in Aristotle and the behaviour of Achilles (say) or Hector will be obvious enough. Aristotle's magnanimous or great-minded man shows a pride in his
superiority over others. He is brave and he is liberal. Indeed, he
practices 'magnificence' (*megaloprepeia*), defined as the appropriate expenditure of large sums of money. Leaving the high ground
of philosophy for a moment, Aristotle also tells us that a great-
minded man maintains his dignity by walking slowly and speaking
in a low voice.[26]

On the other hand, Aristotle's stress on *phronesis* ('prudence' or
'practical intelligence') and self-control (*sophrosyne*, traditionally
translated as 'temperance'), has more in common with Odysseus
than with Achilles, while his emphasis on the doctrine of the
golden mean is distinctly unhomeric. Courage is defined as the
mean between rashness and cowardice, liberality as the mean
between extravagance and parsimony, and so on. Aristotle was
attempting to achieve an equilibrium between opposing forces
within an ethical tradition already riven by conflicts.

Another Greek text deserves to be mentioned here because of its
importance for Castiglione (as indeed for Renaissance humanists
in general). Xenophon's *Cyropaedia* or 'Education of Cyrus' presented Cyrus, king of Persia, as an exemplar of royal and aristocratic virtues, notably self-control, modesty (*aidos*, more literally
'shame') and decorum (*eukosmia*). Cyrus is also said to have
discouraged the Persian nobles from spitting or wiping their noses
in public, and to have encouraged them to wear high shoes, make
up their faces, and, above all, to spend their time in attendance at
his court.[27]

Despite their admiration for Greek culture, the patricians of the
Roman Republic in the age of Cicero did not learn all their values
from Homer. The ideal expressed in Cicero's book 'On Duties'
(*De officiis*), a work of moral education addressed to his son and

25 Lloyd (1967), 206.
26 Aristotle (1926), 4.3.34.
27 Xenophon (1914); cf. Jaeger (1933–45), vol. III, 156–81.

presumably intended for upper-class readers, is rather more flexible. The emphasis falls on what the author calls *decorum*, in other words the adaptation of social behaviour, including posture and gesture, to circumstances and style of life, *genus vitae*. Decorum implies self-control, the control of reason over the passions, and it also implies self-consciousness, especially the conscious avoidance of extremes, such as walking too fast or too slowly, or being either 'soft' or 'effeminate' on the one hand, or 'hard' or 'boorish' (*rusticus*) on the other.[28]

This Aristotelian ideal of a golden mean received its sharpest formulation in Cicero's *Orator*, where the author recommended what he called a kind of 'studied negligence' (*neglegentia diligens*), in which the orator concealed his skill in order to give the audience the impression that he was not using rhetoric at all, but was more concerned with the ideas than with the words chosen to express them. In the next century, the Spanish Roman Quintilian would offer orators similar advice on simulated spontaneity.[29] As speaking in public with the appropriate gestures was one of the most spectacular forms of self-presentation appropriate to adult male Romans of the ruling class, advice to orators tells us a good deal about ideal behaviour at this time.

It would of course be extremely unwise to regard any one text as 'the' expression of ancient Roman culture. Cicero's recommendations for what his contemporaries called 'urbanity' (*urbanitas*) themselves follow a middle path between serious moral philosophy (exemplified by Seneca) and the worldly advice of the poet Ovid.[30]

Seneca stresses what he calls 'constancy' (*constantia*), a virtue which results from rigorous self-discipline (Cicero too had recommended this virtue, but placed less emphasis on it). According to Seneca, the wise man should be able to resist the buffeting of fortune as a mighty tree resists the winds, or a rock the waves. Seneca was thinking of an inner peace of mind (*tranquillitas animi*) but his advice has sometimes been interpreted as a recommendation of cool, aristocratic outward behaviour. The term

28 Cicero (1913), 1.27, 1.32, 1.35–6.
29 Cicero (1939), 23; Quintilian (1921–2), vol. II, 11.2.47; cf. Ramage (1973), 62ff.
30 Ramage (1973), 52, 56, 78, 102.

'stoicism', which originally described the philosophical school to which Seneca belonged, has of course suffered a similar redefinition in terms of suffering without complaining, the stiff upper lip and so on.[31]

Ovid offers a very different vision of the upper-class Roman world, his tone as deliberately frivolous and cynical as Seneca's was moral and serious. Yet he too stresses the calm and negligence which reveal self-confidence. For example, Ovid tells the young man who wants to be successful in the 'art' of love to wear a clean toga, get a good haircut, and clean his fingernails, but – unlike the nobles at the court of Cyrus, described above – not to take too much care of his appearance: 'A casual look suits men' (*forma viros neglecta decet*). Young women are warned against men who take too much trouble with their hair. Again, although women are advised to seek elegance (*munditia*) in the smallest details of their *toilette*, in the way they walk, for example, and the way they laugh, they are also told that 'Art produces the illusion of spontaneity' (*ars casum simulat*). In the much-quoted phrase, 'the point of art is to conceal art' (*ars est celare artem*).[32]

Despite their differences in tone, purpose and generation, all three Roman authors are recognizably participants in the same upper-class culture, and all three remained influential guides to behaviour over the centuries.

In the early Middle Ages, the Roman tradition of good behaviour was reconstructed for the use of the clergy. The central text in this process of reconstruction was written by St Ambrose, bishop of Milan, who told his priests to show modesty (literally 'shame', *verecundia*) in every gesture. As its title, *De officiis clericorum*, suggests, Ambrose's treatise was essentially a rewriting of Cicero, and one which followed its model in many respects, down to the advice on walking in the streets – neither too fast nor too slow.[33]

The rules of early monastic communities also paid attention to behaviour in public, at the table as well as in the church, warning monks not to arrive late for meals, not to talk at the table, not to look around, not to drink greedily or noisily, and not to enjoy

31 Seneca (1917–25).
32 Ovid (1929), 1.509; 3.155, 281–4, 298–9, 433–4; cf. Ramage (1973).
33 Ambrose (1984), 131–2.

what they were eating. The point was to eat 'with discipline', in other words a self-control which had once been associated with the Roman army but now acquired a religious meaning.[34] In the twelfth century, a cluster of treatises suggests that increasing attention was being paid to good behaviour, including posture and gesture. The texts addressed to the clergy include Petrus Alfonsi's *On Clerical Discipline* and Hugh of St Victor's *On the Education of Novices*, both of which develop the ideas of Ambrose and early monastic writers a little further.[35] The treatises of both Ambrose and Cicero were 'abundantly available', so we are told, 'in the cathedral and monastic libraries of the period'.[36]

Max Weber once described the rise of what he called the 'Protestant Ethic' as the secularization of asceticism. The same point might be made about 'discipline' in the Middle Ages. The term *disciplina*, formerly applied to the self-control of monks and other religious groups, was secularized (or more exactly, re-secularized) and adapted to describe refined behaviour among the laity.[37]

For by the twelfth century, if not before, some of the laity had also become concerned with the rules of good behaviour. It was at about this time that the laws of 'chivalry' were formulated for the sake of a relatively new social group, the knights, a code of conduct telling them how to behave on and off the battlefield, to show mercy to a defeated enemy, for example, and to treat women with respect.

The ideal of chivalry was formulated most vividly, memorably and persuasively in the so-called *chansons de geste*, the medieval equivalents of the *Iliad*, in which the heroes, such as Roland, Ogier the Dane, Renaud de Montauban, and the Cid, make themselves conspicuous by their 'prowess', a combination of courage, skill and leadership not far removed from Homeric *arete*.[38] Like Achilles, these heroes show themselves hypersensitive to reflections on their reputation. This point is made with particular clarity

---

34 Pachomius (1845), nos 31–3; Isaia (1851), no. 20: cf. Nicholls (1985), 31; Knox (1991).
35 Nicholls (1985), 16, 36–8; Schmitt (1990).
36 Jaeger (1985), 119.
37 Jaeger (1985), 129ff.
38 Le Gentil (1955); Keen (1984).

in the epic of the Cid, a poem which is organized around the theme of the loss and recovery of the hero's honour.

A medieval historian once drily observed that 'it is impossible to be chivalrous without a horse.'[39] The names of horses as well as their riders recur in the *chansons de geste*, Roland's horse Veillantif, for example, the Cid's Babieca, or Bayard, the marvellous horse which carries the four brothers Aymon, rebels against Charlemagne, to their refuge in the forest of the Ardennes. Just as the word 'chivalry' derives from *cheval*, so the ideal of life it summed up was essentially one for a knight, at once a cavalryman and a gentleman (*caballero*).

The heroes of the *chansons de geste* were conspicuous for courage but not for self-control or refinement. They resembled lions, or the medieval image of lions, easy to rouse but difficult to pacify. A recurrent theme in these epics is that of a violent quarrel over a game of chess. In the course of the Middle Ages, however, the values of chivalry were gradually complemented by a less military quality, or cluster of qualities, including 'good manners' and especially 'courtesy'.

Courtesy has as much to do with courts as chivalry with horses. Nothing has been said about courts so far, and for good reason. The role of 'courtier' did not exist in the Greece of Homer or the Rome of Cicero. Aristotle spent some time at the court of Philip of Macedon, Plato at that of Dionysius of Syracuse, and Seneca at the court of Nero, but they were not courtiers in the medieval or Renaissance sense of the term, even though Castiglione makes Ottaviano Fregoso describe Plato and Aristotle in precisely this way (4.47).[40]

Courtesy has been described as a medieval 'invention'.[41] In the strong sense of the term 'invention', this statement may be challenged by the students of classical or clerical traditions of civility. However, as we have seen (p. 4), it is impossible to draw a sharp distinction between 'invention' and 'adaptation'. It was indeed during the Middle Ages, perhaps around the twelfth century, that behaviour at court became a model for that of other people, that the court became a space, locale or milieu central in what Elias

39 Denholm-Young, quoted in White (1962), 38.
40 Sørensen (1977).
41 Brewer (1966), 54.

calls the 'civilizing process'.[42] The term *curialitas*, 'courtesy', defined by one writer as 'nobility of manners', entered Latin at the turn of the eleventh and twelfth centuries.[43]

It was to this new milieu, that of the court, that the ancient Roman vocabulary of good behaviour – Ovid's as well as Cicero's – was adapted from the twelfth century onwards. 'Courtesy', associated with love as well as with good manners, was opposed to *villania* as *urbanitas* had been to *rusticitas*. It was associated with 'measure' (in the Provençal of the troubadours, *misura*), a sense of discretion leading an individual to avoid excess and follow the mean, a central concept in the courtly system as decorum had been in that of Cicero. A knight was also supposed to be conspicuous for his loyalty, his generosity (*largesse*) and his frankness (*franchise*). He was also required to be 'literate' (*litteratus*) in other words able to compose verses and understand Latin.[44]

This new ideal was not shared by all European elites. There was a clerical tradition of criticism of the court as a place of moral corruption, a critique to which we shall return in chapter 6. All the same, the courtly ideal was spread over much of Europe by the poetry of the troubadours and by the 'courtly romance' (*roman courtois*), a story written about knights, for knights, and not infrequently by knights (the examples of Wolfram von Eschenbach and Sir Thomas Malory, among others, show that the 'literate knight' was not an unrealistic ideal). This new literary genre reveals the fusion, or more exactly, the unstable mixture of chivalry with courtesy, the values of the battlefield with those of the court. The action took place against the background of the idealized courts of Charlemagne and King Arthur, who was presented as an exemplary knight, 'brave and courteous' (*preu et courtois*). These romances bear eloquent witness to the attempt to domesticate the warrior, to tame the lion. The adventures in search of which the heroes set out were designed to test whether or not they possessed the qualities of a good knight in both milieux.

Outstanding examples of the courtly romance from the twelfth and thirteenth centuries are the *Perceval* of Chrétien de Troyes and the *Parzival* of Wolfram von Eschenbach – perhaps the first

42 Elias (1939, 1969).
43 Latham (1965); Ganz (1986).
44 Jaeger (1985).

examples in western history of the *Bildungsroman* – in which the
hero grows up fatherless in a forest and so has everything to learn
when he first encounters the world of knights and ladies.

In Wolfram's poem, for example, the young Parzival is instructed how to speak and how to spend money, and advised to
show mercy in battle, not to deceive women, and to wash his
hands and face after taking off his armour. Thus the wild boy is
'tamed'. What he learns is 'moderation'. Elsewhere in the poem a
squire declares that he never heard any man praised 'if his courage
was without true courtesy'. Sir Gawain in particular is presented
as a knight who exemplifies this ideal.[45]

A major new feature of the value-system associated with courtesy was that it applied to both sexes. Women had been virtually
invisible in the *chansons de geste*. In the courtly romance, on the
other hand, as in the court itself, women had important roles to
play. Marie de Champagne was the patron of Chrétien de Troyes,
while Marie de France composed romances herself. The texts
expressed ideals for ladies as well as for knights, and they had
much to say about relations between the sexes. Prominent among
those ideals was that of courtly love. Ovid's *Art of Love* was being
studied once more. Two free translations of the text were produced in thirteenth-century France, while the poet Garin Lo Brun
drew on Ovid in his instructions to ladies on their *toilette*, their
deportment, and their behaviour to their lovers, emphasizing the
need for *cortesia*.[46]

The contrast between the traditional *chanson de geste* and the
new courtly romance may be made more vivid if we examine some
of the unheroic characters, whose refusal to recognize the ideals
underlying the stories gives them still more emphasis. In the *Song
of Roland*, the greatest of villains is the traitor, Ganelon. In the
romances of Chrétien de Troyes and Wolfram von Eschenbach,
the kind of behaviour to be avoided is illustrated by the discourteous knight Sir Kay, who mocks his colleagues and even strikes
a lady.

The courtly romance appealed to the nobility all over Europe.
In Italy, for example, the fusion of *cavalleria* and *cortesia* may
be illustrated from Ludovico Ariosto's rewriting of the story of

45 Wolfram (1927), sections 170–3, 344, 631, etc.
46 Bornstein (1983), 38–41; Lo Brun (1889), lines 372, 412, 457–60, etc.

Roland in his epic poem *Orlando Furioso*, first published in 1516. From the start Ariosto declares his intention to write about both love and war, knights and ladies (*Le donne, i cavallier, l'arme, gli amori*) and also about courtesy. Ariosto's model of this quality is the knight Leon, son of the emperor Constantine, whose supreme act of courtesy is his yielding of the lady Bradamante to his rival Ruggiero.[47]

In Spain, romances of chivalry seem to have been particularly popular in the early sixteenth century, with at least 157 editions between 1501 and 1550.[48] Here Amadís de Gaula, the hero of a romance of that name published in 1508, was presented as an exemplary knight, *virtuoso caballero*, known not only for his skill and courage in arms, but also for his possession of 'all the other good manners which a good knight should have'. The phrase *buenas maneras* here refers not only to the sphere of what we call 'good manners' but to a wider domain, including that of love. Amadís trembles when he hears the name of his beloved, Oriana, and wastes away with melancholy when she rejects him.[49]

In England, Sir Lancelot was described in Sir Thomas Malory's *Morte D'Arthur* as the most courteous knight who ever bore shield, at once 'the sternest' knight to his mortal foe and 'the meekest' who ever ate in hall among ladies. Of all the knights of the Round Table, however, it was Sir Gawain who was most often presented as a man of courtesy. In the fourteenth-century English poem *Sir Gawain and the Green Knight*, we see Sir Gawain's courtesy put to the test.[50]

The ideal was also spread by a long series of 'courtesy-books', in other words treatises concerned with the correct behaviour of young noblemen, especially at the table of their 'lord', in other words the head of the household in which they were boarded out. These treatises – *The Book of Courtesy, Stans Puer ad Mensam, Urbanitatis, The Babees Book*, and so on – consist in the main of warning readers or listeners against sleeping, breaking wind, scratching, or spitting in the wrong place when seated at table.[51]

---

47 Ariosto (1516); cf. Vallone (1955).
48 Chevalier (1976), 67.
49 Montalvo (1991), esp. 240, 252; cf. Cacho Blecua (1979).
50 Malory (1954), 882; Brewer (1966); Nicholls (1985), ch. 8.
51 Furnivall (1868); Nicholls (1985), chs 3–4.

However, the treatises also have something to say about the positive ideals of 'courtesy', 'urbanity' and 'civility'. Like urbanity, 'civility' (*civilitas, civilité, civiltà*) is a term with urban or civic origins. Already in occasional use from the twelfth century onwards, especially in a political context, it seems to have been launched into popularity by Erasmus, whose *De civilitate morum puerilium* (1530) made a classic synthesis of medieval ideas of discipline and courtesy. His book was often reprinted and it was translated into several vernaculars in the course of the sixteenth century.[52]

Erasmus was no friend of chivalry, or anything connected with war. Like some other Renaissance humanists, from the Florentine Poggio Bracciolini to the Valencian Juan Luis Vives, he was a critic of medieval aristocratic ideals. Vives, for example, declared the romances of chivalry, such as *Amadís de Gaula*, to be 'pestiferous books'.[53] Erasmus was loud in his denunciations of war. For him, letters were everything and arms nothing. The fundamental value of the humanists was of course 'humanity' (*humanitas*), by which they meant a quality which could be taught by following a certain course of study (the *studia humanitatis*). This quality exemplified the dignity of man and his distinction from the animals, who lacked speech and consequently the power to distinguish right from wrong.

By the end of the Middle Ages, then, the classical tradition of good behaviour – itself multiple rather than monolithic, as we have seen – had been reconstructed several times for the sake of different social groups in various milieux in many parts of Europe. This chapter has concentrated on the ideals of urbanity, chivalry and courtesy, ideals which were most closely associated with the city, the battlefield, and the court. Despite the tension between these three traditions, they influenced one another, as we have seen, especially in the later Middle Ages. They are all present to some degree in Castiglione's *Courtier*, as the following chapter will attempt to show.

52 Erasmus (1530); Elias (1939).
53 Vives (1524), 24.

2

The Courtier *in its Time*

There is little point in discussing the reception of a text without first offering an interpretation of that text as a base-line from which to measure deviations. Such an interpretation cannot avoid being controversial, but it can avoid being arbitrary, by taking into account the literary genre to which the text belongs, the personality of its author, and the occasion of its production.

The Genre

To understand a text, we have to concern ourselves not only with its content but also with its form. Castiglione could perfectly well have written a plain treatise on the courtier if he had wanted to do so, modernizing and amplifying the precepts of the late medieval courtesy-books discussed in the previous chapter. He could have expressed his ideas in the form of a romance, allowing the moral to emerge as the story unfolded. The form Castiglione chose, however, was the dialogue, an unusually flexible and 'open' literary form, a 'frozen conversation', as the Cambridge classicist Lowes Dickinson once called it, in which different voices expressing different viewpoints are given a hearing, while there is no need to come to any definite conclusions.[1] The form was well suited to

1 Dickinson (1931), 56; Bakhtin (1981), 259–422; Eco (1981); Gay (1966), 171–2.

the author's aim of confronting and mediating between opposed views of the ideal courtier, the tensions within the traditions of urbanity, chivalry and courtesy. The dialogue was also, in early sixteenth-century Italy, a fashionable genre.

Dialogues had of course been written throughout the Middle Ages. What was new in the Renaissance was the revival of the classical forms of the genre. The term 'forms' has to be used in the plural because several types of dialogue were composed by ancient Greeks and Romans. Plato's dialogues themselves vary between two extremes. Some are little more than monologues by Socrates, in which the function of the other characters is either to agree with the main speaker or to ask him questions. Other Platonic dialogues, notably *Protagoras* and the *Symposium*, are more dramatic, more relaxed and more playful. They represent a genuine debate between the different characters in a particular social setting, such as the drinking-party from which the *Symposium* derives its name. The late arrival of Alcibiades at the party adds a final touch of theatre to the dialogue.

How 'open' the Platonic dialogues are intended to be remains a matter for controversy. According to the Russian critic Mikhail Bakhtin, 'the multiplicity of voices is extinguished in the idea'. For the German scholar Werner Jaeger, on the other hand, some at least of the dialogues exemplify the belief of Socrates that virtue cannot be taught, and that all one can hope to do – as the famous image of the teacher as midwife suggests – is to help others to draw their own conclusions. More recent studies have placed increasing emphasis on the different interlocutors in Plato's dialogues and on the need to interpret their utterances in context.[2]

Cicero's didactic dialogues, the *Academica*, for example, the *Orator* or the *Tusculani* ('Discussions at Tusculum') followed Plato's model. Indeed, the discussions at Tusculum are presented as an example of the Socratic method. The dialogues were less playful than Plato's, but they did include individualized characters such as Crassus, Antonius or Varro. They also allowed readers to see both sides of the questions under discussion. The Greek satirist Lucian wrote even more dramatic dialogues, *Charon*, for example,

2 Bakhtin (1929), 279; Jaeger (1933–45), vol. II, 107–25, 179. Cf. Andrieu (1954); Guthrie (1975), 56–65, 215, 380; Stokes (1986), ch. 1.

or the *Dialogues of the Courtesans*, in which the ideas expressed
mattered less and the personalities presented mattered more.

In the course of the Italian Renaissance, the dialogues of Plato,
Cicero and Lucian were all rediscovered, studied and imitated,
first in Latin works and then in the vernacular. Such leading
fifteenth-century humanists as Leonardo Bruni, Poggio Bracciolini
and Lorenzo Valla expressed their ideas on ethics and politics in
the form of Latin dialogues in which the leading roles were played
by their friends. The vernacular dialogue seems to have been
considered less important in fifteenth-century Italy. Leonbattista
Alberti's *Libri della famiglia*, most of which was written in the
1430s, was not published until the nineteenth century. It was after
1500 that Pietro Bembo put the vernacular dialogue on the literary
map.[3]

Pietro Bembo was a Venetian patrician well known for his
enthusiasm for the philosophy of Plato, for the Latin of Cicero,
and for a 'classical' literary Italian based on the practice of the
three great Florentine writers of the fourteenth century, Petrarch,
Boccaccio and to a lesser extent Dante. He put forward his ideas
in two Italian dialogues, the *Asolani* (published in 1505) and the
Prose della volgar lingua (1525).

The *Asolani* ('Discussions at Asolo', on the model of Cicero's
'Discussions at Tusculum'), represents a conversation about love
lasting three days and involving three young men and three young
women in the garden of the Queen of Cyprus at Asolo, not far
from Venice. One of the protagonists, Perottino, speaks against
love; another, Gismondo, speaks in favour of worldly love; the
third, Lavinello, concludes (like Socrates in the *Symposium*) in
favour of a love and a beauty which is spiritual, divine or platonic,
quoting the words of a hermit who explained to him the need to
ascend from the visible world to that which is invisible. The three
women, Berenice, Lisa and Sabinetta, are not exactly mute, but
they are given relatively subordinate roles. The dialogue echoes
not only the *Symposium* and the *Tusculani* but also Boccaccio's
Decameron, in which the hundred stories are framed by a conversation about love in a group of young men and women in a
garden.

3 Dionisotti (1952).

By contrast, Bembo gave his *Prose della volgar lingua* ('Writing in the Vernacular') an indoor setting, around the fireside in a Venetian house before and after dinner on three successive evenings. The time is the year 1502. The four characters are Carlo Bembo, the author's brother; Giuliano de' Medici, a cousin of Pope Clement VII; Federico Fregoso, a Genoese patrician; and the poet Ercole Strozzi of Ferrara. Carlo, Federico and Giuliano take it in turns to expound their views, while Ercole's role is that of asking awkward questions. What the four men are discussing is the so-called *questione della lingua*, in other words how to write good Italian, and especially what model to imitate – tradition, or the speech of ordinary people, or the example of the great Florentine writers of the past.

In these two dialogues, as well as a lesser-known one set at the court of Urbino, Pietro Bembo provided a model for Castiglione, who took over some of his characters, such as Federico Fregoso, Giuliano de' Medici, and the Lady Emilia, and modelled the final speech in the *Courtier* on the hermit's speech at the end of the *Asolani*, acknowledging his debt with elegance by making his spokesman Bembo himself, who in turn declares his need to consult 'my Lavinello's hermit' (4.50).[4] Bembo was also a leading member of Castiglione's social circle, as we shall see.

The Author

Baldassare Castiglione was born in 1478, so that he was fifty years old when the *Courtier* was published. He was a nobleman from the region of Mantua, in northern Italy, where his family had an estate. Following the custom of his class, his father sent the young Baldassare to be brought up at the court of the flamboyant Lodovico Sforza in Milan. He returned home only on the death of his father in 1499, to enter the service of the marquis of Mantua, Francesco Gonzaga. Castiglione served as a soldier, on campaign in the south of Italy, but his relations with the marquis became somewhat difficult, and in 1504 he was transferred at his own request to another small court, that of the dukes of Urbino. At

4 Floriani (1976), 33–49.

Urbino he was employed as a diplomat by Guidobaldo di Montefeltro and his successor, Francesco Maria della Rovere. He visited England and met the king of France at Bologna. He also spent a good deal of time as ambassador in Rome, looking after the interests of the duke of Urbino and of the new marquis of Mantua, Federigo Gonzaga.

It was in the years from 1513 to 1518, when Castiglione was in his late thirties, that he wrote most of the first draft of the *Courtier*, at much the same time as his friend Bembo was writing his *Prose*. Castiglione asked Bembo, who was already an authority on literary matters, for advice on the revision.[5] The second draft he wrote in his forties, in Rome, in the early 1520s. Soon afterwards, in 1524, Clement VII sent him to Spain as a papal ambassador, or *nuncio*, where he followed the court of the Emperor Charles V to Burgos, Valencia, Madrid and other cities.

Castiglione was still in Spain at the moment of the sack of Rome in 1527 by the troops of Charles V, in other words at a time of open if unofficial hostilities between his new master and the ruler to whom he was accredited. When Alonso de Valdés, a follower of Erasmus and one of the emperor's secretaries, wrote a dialogue in the style of Lucian, blaming the pope for the sack of Rome and criticizing the corruption of the Church, Castiglione responded with a long letter of unwonted violence, accusing him (as Valdés complained to Erasmus), not only of falsehood but also of heresy. He died in Toledo on 8 February 1529, shortly after the publication of his book in Venice and his election as bishop of Avila in Spain.[6]

Charles V paid Castiglione the tribute of describing him, in a much-quoted phrase, as 'one of the best knights in the world' (*uno de los mejores caballeros del mundo*), a phrase which might have come from the pages of *Amadís de Gaula*, in which the knight Arcalaus is indeed described by a hermit as 'the best knight in the world'.[7] In similar fashion, Castiglione's friend Jacopo Sadoleto described him in a letter of 1529 as someone whose achievement in both arms and letters was to be admired, and as a universal man

5 La Rocca (1978), 383–4.
6 Cian (1951); Cartwright (1908); Woodhouse (1978), 6–38.
7 Montalvo (1991), 263.

knowledgeable about all arts and forms of learning.[8] In a biography published later in the century, Castiglione was described as 'an example of perfection' for readers to imitate.[9]

As a courtier, however, Castiglione does not seem to have been an enormous success. He had difficulties with at least two of the princes whom he served.[10] His military career was an undistinguished one.[11] As a diplomat, he suffered from misfortune, at least at the end of his career. One might even hazard the suggestion that he died of embarrassment at the impossible position in which the emperor and the pope had placed him.

The comparison which suggests itself at this point is with Castiglione's contemporary, Machiavelli. Machiavelli was not a great success in the Florentine chancery. He spent his time organizing a rural militia which ran away when the Spanish army arrived, bringing back the Medici and thus leading to Machiavelli's exile to the country estate where he wrote the *Prince*. It may not be not implausible to suggest that both men turned to theory, to contemplation, to compensate for disappointments in the life of action, although Castiglione still had reason to view himself as a successful diplomat at the moment when he was making the final revisions to his text.

Castiglione had more positive qualifications for writing the *Courtier*. He was a well-read man, even by the standards of the time – he knew Greek as well as Latin. The references in the text itself show the author's familiarity with the classics, notably the work of Homer, Plato, Aristotle, Xenophon, Plutarch, Cicero, Horace, Virgil, Quintilian and Ovid. Among modern writers, he made references or at least allusions not only to Dante, Petrarch and Boccaccio, but also to Poliziano, Lorenzo the Magnificent and the neoplatonist Francesco Cattani da Diacceto (1.37).

Castiglione also had experience in writing. In Urbino, at the age of twenty-eight, he had collaborated with his cousin Cesare Gonzaga on a dramatic eclogue for the Carnival, both writing and acting out a play in which nymphs and shepherds disguised topical

8 Sadoleto (1737), vol. I, 119.
9 Marliani (1583), 'To the readers'.
10 Dionisotti (1952).
11 Hale (1983).

references to individuals at the court.[12] He was an accomplished poet in Latin as well as Italian, his works including an elegy on the death of Raphael, to whom he had sat for his portrait in 1517 or thereabouts. Like his friends Bembo and Raphael, Castiglione was a participant in what is known as the 'high' Renaissance, the phase in the movement (centred on Rome in the early sixteenth century), in which most emphasis was placed on rules – whether rules for art, rules for language, or rules for behaviour. It is to the rules followed by the perfect courtier, or more precisely to the discussion of these rules, that we must now turn.

The Text

Before we can proceed to interpretation, the text needs to be summarized – or at any rate described, since a true dialogue does not lend itself to summarization. Treating the *Courtier* as a play rather than as a treatise, it is time to describe its setting and its characters before turning to what they have to say.[13]

The setting of the dialogue is the ducal palace of Urbino, a magnificent Renaissance building which is still to be seen much as it was in Castiglione's day. The time is the year 1507, about six years before the author began to write but more than twenty years before the dialogue was published. The four books of the *Courtier* correspond to four acts of a play, four successive evenings during which the court surrounding the duchess, Elisabetta Gonzaga (the duke, who is sick, having retired to bed early), is employed in the pastime of discussing the qualities of the perfect courtier.

As for the *dramatis personae*, there are more than twenty of them, an unusually large number for a dialogue (even Plato's *Symposium* included only eight participants).[14] To allow variety while avoiding fragmentation, Castiglione gives the main role to several speakers in turn, all friends and acquaintances of his. The task of describing the perfect courtier is first allotted to a nobleman from Verona, Count Lodovico da Canossa, whose discourse

12 Guidi (1977).
13 Rebhorn (1978); Arbizzoni (1983); Clubb (1983).
14 Rebhorn (1978), 179ff.

is cut short by the late arrival of Francesco della Rovere, like that of Alcibiades in the *Symposium*. On the second evening, Federico Fregoso, the Genoese patrician who had been given a role in Bembo's *Prose*, is the main speaker, handing over in his turn to the Florentine Bernardo da Bibbiena. On the third evening, the protagonist is Giuliano de' Medici (like Fregoso, a participant in Bembo's dialogue). The fourth and last session is begun by Ottaviano Fregoso (Federico's brother) and concluded by Pietro Bembo – if it can be said to be concluded at all, since the discussion is represented as breaking off at dawn with the intention of reconvening the following day.

The protagonists are not allowed to speak without pause. They are frequently interrupted and questioned by other participants, notably Gasparo Pallavicino, a Lombard nobleman who is given the role of objector (like Ercole Strozzi in Bembo's *Prose*). Gasparo finds the idealization of the courtier and the court lady implausible, or as we might say, 'utopian'. His function is to bring the discussion down to earth. Significant roles are also played by Castiglione's cousin Cesare Gonzaga, whose questions and objections are less obtrusive; by the Duchess Elisabetta herself; and by Lady Emilia Pia, who chairs the assembly as Elisabetta's 'lieutenant' (1.6), calling on others either to speak or to be silent. Although neither woman intervenes very often or at great length in the dialogue, when they do so they are presented as effective in changing its course.[15] In earlier versions of the text, serious speaking parts were also given to two other women, Costanza Fregosa and Margherita Gonzaga.[16] Absent friends are sometimes quoted, as in the case of the jokes attributed to Jacopo Sadoleto and to Raphael (2.63, 2.76), giving the dialogue more resonance in the author's own circle.

Some at least of the characters are brought to life as individuals; the facetious Bibbiena, for example, or the mocking Gasparo, who likes to play the role of misogynist. With great skill and in a manner almost without parallel in the Renaissance dialogue, Castiglione creates an atmosphere of relaxation by allowing participants to tease one another, to engage in repartee and to express

15 1.6, 1.9, 1.39–40, 3.2, 3.4, 3.17, 3.32, 3.60, 3.77, 4.50, etc.
16 Guidi (1980), 56, n. 69.

their emotions as well as speaking to the point. On one occasion, for example, the Lady Emilia nearly loses her temper with Bembo (4.50). 'He said, laughing as he did so' (*disse ridendo*) or 'laughing, he replied' (*suggiunse ridendo*) are recurrent phrases in the text (3.7, 3.10, 3.13, etc.). Like Plato, Castiglione manages to be at once serious and playful. Like Socrates, he refuses to give direct instruction. Despite didactic passages, the tone of his dialogue is not far removed from *Love's Labour's Lost* (say) or *Much Ado about Nothing*. The argument that the Beatrice and Benedick of *Much Ado* are derived from Castiglione's Emilia and Gasparo may fail to carry conviction, but the exchanges are certainly in the same mood and style.[17]

The content is of course very different. Despite its appearance of spontaneity and free association, the dialogue develops in an ordered manner. The discussion of the perfect courtier begins with the question of nobility (in other words, the importance of 'worth' versus birth), followed by that of fighting (more exactly, arms versus letters). The description of the literary skills required by a perfect courtier leads to a debate on 'the language question', in other words the advantages and disadvantages of speaking and writing Tuscan compared with those of a hybrid 'courtly language'. Again, the requirement that the courtier have a good knowledge of the visual arts turns into a discussion of the relative merits of painting versus sculpture. These binary oppositions were at once traditional and appropriate to the dialogue form.

In this way the first book has already raised four of the major socio-cultural problems discussed in Italy at this time. It contains little to surprise anyone familiar with these traditions, apart from Count Lodovico's suggestion, introduced with an air of apology, that a courtier ought to know how to draw. The second book moves more quickly from one topic to another, but it has a good deal to say about the art of conversation and more particularly about the conventions of joking, with whom and in what manner the courtier is permitted to joke about what if he wants to display grace.

The third book is devoted to the qualities of the ideal court

17 Scott (1901).

lady (the *donna di palazzo*, so called to distinguish her from the *cortegiana*, or courtesan). The discussion centres on the knowledge of literature, music and painting necessary to a lady of the court, as well as on the way in which she should walk, gesture, talk, dance, and so on. This topic naturally leads to a topical debate of the time, on the merits, equality or 'dignity' of women as compared to men. Gasparo Pallavicino argues in his usual provocative style that women are 'a mistake of nature', while Giuliano de' Medici counters with the classic examples of feminine achievement (Artemisia, Cleopatra, Semiramis, etc.) as well as modern ones such as Isabella d'Este (3.36), and Queen Isabella of Spain (3.35). While Giuliano claims that females can understand as much as men can, Cesare Gonzaga declares that their function is to inspire male achievement and that the joy and splendour of courts depends on them (3.3). This debate on women has recently received a good deal of attention, above all from feminist scholars.[18] It has been pointed out that Castiglione had already offered a defence of women as early as the years 1506–9, in the form of a letter to his friend Nicolò Frisio, who was later allocated some misogynistic remarks in the *Courtier*.[19]

The fourth book, changing both subject and tone rather abruptly, addresses the problem of the relation between the courtier and the prince. Ottaviano Fregoso argues that the courtier needs to win the favour of his master so as to be able to give him good advice, and he also makes some pungent comments about the ignorance and conceit of princes (it should be remembered that the speaker is a Genoese, in other words a citizen of a republic). Towards the end of the evening, however, the discussion returns to the nature of love, allowing Pietro Bembo to have the last word, making a passionate speech in favour of spiritual love as the light of dawn begins to enter the room.

In the previous chapter, the description of changing ideals of aristocratic behaviour depended on an analysis of changes in the vocabulary used to describe that behaviour over the centuries. What then of the vocabulary of the *Courtier*? Turning back to the

18 Battisti (1980); Guidi (1980); Zancan (1983); Finucci (1989); Jordan (1990), 76–85; Benson (1992), 73–90.
19 Ghinassi (1967), appendix.

text with this question in mind, it is difficult not to be struck by the richness of the author's language, the fine shades of meaning and the subtlety of the distinctions drawn by the speakers, especially in the domain of the body, its appearance, postures, gestures, and what the sociologist Pierre Bourdieu (following the medieval translators of Aristotle) calls 'habitus', in other words a particular style of behaviour.[20] Earlier Italian treatises on behaviour, especially female behaviour, like the anonymous *Decor puellarum* and Francesco da Barberino's *Reggimento e costumi della donna*, had already discussed proper gestures, but they had done so in a less elaborate or sophisticated way. The *Courtier* was at once more sophisticated than conduct-books of this kind and more concrete than earlier philosophical discussions.

Many of the terms employed by classical, medieval and earlier Renaissance writers to describe good behaviour may be found in the *Courtier* at some point. Men and women alike should cultivate *gravità*, in other words the quiet dignity valued in Cicero's Rome (2.20, 3.5). The term 'chivalry' appears in the text (*cavalleria*, 4.48), and so does 'courteous' (*cortese*, 2.30, 2.98), even if courtesy in the strict sense of the term receives little emphasis.[21] *Gentilezza*, or a *gentil maniera*, is another medieval term of praise to be found in the *Courtier* (2.10, 2.17), and following medieval tradition, it is associated with the service of ladies (3.73). 'Honour' is described as necessary, and the speakers condemn what is 'dishonourable' (*disonesto*, 2.23, 3.57). Both ladies and gentlemen are supposed to have a sense of shame (*vergogna*, 2.22, 3.40), and also a sense of 'modesty' (*modestia*, 2.21, 3.5). There are several approving references to *mediocrità*, not in its modern meaning of 'mediocrity', but in the sense of following the golden or Aristotelian mean (2.16, 2.41). Liberality is praised, and so is magnanimity, at least for princes (2.10, 2.30, 4.18). 'Urbanity' is recommended, like elegance, and these qualities are contrasted with behaviour which is 'wild' (*selvatico*, 2.43, 3.5), or 'rustic' (*contadinesco*, 2.32). The humanist virtue *par excellence*, that of being 'humane' (*umano*), is also praised more than once (1.17, 2.30).

20 Bourdieu (1972), 78–87.
21 Loos (1955), 173ff.

Together with these traditional terms, however, we find behaviour described in the *Courtier* by a number of new words or clusters of words. The ideal courtier should be 'affable', for example, 'amiable', and 'pleasing' (*affabile, amabile, piacevole,* 2.20, 2.17, 2.22). This quality of pleasing others may have been implied by the traditional term 'urbanity', but the implication is both developed and emphasized in Castiglione's text. A second cluster of words amplifies the Aristotelian keyword of 'prudence'. The courtier is advised, for example, to be 'discreet' (*discreto,* 1.18, 1.22), and even to employ 'a certain circumspect dissimulation' (*una certa avvertita dissimulazione,* 2.40), although the term 'deceits' (*inganni*) is generally used in a pejorative sense by the different speakers (2.2, 2.40).

A third cluster of terms develops the idea of 'modesty', especially in the sense of an avoidance of ostentation or affectation. The courtier is therefore advised to be *rimesso, riposato,* and *ritenuto* in his behaviour (2.19, 2.27, 1.17). Behaviour includes appearance (*lo aspetto*), posture (*lo stare*) and gestures (*i movimenti*). In all these respects, ladies and gentlemen alike should cultivate 'grace' (*grazia*), a term with which Castiglione has become identified in the eyes of posterity, so important a function does it perform in his text. It is here that Castiglione's concern with the aesthetics as well as the ethics of behaviour – with the tradition of Ovid as well as the tradition of Aristotle – is at its most obvious. One section of the discussion of the perfect lady keeps particularly close to Ovid (3.50).

Grace, or charm (*charis, gratia*), was a term which had been employed by some ancient writers, such as Pliny and Quintilian. However, the context was usually a discussion of literature or art – the style of the Greek painter Apelles, for example. Among the neoplatonists of the Renaissance, Marsilio Ficino and Pietro Bembo both discussed the link between grace and beauty. The first writer to make grace central to a discussion of behaviour was Castiglione himself.[22]

Grace leads us to what is now the most famous concept in the dialogue: *sprezzatura*. It is presented as a new coinage. Count Lodovico da Canossa, explaining the need to avoid affectation,

22 Monk (1944), 138–40.

declares that the courtier must, 'if I may use a new word, use
in every action a certain *sprezzatura*, which conceals art, and
presents what is done and said as if it was done without effort and
virtually without thought' (1.26). *Sprezzatura* was not, literally
speaking, a new word at all, but rather a new sense given to an old
word, the basic meaning of which was 'setting no price on'. A
more traditional term which the author occasionally uses in its
place is *disinvoltura* (1.26), 'calm self-confidence', the Italian version of the *desemboltura* ascribed to the chivalric hero Amadís de
Gaula.[23] However, *sprezzatura* means more than this. It also in-
volves giving the impression of acting 'on the spur of the moment'
(*all'improviso*, 2.34). This contrived spontaneity is a more dramatic version of the *neglegentia diligens* which both Cicero and
Ovid advocated in their different ways, as we have seen. Aristotle's
magnanimous man has also been described, retrospectively but
with justice, as having 'more than a touch of *sprezzatura*'.[24] Despite these precedents, the stress on this quality in the *Courtier*,
like the twist given to the word, is new.

The use of this term is one sign among several of an increased
interest in what Jacob Burckhardt called 'self-consciousness' and
Erving Goffman 'the presentation of self' or the art of 'impression
management'.[25] Castiglione does indeed discuss the importance for
the courtier of 'giving a good impression of himself' (*dar bona
impression di sé*), and especially of the 'first impression' (2.26,
1.16). He is well aware that he is instructing his readers how to
play a role, how to 'become another person' or better, perhaps, to
'put on a different mask' (*vestirsi un'altra persona*) when the
occasion demands it (2.19). 'Courtier' is itself such a role, and one
which was becoming institutionalized into what Castiglione himself calls a 'profession' (2.10), in other words an art or discipline
(*arte e disciplina*).[26] Hence his coinage of another term to describe
the subject of his dialogue: 'courtiership' (*cortegianía*, 1.12, 1.54).

The author himself practised what his characters preached.
The *Courtier* is itself a work of art which conceals art under the

23 Montalvo (1991), 267.
24 Barker (1948), 145.
25 Goffman (1956).
26 Ghinassi (1971).

appearance of spontaneity. Castiglione claimed to have written it 'in a few days' (1.1), although we know that he rewrote and elaborated it over a number of years. The text exemplifies grace and *sprezzatura* as well as discussing these qualities. Some of its most important points are made casually, as if in passing. Although it is not remarkable for originality, the book is a remarkably skilful synthesis of classical, medieval and Renaissance ideas on good behaviour.

In some cases the author makes explicit reference to the past. He knows his Plato, his Aristotle and his Cicero, and doubtless expects his readers to recognize the allusions. In the case of medieval traditions, the references are less explicit, though it would have been odd indeed if a north Italian nobleman of Castiglione's generation had not been familiar with at least some romances of chivalry, and he did include a reference to *Amadís de Gaula* (3.54).[27] The *Courtier* is most original in its emphases, notably in its stress on the aesthetics of behaviour, on the construction of the self as a work of art, and on the dignity of women (even if the space allotted to them remains minimal compared with what is given to men.[28]

What then is Castiglione's message? The purpose declared by the author in his prefaces, in the form of letters to two friends, is to describe the perfect courtier as a model for real courtiers. However, this purpose is ambiguous or, more exactly, paradoxical. The book professes to teach what cannot be learned, the art of behaving in a naturally graceful manner. One is reminded of Socrates and his belief that virtue cannot be taught – at least, not directly. A second paradox arises from the fact that the very people expected to read the dialogue, the well-born ladies- and gentlemen-in-waiting at courts, are supposed not to need it. The book appears to inform those already in the know. The gap between the apparent and real purposes and audiences of the *Courtier* is filled, or at least papered over, by a playful form of presentation which suggests entertainment rather than instruction.

27 Guidi (1978), 161.
28 Williamson (1947); cf. Greenblatt (1980).

The *Courtier* in its Contexts

What, then, was the author's intention in writing this book? What was its intellectual context? It might be wise to use both terms, 'intentions' and 'contexts', in the plural, and to treat the work as 'overdetermined', as Freud used to say. Many of the suggestions debated by modern scholars as if they were alternatives are in fact compatible with one another, and might well be combined in a synthesis.

The immediate occasion of the dialogue seems to have been provided by Vittoria Colonna, marchioness of Pescara and niece of Duke Guidobaldo of Urbino. It was she who apparently encouraged Castiglione to write – he referred in a letter of 1525 to her 'implicit command' (*tacito commandamento*), a request from a lady which it would have been uncourtly if not downright discourteous to refuse.[29]

In the course of writing, however, the author responded to a number of other imperatives, internal and external. According to some scholars, emphasizing the nostalgic reflections in the author's prefatory letter to his friend the bishop of Viseu, the book was primarily intended as an exercise in autobiography, a Proustian evocation of a time now lost when the author was in the 'flower' of his youth, a resurrection of departed friends and a loving recreation of the court of Urbino as it had been in 1506, before its calm was shattered by war.[30] The *ubi sunt* theme is given considerable emphasis, with references to the death of Giuliano de' Medici, of Bernardo Bibbiena, of Ottaviano Fregoso, and above all of Elisabetta Gonzaga, the duchess of Urbino. The *Courtier* might indeed be described as the author's 'Book of the Duchess', a tribute to Elisabetta, to whom he was closer than to the duke (after all, Castiglione was half a Gonzaga himself).

According to other scholars, writing the *Courtier* was essentially a political act, an attempt (as it happens, unsuccessful) to defend the duchy of Urbino and its ruling house, the Montefeltro,

29 Serassi (1769–71), vol. I, 167.
30 Cian (1951), 27.

at a time when they were threatened by two successive popes, Julius II and Leo X, both of them intent on carving out Italian principalities for their relatives, the della Rovere and the Medici respectively.[31]

The *Courtier* also needs to be placed in other, wider contexts. One way of summarizing its author's achievements in a sentence would be to say that he helped adapt humanism to the world of the court, and the court to the world of humanism. Early Italian humanism was the product of independent city-republics, especially that of Florence. It was, in the famous phrase of the scholar Hans Baron, a 'civic' humanism.[32] By the early sixteenth century, however, most of these city-republics were in decline. Italy was 'refeudalized', as some historians put it. From both the political and the cultural point of view, principalities were increasingly important. So when Count Lodovico da Canossa suggested that the ideal courtier should be reasonably learned 'in those studies which we call humanities' (1.44), he was building a bridge between the cultures of the nobleman and the humanist.

However, the Italian principalities had won their conflict with their republican rivals only to confront a more serious threat to their existence. Born in 1478, Castiglione was sixteen in 1494, the year in which the French invaded Italy, destroying the delicate balance of power between Milan, Venice, Florence, Rome and Naples, turning the peninsula into a battlefield for more than sixty years, introducing new methods of war (including a greater emphasis on guns), and forcing the Italians to realize their weakness relative to foreign states, especially France and Spain. Like Machiavelli (born in 1469), Ariosto (born in 1474) and Guicciardini (born in 1483), Castiglione belonged to what might be called the 'generation of 1494', young enough to be marked for life by the experience of invasion, military impotence and political crisis.[33] He personally witnessed the entry of the French into Milan in 1499, after his former master Lodovico Sforza had been driven out, expressing his regret that a city which had recently housed a flourishing court was now full of taverns and the smell of dung.[34]

31 Loos (1955); Guidi (1983).
32 Baron (1955).
33 Burke (1972), 233–4.
34 Serassi (1769–71), vol. I, 5; La Rocca (1978), 6.

There would seem to be a case for arguing that despite its apparent serenity, the dialogue was a response to a time of political crisis and social change, when norms which had been taken for granted needed to be adapted and made explicit. It was an attempt to redefine the identity of the Italian nobles at a time when their traditional roles were under threat. Their military functions and values were threatened by the increasing importance of gunpowder, a theme explored by Ariosto in *Orlando Furioso*. As for the political role of the nobility, it was being undermined by the rise of what historians call 'absolute monarchy'. No wonder that the work of Ariosto and Castiglione alike is informed by a sense of irony.

Studied closely, the apparently smooth surface of the dialogue reveals traces of bitterness, conflict and above all of ambivalence. Bitter, for example, are the observations of Lodovico da Canossa on the ruin of Italy and the collapse (if not the death) of Italian valour (1.43), or the remarks of Ottaviano Fregoso on the corrupt princes of today and their false image of themselves, thanks to the crowd of courtiers who flatter them (4.9), or the admission by the Fregoso brothers that 'poor Italy' has become the prey of foreigners, 'so much so that little rests to be taken, but they still do not rest from taking' (2.26, 4.33).

It is with respect to these foreigners, especially the French and the Spaniards, that the ambivalence of the dialogue and its author is most apparent. On the one hand, like a good Renaissance Italian, Castiglione considers Italy to be the centre of culture and other parts of Europe to be the periphery, inhabited by 'barbarians'. He wrote a sonnet in 1503 lamenting the fact that Italy was under the 'barbarous yoke' of France and Spain.[35] In the *Courtier*, the French were characterized as 'ignorant of literature' (1.43), just as the young Charles VIII, who invaded Italy in 1494, was described by the historian Guicciardini as virtually illiterate.

On the other hand, despite their inferiority in the domain of letters, these barbarians are recognized as superior to the Italians in arms. They dominate Italy. Some foreigners are praised, especially princes and princesses such as François I of France, Isabella of Spain and Margaret of Austria. Some French noblemen

35 Guidi (1982), 102.

are described as 'courteous' (in their own way, without standing
on ceremony), while one speaker describes the Spaniards as 'masters of courtiership' (*maestri della cortegianía*, 2.21). The cultural
problem arising from this contrast between good and bad foreigners is that of imitation. Are the Italians who dress like Frenchmen
or Spaniards right or wrong, or is the matter indifferent? Should
the courtier learn Spanish and French? Should he introduce French
or Spanish words into his Italian? Will the French, now that
the age of François I has arrived, be able to imitate Italian
achievements in the arts (2.26, 2.27, 1.34, 1.42)?

These questions are of course raised by individual speakers in
the dialogue and they are as usual left unresolved. All the same,
Castiglione has left us some clues about his own attitudes. It has
already been pointed out that the text of the *Courtier* as it was
published in 1528 was the result of a process of writing and
rewriting which had been spread over some twelve years (1513–
24). Two drafts of the text have survived, and a close study of the
process of revision has revealed a number of significant changes.
For example, scholars have caught Castiglione the author in the
act of deleting references to France and inserting references to
Spain at the time when Castiglione the diplomat was advocating
an alliance between the pope and Charles V. The author also gave
increasing space to noblemen at the expense of the ladies and also
of commoners, such as the sculptor Giovan Cristoforo Romano,
whose roles shrank in successive versions of the text.[36]

Thus the ambiguities of the *Courtier* may not all be intentional.
For example, the revisions made in the 1520s, when Castiglione
had shifted to a semi-clerical career and the need for moral reform
was under discussion, made the work a more serious one by
removing some jokes and by adding a fourth book, discussing
spiritual love and the courtier's duty to advise his prince.[37] The
original discussion of divorce was also removed, perhaps because
it seemed tactless at a time when Henry VIII was attempting to
abandon Katherine of Aragon.[38] Like several of the friends he
portrayed in the *Courtier*, Castiglione had adapted himself to a

36 Ghinassi (1967, 1971); Guidi (1978, 1982); Floriani (1976), 50–67.
37 Ghinassi (1967, 1971); Ryan (1972); Woodhouse (1979).
38 Guidi (1982), 105, 111.

new age. Bernardo da Bibbiena, Federico Fregoso and Lodovico da Canossa all became bishops, while Bibbiena and Bembo ended their days as cardinals.[39]

A clerical career was of course a traditional one for intellectuals, but some of these men were involved in the movement to reform the Church from within that historians now call the 'Counter-Reformation'. Federico Fregoso was the probable author of a commentary on the Psalms expressing regret at having had trust in princes and their favour.[40] Lodovico da Canossa was a friend of Gianmatteo Giberti, the reforming bishop of Verona. Bembo was a friend of other supporters of reform such as Jacopo Sadoleto, another humanist turned bishop, and the English Cardinal Reginald Pole. Castiglione was also a friend of Sadoleto's – indeed, he had submitted a draft version of the *Courtier* to him in 1518.[41]

In other words, the middle-aged bishop-elect of Avila was not the same person as the young man who served the duke of Urbino, and the *Courtier* we read today is different in a number of important respects from the book Castiglione originally wrote. The dialogue form and the long process of revision in a constantly changing context produced between them a text which is both ambivalent and ambiguous. As in the case of Leonardo's *Mona Lisa*, it might be argued that its polysemy, its capacity to lend itself to different interpretations, is an essential reason for the dialogue's popularity over the centuries.[42]

In other words, I am inclined to agree with those modern readers who find the *Courtier* what is sometimes called an 'open' work, that is, one which is not only ambiguous but deliberately so, in the manner of a play.[43] 'I can only praise the kind of courtier I most appreciate myself', so Count Lodovico da Canossa explained at the beginning of the dialogue. 'I shall not claim that mine is better than yours' (1.13). In the words of a recent commentator, the text is 'a drama of doubt'.[44] Count Lodovico's remarks may be interpreted not only as an example of courtly manners, but as a

39 Clough (1978).
40 Prosperi (1980), 79–80.
41 La Rocca (1978), 383.
42 Boas (1940).
43 Eco (1981).
44 Cox (1992), ch. 5.

hint to the reader how to interpret the remainder of the text. The dialogue form was exploited by the author in such a way as to leave fundamental questions in suspense, rather than to articulate a consensus.[45] It was for this reason that I devoted more space to the description of the different speakers and to the vocabulary they employed than to a summary of the arguments they put forward.

One powerful argument in favour of the 'open' interpretation draws attention to the many 'self-subversions' of the text.[46] It is indeed difficult to think of any major objection raised by later critics which is not anticipated at some point by some speaker within the dialogue – the idea that *sprezzatura*, far from avoiding affectation, is simply a form of affectation, for example (1.27), or the debate on dissimulation, which is recommended by Federico Fregoso but condemned by Gaspar Pallavicino (2.40). Thus the dialogue was a response to both past and future criticisms of courts.[47]

All the same, many sixteenth-century readers appear to have seen a clear and distinct message in the book, as the following chapters will attempt to demonstrate.

45 Contrast Patrizi (1984), 862.
46 Greene (1983), 61; Rebhorn (1978), 186. Cf. Guidi (1982), 99; Quondam (1980), 17.
47 Kiesel (1979), 77–88.

3

The Courtier *in Italy*

The reception of the *Courtier* began even before the text was published. From about 1518 the text, or some portions of it, had been circulating in manuscript among Castiglione's friends and acquaintances. In 1519, for example, a Milanese poet named Girolamo Cittadini wrote to Isabella d'Este's secretary, Mario Equicola, saying that if there were a chance of seeing a copy of the dialogue, 'I should be very glad to read it.' A year later a French nobleman in Milan, Odet de Foix, approached the marquis of Mantua with a similar request. This suggests that the *Courtier* was already well known in Lombardy by this time, at least by reputation.[1]

Indeed, Castiglione's manuscript was circulating even more widely, since Vittoria Colonna, who read it twice in 1524, had the text transcribed without his knowledge. The author's annoyance at this betrayal is manifest in the preface to the book itself as well as in his politely cutting letter to the marchioness, which speaks of 'theft' and the 'fragments of the poor *Courtier*' to be seen in the hands of various people in Naples. Unlike nine other noble ladies of the author's acquaintance, Vittoria did not receive a presentation copy of the printed version.[2]

By the standards of the time, writing a book and having it printed was a somewhat ambiguous activity for a courtier. Publi-

1 Danzi (1989), 293, 301; Kolsky (1991), 184n.
2 Serassi (1769–71), vol. I, 172; Colonna (1889), nos 19, 34.

cation was associated with profit as well as fame (when he did
publish his dialogue, Castiglione did his best to sell four hundred
copies on his own account at a profit).[3] This made association with
the press inappropriate for noblemen, at least in the eyes of some
contemporaries. In the previous century, Federico of Urbino, the
father of Guidobaldo and a great collector of manuscripts, had
been said to despise printed books and to refuse to have them in
his library. These prejudices were not universal. As we have seen,
Ariosto published his poem *Orlando Furioso* in 1516, and Bembo
published his dialogues in 1505 and 1525. All the same, publishing a book did not quite fit the image of the aristocratic amateur,
the dilettante portrayed in the pages of the *Courtier*.

The *Courtier* edited

Having made his decision, Castiglione took considerable interest
in the process of publication. Like his friend Bembo, Castiglione
turned to the firm of Aldo Manuzio in Venice, which was still
flourishing despite the death of its founder in 1515. This firm of
printers, or publishers – the distinction between the two roles was
only beginning to develop at this time – was the most famous in
Venice, while Venice was the city best known for its printed books
in the Europe of the day. Living as he was doing in Spain, at the
court of Charles V, Castiglione had to rely on friends to see his
book through the press, notably Bembo (despite their disagree-
ments over the best form of written Italian), and Gianbattista
Ramusio, a Venetian civil servant best known for his later edition
of an anthology of accounts of voyages around the globe.[4] In April
1528, the *Courtier* was published as a handsome folio volume
printed in Roman type, in an edition of 1030 copies, thirty of them
printed on special paper to make more impressive gifts (in fact the
author planned to give no fewer than 130 copies to friends and
relatives).

The demand for the *Courtier* must have been considerable, for
it was quickly reprinted, the second time without a place of

3 Cartwright (1908), vol. II, 373–5.
4 Cartwright (1908), vol. II, 376–8.

publication, which suggests that someone was ignoring Aldo's privilege (for a full list of editions, see appendix 1). Around sixty-two editions of the text were published in Italy in the sixteenth and seventeenth centuries; three or four in the 1520s, rising to thirteen in the 1530s, another thirteen in the 1540s, ten in the 1550s, and nine in the 1560s, declining to four in the 1570s, four more in the 1580s, two in the 1590s and three in the 1600s (the last before 1733).

Of these sixty-two Italian editions, at least forty-eight were printed in Venice. Five editions came from the press of the original publishers, the firm of Aldo, while no fewer than sixteen, from 1541 to 1574, came from the rival press of Giolito, which also printed many editions of Petrarch and Ariosto. The remaining twenty-seven were split between fourteen Venetian firms – in chronological order, Curtio, Torresano, Robani, Tortis, Giglio, Fagiani, Cavalcalovo, Domenico, Comin, Farri, Basa, Mimima, Ugolino and Alberti.

In these successive editions, the book gradually changed its appearance. The folio version of 1528, impressive to look at but difficult to handle, was replaced by smaller and more manageable octavos, or even tiny duodecimos like the Giolito editions of 1549 and 1551, true 'pocket-books'. Page numbering was introduced in the Florentine edition of 1529. From 1533 on, many editions were printed in the new and elegant italic type.

The way in which the book was advertised on its title-pages suggests competition between publishers to produce the most attractive version of this best-selling text. Two Venetian editions of 1538 claimed to be 'newly revised'. The Giolito edition of 1546 capped earlier claims by declaring itself 'revised with extreme diligence'. The firm of Aldo responded in 1547 with the claim that their edition had been 'collated once more with the original manuscript, written in the author's own hand'. Giolito riposted in 1552 with an edition which claimed to be 'corrected according to the author's own copy' as well as being revised by Ludovico Dolce, a professional editor in the service of the firm (revision, as often in this period, included what the editor considered to be linguistic improvements).[5] Other books published by Giolito drew attention

5 Cian (1887), 709; cf. Richardson (1994).

to the *Courtier*, notably works by Dolce, Domenichi and Doni which appeared between 1545 and 1550.[6]

The book also acquired an increasingly elaborate 'paratext', to use a recently-coined but convenient term for describing material such as prefaces and notes, whether they precede or follow the text itself.[7] The 1528 edition had already included Castiglione's prefatory letters to the bishop of Viseu and to Alfonso Ariosto, no mere decoration but – as the author's careful revisions demonstrate – part of a careful strategy for the presentation of the text to the public.[8] The Giolito edition of 1541 added an elaborate 'table' (*tavola*) 'of all the matters contained in the present book' in the order of their appearance in the text, from 'the author's excuses' to 'whether ladies are capable of divine love'.[9] The Aldine edition of 1547 included an index 'of all the matters worthy of notice', arranged in alphabetical order, from 'Accident' to 'Zeuxis', together with a concluding summary of the book in the form of a brief list of the qualities of the courtier, a summary which was advertised on the title-page.

The Giolito edition of 1556 went one better than Aldo by boasting that it was 'annotated in the margins' (*nel margine apostillato*), an increasingly common procedure at this time. These annotations were generally summaries of the relevant section, but at times they took the form of editorial notes, pointing out, for instance, that the opening remarks by Castiglione to Alfonso Ariosto were an imitation of the prologue to Cicero's *Orator*. Editions of 1559 and 1573 prefaced the book with Giovio's life of the author, while Basa's 1584 edition replaced it by a new life of Castiglione by Bernardo Marliani. The Giolito edition of 1560 appeared with a new index (from 'A chi nasce aggratiato' to 'Utilità del riso') and also 'with the addition of summaries (*argomenti*) for every book', an innovation which other Venetian publishers quickly copied. The 1574 edition published in Venice by Farri included a particularly elaborate paratextual apparatus. In short, in the course of their competition for readers, sixteenth-

6 Dolce (1545); Domenichi (1549); Doni (1550).
7 Genette (1981, 1987).
8 Guidi (1989).
9 Ossola (1987), 44 ff.

century publishers and their editors combined to transform the *Courtier*.

Readers familiar with the layout of sixteenth-century books are unlikely to be surprised by this account of the editions of the *Courtier*. Elaborate prefaces and dedications, like complimentary verses by the author's friends, were common conventions of the time. Editors not infrequently divided texts into chapters, or added marginal notes, or various kinds of index. Giovanni Della Casa's *Galateo*, for instance, was not divided into chapters in its first edition. The divisions were made by later editors in order to make the book easier for its users to consult. Again, the text of Ariosto's *Orlando Furioso* was provided with a whole apparatus of 'expositions', 'annotations', 'declarations' and 'notes' by some of its editors, including Ludovico Dolce, who went on to treat the *Courtier* in a similar manner.[10]

Dolce offers a good example of a new profession made possible by the invention of printing, that of the 'polygraph' (*poligrafo*), in other words the man of letters who made a living by working for a publisher, editing, translating and plagiarizing the works of others as well as producing some of his own. Among Dolce's 358 productions were several romances of chivalry, furnishing one more illustration of the sixteenth-century synthesis of chivalry and courtesy.[11] If there is a difference between Dolce's treatment of the *Courtier* and that of other books he edited, it is only a matter of degree.

These bibliographical details may seem to be of merely antiquarian interest, but they do have a wider significance. Critics used to draw a sharp distinction between the content and the form of a book, but some now argue that the form is part of the content, in the sense that the physical appearance of a book helps shape the expectations and perceptions of its readers.[12] In this case, the paratext helped transform the *Courtier* from an open dialogue, probably designed to be read aloud, into a closed treatise, an instruction manual, or one might even say a 'recipe-book'.[13] It is likely that the tradition of the courtesy-book, discussed in

10 Quondam (1983); Hempfer (1987).
11 Guidi (1983); Ossola (1987), 43ff; Bareggi (1988), 58ff.
12 McKenzie (1986).
13 Cf. Quondam (1980), 17–19.

chapter 1, also shaped the expectations of readers. One might say that – as in the case of other works of the period, notably More's *Utopia* – the author thought of his book as an example of one genre, while editors and many readers placed it in another. Despite Castiglione's concern to control the production of the first edition, the book was taken out of his hands thereafter, thus illustrating in a dramatic way the inevitable process of the detachment or distanciation of a printed text from its original context or milieu.[14]

The buyer of one of the later sixteenth-century editions scarcely needed to read the book to be instructed. Turning to one of the indexes, he or she would have found no fewer than forty-six references to 'courtier'. Alternatively, the customer could have begun at the end of the book, and found there (from 1547 onwards) a summary of the qualities of the perfect courtier and lady of the court. A third possibility would have been to browse through the volume, guided by the marginal annotations.

It hardly mattered which procedure the reader adopted, since the marginalia, index, table of contents and final summary echoed one another rather than the author's text. These additions by the editors generally took the form of rules: 'The courtier ought to abominate affectation', 'The courtier ought to be able to speak well', 'The courtier ought to know how to draw', 'The courtier should avoid praising himself', and so on. Again, in the index under 'how', we find 'how the courtier has to govern himself in speaking and writing', 'how he has to dress', 'how he has to choose friends', etc. The predominant mood of the paratext was the imperative of the instruction manual.[15] The book was also presented as a treasury of witty and wise sayings. Dolce's index referred to fifty-one pieces of advice, twenty repartees, eleven remarks and seven jokes.

In short, Castiglione's dialogue was flattened and decontextualized by its editors. A specific observation made by a certain character at a certain point in the discussion, to which another character replies, was often transformed into a general rule. In the original text, the existence of such maxims for the behaviour of the courtier was left in suspense. Federico Fregoso indeed declared his

14 Ricoeur (1981).
15 Ossola (1980), 32.

wish that 'our courtier' should make use of 'some universal rules' (*alcune regole universali*), but he was immediately interrupted by a speaker who dismissed his rules as useless because circumstances differ (2.7–8). The compilers of the tables of contents, marginalia, and so on, guillotined these debates and imposed their own views on the readers.

A recent study of the Renaissance dialogue has argued that it became increasingly closed in the sixteenth century, attributing the change partly to the mood of the Counter-Reformation, and partly to the fixing effect of print.[16] The argument is a plausible one, and suggests that we should not place too heavy a load of responsibility on Dolce and his editorial colleagues. They were responding to as well as reinforcing wider movements.

The *Courtier* as a Parlour-game

The idea of a manual or recipe-book, however important, may not be sufficient as a description of the cues which the printed text gave its readers. A second important idea is that of the game. Some modern critics have written perceptively about the *Courtier* as a game.[17] The problem I should like to address now is whether the text was received or perceived in this way in the sixteenth century itself.

One of the many consequences of the invention of printing, and one which has not received much attention, is its effect on the organization of leisure, in particular the place of the book in the rise of what came to be known as 'parlour-games'. Printed books helped to codify and standardize ludic practice, and new games were invented in which books were central. These games drew on popular pastimes for winter nights, on the medieval traditions of courtly love, and on aspects of Renaissance culture. In Lorenzo Spirto's 'Book of Divination' (1476), or Sigismondo Fanti's 'Triumph of Fortune' (1527), or Francesco Marcolini's 'Ingenious Fates' (1540), for instance, we see the printed book employed as an instrument of divination, apparently as a pastime.

16 Cox (1992), chs 6–9.
17 Greene (1983).

Other guides to games drew on intellectual debates. The 'book of a hundred games' compiled by Innocentio Ringhieri and published in 1551 began with 'the game of the knight', in which participants had to discuss whether it is better 'to love men of letters or men of arms'.[18] The 'Dialogue on Games' (1572) by Scipione Bargagli cited Castiglione and described games in which men and women sit alternately, as in the *Courtier*, discussing which characters in *Orlando Furioso* behaved best or composing verses or witty repartees.[19] Another dialogue by Bargagli, 'The Entertainments' (1587), included the 'game of questions of love', in which participants debate the superiority of arms or letters, art or nature, mind or body, in a manner reminiscent of Castiglione's courtiers. The author did not forget to acknowledge what he calls 'the most worthy example' of 'the elegant and magnanimous court of Urbino' in this respect.[20]

Another institution with combined a playful manner with serious topics, and one which multiplied in sixteenth-century Italy, especially from the 1540s onwards, was the 'academy', in other words a discussion group with a fixed membership and regular meetings.[21] Some of these academies were open to ladies, and some of the topics they discussed, like neoplatonism or the comparison between the merits of painting and sculpture, echo the conversations in the *Courtier*. Scipione Bargagli went so far as to describe the court of Urbino as an academy.[22] The Venetian writer Francesco Sansovino also called the court of Urbino 'the famous academy'.[23] If he was able to view the *Courtier* as something like the minutes of the meetings of an academy, it is plausible to suggest that academicians may sometimes have been following the model of the dialogue.

Despite the editorial interventions which encouraged readers to view the dialogue as a manual, the existence of this ludic tradition may have allowed some of them to treat the *Courtier* more playfully. A certain Mario Galeota, who declared he would rather have

18 Ringhieri (1551), no. 1.
19 Bargagli (1572), 34–5, 65–6, 128, 167.
20 Bargagli (1587), 118.
21 Quondam (1982).
22 Quondam (1982), 832.
23 Sansovino (1582), 70 verso, 169 verso.

written the *Courtier* than the *Decameron*, seems to have taken this point.[24]

Responses to the *Courtier*

The number of Italian editions of the *Courtier* in the sixteenth century, around fifty-eight of them, suggests an extremely warm reception for Castiglione's book. One reason for this warmth is surely the fact that the author had included something for everyone among the Italian upper classes. The speakers came from different parts of Italy. Men and women, soldiers and scholars, the already established and the upwardly mobile could all find arguments to suit them and characters with which to identify. Although the dialogue described the world of the court, it was not necessarily antipathetic to citizens of republics. After all, three of the speakers (Federico and Ottaviano Fregoso and Gaspare Pallavicino) came from the republic of Genoa. It should not surprise us too much then, to discover that two of the Venetian editions were dedicated to patricians of the city, Alvigi Giorgio (in 1538), and Giorgio Gradenigo (in 1565), the former described as a young nobleman with most of the 'ornaments' of the ideal courtier.

At this point it may be useful to pick out some faces from the crowd of readers, drawing on the list in appendix 2. Despite the problems discussed in chapter 1, it may be worth examining those few sixteenth- and seventeenth-century Italians – eighty-nine of them altogether – who are known to have owned the *Courtier*, or who made some reference to the text or its author.

It turns out that this group was quite a social mixture. It is no surprise to find that they include men of Castiglione's own class. Among the Italian men of letters of noble birth, who cited the dialogue with approval were Ludovico Ariosto, Annibale Romei and Torquato Tasso, all of Ferrara; Giangiorgio Trissino, of Vicenza; Alessandro Piccolomini, of Siena; and Stefano Guazzo, of Casale in Monferrato, the author of a well-known dialogue on conversation, which refers the reader for a

24 Cian (1887), 663n.

discussion of courts to 'the polished pen of the man who created the perfect courtier'.[25]

Castiglione's dialogue also appealed to readers who did not belong to the nobility. It was praised, for example, by the Florentine critic Benedetto Varchi and the Venetian writer Francesco Sansovino (the illegitimate son of the sculptor-architect Jacopo Sansovino), and it was used as a source by the physician-philosopher Agostino Nifo in his own book on the courtier. Artists conversant with the text included Rosso Fiorentino, who already owned a copy in 1531, and Giorgio Vasari. By the end of the century, the book could also be found in the libraries of lawyers such as the Sicilian Argisto Giuffredi, and merchants such as Giovanni Zanca, of Venice, who owned a 'Cortegiano in ottavo', in 1582.

Among the clergy, apart from the censors, to be discussed below (pp. 100–6), Castiglione's readers included the Benedictine monk Vincenzio Borghini, who was also a Florentine patrician and one of the leading scholars of his day; Giovanni Andrea Gilio da Fabriano, himself the author of a treatise on courtiers, who praised the style of the dialogue; and the humanist bishop Paolo Giovio, who described the book more ambivalently as an anthology of classical ideas, written in the vernacular in order to please women.

Ludovico Dolce's treatise on the lady also recommended female readers to turn to the *Courtier*. As we have seen, Vittoria Colonna read it with enthusiasm. So, in all probability, did Isabella d'Este. In any case the author presented Isabella with a copy, together with eight other ladies; Aloysia Gonzaga Castiglione; Margherita Trivulzio, countess of Somaglia; Eleonora Gonzaga; Emilia Pia; Ippolita Fioramonda, marchioness of Scaldasole; Margherita Cantelma; Margherita di San Severino; and Veronica Gambara.[26]

Of these ten ladies, the choice of the author's mother, of Emilia Pia, and of Isabella d'Este (who may have helped reconcile her husband with Castiglione) was only to be expected. Eleonora Gonzaga was the new duchess of Urbino. Veronica Gambara was a well-known poet and a friend of Bembo's. Margherita di San

25 Guazzo (1574), f.252b.
26 Cartwright (1908), vol. II, 378–83.

Severino was the sister of Emilia Pia. Margherita Trivulzio came from the Lombard nobility and her family included other learned ladies. Ippolita Fioramonda was mentioned by Giovio for her elegance and the boldness of her *impresa* (an enigmatic allegorical device).[27] As for Margherita Cantelma, née Margherita Maloselli, she was the daughter of a rich notary from Ferrara and the wife of a noble from Mantua, Sigismondo Cantelmo. She was a friend of Isabella d'Este, and a manuscript defence of women by a certain Agostino Strozzi was dedicated to her.[28]

Later in the century, we learn that Irene di Spilimbergo, a noblewoman from Friuli, had a copy of the *Courtier* as one of her constant companions, alongside volumes of Petrarch and Bembo.[29] She was probably not alone in her tastes. Although it is impossible to prove this assertion, I think it extremely likely that the *Courtier* was read widely by ladies in Italy, especially in the middle years of the sixteenth century. It is of course impossible to use the usual evidence of library inventories to support this claim because inventories were usually in the name of husbands, who were also the ones to write their names in books.

To justify the assertion, it will therefore be necessary to digress a little and consider the question of the 'learned lady', fact or fiction, concentrating on the knowledge of 'letters' recommended to the *donna di palazzo* in book III, in other words on literary skills in the vernacular rather than Latin and Greek. How widespread was this knowledge of letters?

Two mid-sixteenth-century Italian anthologies were devoted entirely to the literary works of women. The first was the 'Letters of Many Worthy Women' (1548) edited by Ortensio Lando, including the work of 181 ladies – though it is only fair to add that doubts have been expressed about the authenticity of some letters. The second was the 'Various Verses of some Noble and Talented Women' (1559), comprising fifty-three female poets, edited by a professional man of letters, Ludovico Domenichi.[30] To this evidence we may add the sixteenth-century writers mentioned in

27 Giovio (1555), 16.
28 DBI, s.v. 'Cantelmo, Sigismondo'; Fahy (1956), 36–44.
29 Atanagi (1561), preface; cf. Schutte (1991).
30 Dionisotti (1965), 237–9; Piéjus (1982).

Francesco della Chiesa's 'Theatre of Learned Ladies' (1620), or represented in an eighteenth-century anthology of women poets, more than 400 ladies altogether.[31]

These ladies were sometimes courtesans, sometimes commoners, occasionally Jewish and more often nuns, but the majority of them were lay noblewomen. Their names read like a roll-call of the Italian noble families of the time (sometimes whole dynasties in the maternal line). The names include those of several families associated with Castiglione's book. Batista da Montefeltra, for instance, daughter of Federico, a nun who wrote religious poems; Egeria da Canossa; and Beatrice Pia. Ironically enough, given Gasparo's notorious misogyny, the Pallavicini contribute four ladies to the list. The Gonzagas, however, contribute no fewer than ten. There is also a Paula Castiglione from Milan, and three Torellis, the family of Castiglione's wife, who might have been considered to deserve a place in this list herself.

Another point concerns publishers. The anthology of letters by women was published by Giolito of Venice, the firm which published most editions of the *Courtier*. It ends with poems by Dolce and others in honour of 'the studious and illustrious ladies' and their 'learned letters'. Giolito also published the poems of Tullia d'Aragona (1549) and Vittoria Colonna (1552), and both the poems and a discourse on Ariosto by Laura Terracina. The same firm was responsible for a series of anthologies of poetry which included contributions by ladies, some of them edited by the indefatigable Dolce. Giolito also published Dolce's 'Education of Ladies' (1545), which recommends the *Courtier*, and Domenichi's 'Nobility of Ladies' (1549), with its list of illustrious women and its reference to Castiglione as a predecessor. Another writer in Giolito's service, Giuseppe Betussi, translated Boccaccio on famous women and wrote a dialogue on love which features the Venetian poet Francesca Baffo.

These details suggest two conclusions. In the first place, it seems reasonable to argue that the rise of the learned lady in Italy between 1540 and 1560 shows the influence of Castiglione's dialogue, which may well have given women courage to write and to publish. In contrast to tradition, the *Courtier* presents ladies in a

31 Chiesa (1620); Bergalli (1726).

role other than that of mother, daughter or wife. In the second place, there seems to have been a campaign, centred in Venice in the 1540s and 1550s, to draw attention to women's writing. More cynically, one might describe the campaign as an attempt to appeal to a female market which the *Courtier* had helped to legitimate, and which in turn encouraged the reprinting of the book. However, for the market to exist and the books to sell, as they apparently did, there must have been a reasonable number of ladies whose tastes corresponded to the publisher's expectations.

What did they find in the dialogue to please them? If the text was viewed as a kind of cook-book, what were the readers' favourite recipes? One might start from a closer inspection of the one-page summary of contents on the final page of several editions from 1547 onwards. It lists twenty-two qualities for the courtier and thirteen for the lady. In the case of the lady, 'nobility' and 'goodness' head the list, followed by 'good management' (*bon governo*), presumably that of the household; 'prudence', 'honour' and 'affability'. Then come 'vivacity of mind', 'strength of soul', 'beauty and elegance of body', 'literature', 'music', 'painting' and finally 'dancing'.

The qualities of the male courtier begin with 'nobility' and 'wit' (*ingegno*) – there is no mention of goodness this time. Then come 'beauty and grace' and 'skill in arms'; 'ardour', 'loyalty', 'prudence', 'magnanimity', 'temperance' and 'strength and agility of body'. Next on the list are knowledge of duelling, dancing, wrestling, running and jumping. After these physical skills we finally reach 'letters', 'music', 'painting' and the 'knowledge of foreign languages'. The list ends with 'hunting' and 'every praiseworthy exercise'. One might summarize the summary as a list of five moral qualities, five intellectual qualities, and eight physical qualities. Readers might like to ask themselves whether or not such a stress on physique accurately describes their memories of the text.

Another way to discover what contemporary readers saw in the *Courtier* is to collect their brief descriptions of the dialogue and to try to make a mosaic out of the fragments. For instance, one reader, Vittoria Colonna, emphasized Castiglione's 'profound maxims'. This may not be what a modern reader first notices in the *Courtier*, but the love of aphorisms seems to have been widespread. Some editions of Guicciardini's 'History of Italy', for example, included a 'gnomologia' or index of aphorisms. Colonna was also far from alone in making special mention of Castiglione's jokes (below, pp. 79, 152). Other Italian readers seem to have turned to the text for practical advice rather than reading it as a work of literature. The lawyer Argisto Giuffredi advised his sons to observe the precepts of both the *Courtier* and the *Galateo*, as if the two books belonged to the same genre.[32]

Imitations of the dialogue or of passages from it are another sign of enthusiasm for Castiglione. Alessandro Piccolomini wrote a dialogue on the education of ladies, sometimes known after one of the speakers as *La Raffaella* (1539), and followed it with a treatise on the education of noblemen.[33] The books for ladies published by Dolce and Domenichi and mentioned a few paragraphs back were also indebted to the *Courtier* for details as well as general inspiration.

For an example of what it was that appealed to later Italian writers, and how they recontextualized the *Courtier* by embedding passages from it in discussions of their own everyday concerns, we might take the twin concepts of *grazia* and *sprezzatura*. The philosopher Agostino Nifo, for example, devoted a chapter of his treatise on the courtier to 'grace', and defined it in terms of 'negligence and contempt' (*neglectus atque contemptus*).[34] Stefano Guazzo and Torquato Tasso followed Castiglione still more closely in their dialogues, the former writing *negligenza o sprezamento* and the latter *isprezzatura cortegiana*.[35] Although he avoided the word, the riding master A. Massario Malatesta made a similar point in his *Compendium* (1600), when he told apprentice riders to try to give the impression of 'natural grace', 'without work and effort' (*senza fatica e sforzo*).[36]

Castiglione's new term had even more resonance in writings on music. For composers around 1600, it seems to have become a technical term, employed to describe and also to legitimate the new style of singing in which monody replaced polyphony and the intelligibility of the words was considered more important than

32 Giuffredi (1896), 83.
33 Piccolomini (1539); cf. Piéjus (1980).
34 Uhlig (1975), 29–33; Hinz (1992), 228.
35 Guazzo (1574), 83b; Tasso (1958), 3–113.
36 Quoted in Hale (1976), 245, n. 62.

the demonstration of virtuoso ornamentation. Giulio Caccini, for instance, one of the pioneers of opera, described his method of composing as *una certa sprezzatura*, which he associated with nobility and grace, while his colleague Marco da Gagliano made a similar point about allowing the singers to show *sprezzatura*.[37]

The words *sprezzatura* and *grazia* were also to be seen in writings on art. Ludovico Dolce, whom of all people one might have expected to know Castiglione's text well, introduced the first term into art theory in his dialogue *L'Aretino* (1557), in which Fabio speaks of *una certa convenevole sprezzatura* in a passage recommending painters not to give their figures too much polish (*politezza*).[38] In his lives of Italian artists, Giorgio Vasari often used the word *grazia*. Indeed, it has been said that he 'only applied to the arts the conception of grace . . . evolved by the writers on manners'.[39] It is difficult to imagine that Vasari was not thinking of Castiglione when he praised Michelangelo for a grace defined as the ability to overcome difficulties so easily that his works 'appeared to be effortless' (*non paion fatte con fatica*).[40] Vasari, himself a successful courtier, also complimented some artists for their graceful manners, notably Castiglione's friend Raphael, an exemplar of 'graceful affability'; Rosso, singled out for his 'presence' and his intellectual interests as well as for his 'facility' in painting; and Giulio Romano, the heir of Raphael in his manners as well as his art. We have already noted that Rosso owned a copy of the *Cortegiano*. As for Giulio, he was an acquaintance of Castiglione's, and it has been suggested that his interest in leaving works unfinished was itself a form of *sprezzatura*.[41]

Again, in a treatise on art theory by Gian Paolo Lomazzo, we find not only an explicit reference to Castiglione's praises of painting, but a description of an artist, Gaudenzio Ferrari, whose facility was such that 'his works seemed to have been made without art'.[42] As in the case of Vasari, one might speak of a kind of

37 Caccini (1600), dedication; Caccini (1601), To the readers; Gagliano (1608), To the readers.
38 Dolce (1557), 156.
39 Blunt (1940), 97.
40 Vasari (1564), vol. VI, 108.
41 Vasari (1550), 610–11, 828, 749–51; Gombrich (1986), 167.
42 Lomazzo (1590), chs 7, 15.

circular tour, in other words the return to the domain of art of a concept which Castiglione had originally borrowed from art in order to analyse behaviour. Finally an eighteenth-century art critic, Luigi Lanzi, used the term *sprezzatura* to refer to the style of a Renaissance painter, Giorgione.[43]

Modern art historians like to use the term 'Mannerism' to describe the self-conscious elegance or stylishness of such artists as Rosso or Parmigianino. They were active at a time when 'style' (*maniera*) was a subject of intense debate among Italian men of letters. The *Courtier* echoes these debates, in its discussion of painting as well as literature. At one point (1.37), creatively imitating Cicero's discussion of oratory, Castiglione allows one of his characters to suggest that Leonardo da Vinci, Raphael, Michelangelo and other painters were each perfect in his own style. Although it was used by Dolce to combat mannerist tendencies in art, notably excessive polish, the *Courtier* itself looks like an example of Mannerism in some respects, as well as a model for later discussions of *maniera*. Mannerism was of course an international movement. It is time to turn to the international reception of Castiglione's book.

43 Lanzi (1795–6), vol. III, 76.

4

The Courtier *Translated*

————————◆————————

The early sixteenth century seems to have been a time when the debate on the court reached its peak, thanks perhaps to the recent accession of three young monarchs, Charles V, François I and Henry VIII. Erasmus's *Education of a Christian Prince*, like his friend Thomas More's *Utopia*, appeared in print in 1516, at a time when Castiglione was writing his dialogue. Both men discussed the problem of counsel, as Castiglione would do, Erasmus from the point of view of the prince, and More from his own point of view, that of an intellectual who is summoned to the court. Two famous critiques of the court were published in 1517–18, Pope Pius II's letter *On the Miseries of Courtiers* (written in 1444), and Ulrich von Hutten's dialogue *The Court*. In the European as well as the Italian context, Castiglione's book was surely a topical one.

Grand claims have been made for the effects of the *Courtier* outside Italy. One scholar has claimed that the English translation 'became the breviary of every gentleman and of every lady', while another has asserted that Castiglione's influence on Elizabethan taste 'can hardly be exaggerated'.[1]

We may at least agree that interest in the *Courtier* was as intense outside Italy as it was in the peninsula. As appendix 1 shows, about sixty editions of the text in languages other than Italian were published in the ninety-two years 1528–1619. In any case,

1 Praz (1943), 196; Buxton (1954), 19.

some foreigners read Castiglione in the original, at a time when the prestige of Italian culture made knowledge of Italian highly desirable, if not absolutely necessary for anyone with pretensions to a good education.

It is likely that Italian was the first modern foreign language to be learned in France, England and Spain alike. The language was certainly becoming more accessible to the English from the middle of the sixteenth century onwards. Sir Thomas Hoby, the translator of the *Courtier*, wrote an Italian grammar for the use of Sir Henry Sidney, while grammars of the language were published by William Thomas (1550), Claudius Hollyband (1575) and John Florio, the son of an Italian Protestant exile (1578).[2] It was thanks to the the grammars of Thomas and Florio that Gabriel Harvey, for instance, learned Italian in the 1570s.[3] Florio taught Italian at Oxford at one point, and Italian grammars can be found in the possession of some members of the university in this period.[4]

In the introductory comments to his translation of Castiglione, Sir Thomas Hoby declared that the English courtier ought to be competent in languages, or as he put it, 'seen in tongues', especially in Italian, French and Spanish. According to her tutor, Roger Ascham, Queen Elizabeth had 'perfect readiness' in these three languages.[5] A number of her courtiers also seem to have reached this standard. Sir Philip Sidney, for example, went abroad in 1572 to learn languages, and seems to have been fluent in Italian, French and Spanish. So was Henry Howard, later earl of Northampton. Sir Walter Raleigh owned books in these three languages.[6] The earl of Leicester, Lord Burghley and Sir Francis Walsingham all knew Italian at least.[7] As for the ladies, the five Cooke sisters and Lady Jane Grey are all known to have studied French and Italian.[8]

It is not easy to discover how common a reading knowledge of Italian would have been in different countries in the sixteenth

2 Hale (1954).
3 Stern (1979), 156.
4 Curtis (1959), 140–1.
5 Ascham (1568), 21.
6 Peck (1982).
7 Firpo (1971), 38.
8 Warnicke (1988), 42–6.

century. The problem would make a good subject for a mono-graph, but the research has not been carried out. My own im-pression, based principally on library inventories, is that such a reading knowledge was not uncommon among European nobles, at least those whose first language was French, German, Spanish, Czech, Polish or Hungarian. Examples from these language areas include Montaigne, Garcilaso de la Vega, Willibald Pirckheimer, Karel Zerotin, Jan Zamojski and Bálint Balassa.

A number of conduct books testify to the desirability of these skills. For instance, in Łukasz Górnicki's 'Polish Courtier' (1566), to be discussed below, the reader was told to learn German, Italian, French and Spanish, in that order. In Louis Guyon's essay on the courtier (1604), French readers were advised to learn Italian, Spanish, 'and even German, if that is possible'. In Nicolas Faret's *Honnête homme* (1630) the languages recommended to French gentlemen were Italian and Spanish, 'which are more widely current than any others in Europe, and even among the infidels'.[9]

Given this knowledge of Italian among the European nobility in this period, foreign responses to the *Courtier* in its original lan-guage deserve to be examined in some detail before we reach the various translations of the text and their reception in different parts of Europe.

The Diffusion of the Text

In a letter to his mother in 1528, Castiglione asked for seventy copies of his book to be sent to him in Spain, doubtless for distribution to his friends and acquaintances there. In any case, Spanish interest in his dialogue was encouraged by the involve-ment first of Aragon and later of Castille in the affairs of Italy. The frequent references to Spain in the *Courtier*, especially prominent in the final, printed version of the text, have often been noted, including the discussion of the propriety of borrowing Spanish words and phrases, such as *acertar*, 'to succeed', or *criado*, 'ser-vant' (1.31).[10] In any case, there is good evidence for Spanish

9 Górnicki (1566), 100; Guyon (1604), 194; Faret (1630), 31.
10 Guidi (1978).

interest in the dialogue. A bookseller of Barcelona owned no fewer than twenty-four copies of the *Courtier* in Italian at his death in 1561, despite the fact that a Spanish translation had been in circulation for decades (since he regularly imported books from Lyon, we may assume his stock to have been one of the Italian editions published there).[11] A number of Spanish noblemen are known to have owned what one inventory calls 'el cortegiano en italiano'.[12] So, of course, did the multilingual Emperor Charles V, to whom is attributed the famous remark that Italian was the right language to use to friends, French to women, German to horses and Spanish to God. It was claimed that the emperor 'loved to read only three books' – Castiglione's *Courtier*, Machiavelli's *Discourses*, and the work of the ancient Greek historian Polybius.[13]

In the case of Portugal, the obvious person with whom to begin is Castiglione's friend Miguel da Silva, bishop of Viseu, to whom the dialogue was dedicated. Dom Miguel leads us to his acquaintance Francisco de Holanda, best known for his writings on art, and Holanda in turn to the religious writer Frei Heitor Pinto. The fact that the Lisbon Index of 1624 discusses an Italian edition of the *Courtier* in some detail confirms that the text was reasonably well known in Portugal at that time.[14]

In the case of France, the most famous reference in Castiglione's dialogue is an uncomplimentary one. Count Lodovico da Canossa claims that the French 'not only fail to appreciate letters, but hate them, and despise writers'. He is contradicted, however, by Giuliano de' Medici, who declares that times have changed and that if 'Monseigneur d'Angoulême' succeeds to the throne (which he did, as François I, in 1515, long before the dialogue was published), letters will flourish as much as arms (1.42). In the first draft of his book, Castiglione claimed that the king, whom he met on two occasions, had encouraged him to go on working on the dialogue.[15]

Three Italian editions of the *Courtier* were published in Lyon between 1553 and 1562. Since Lyon was a city in which consider-

---

11 Kamen (1993), 412 (Joan Guardiola).
12 Le Flem (1973), nos 424–5.
13 Sansovino (1567), 21.
14 Deswarte (1989, 1991).
15 Clough (1978), 24–5.

able numbers of Italian merchants resided, we are left in doubt whether the volumes were intended for Italians abroad, for Italianized Frenchmen or indeed for export to Spain and Portugal. Fortunately there is more direct evidence for French readers of the Italian text.

Jean Groslier (*c*.1486–1565), for example, was a civil servant who collected books on a grand scale. Groslier studied with an Italian humanist in Paris before becoming secretary to King Louis XII. He lived in Italy in the 1510s, as royal treasurer in Milan, and he also became acquainted with Bembo and with the printer Aldo Manuzio. It was through the Aldine connection that Groslier came to own a manuscript of the *Courtier*, not to mention six copies of the first edition and five of the 1533 edition (published by the same firm).[16]

Another French owner of the *Courtier* in Italian was the nobleman Nicolas d'Herberay, Seigneur des Essarts, an artilleryman by profession, but a man who combined arms with letters, like Castiglione himself. Herberay is best known to posterity as the man who translated the romance of chivalry *Amadis de Gaule* into French at the request of François I, yet another sign of the compatibility between the values of chivalry and courtesy, or at least their mutual interaction at this time. Again, the historian Jacques-Auguste de Thou owned two copies of Castiglione in Italian, one of which is now in the Bodleian Library.[17] Montaigne's friend Etienne La Boétie celebrated his own beautifully bound and gilded copy in a sonnet: 'I have a Tuscan book with its spine richly decorated in beaten gold. The outside shines with gold and inside is Count Balthasar's art of courtiership.'

> J'ai un livre Tuscan, dont la tranche est garnie
> richement d'or battu de l'une et l'autre part;
> le dessus reluit d'or; et au dedans est l'art
> du comte Balthasar, de la Courtisanie.[18]

A similar copy of the Venetian edition of 1545, bound in fine red morocco, was owned by the statesman Cardinal de Granvelle,

16 Austin (1971).
17 Thou (1679), 400; cf. Coron (1988).
18 La Boétie (1892), 275.

who came from Besançon in Franche-Comté.[19] In Austria and
Germany, Italian editions of the *Courtier* occur in library catalogues.[20] Bohemian and Hungarian nobles such as Hans
Dernschwam, the Lobkovič family and Miklós Pázmány also
owned Italian editions.[21]

In England too there were a number of references to the
Courtier before its appearance in English dress in 1561, confirming its translator's comment in his preface that 'this *Courtier* hath
long strayed about this realm.'[22] The earliest of these references
dates from 1530, only two years after the first Italian edition was
published. In that year a young diplomat called Edmund Bonner
(later bishop of London and a leading opponent of the Reformation), asked Thomas Cromwell for the loan of 'the book called
Cortigiano in Italian'.[23] That the busy secretary to Cardinal
Wolsey and to Henry VIII should have owned a copy of the
dialogue becomes less surprising when we learn that Cromwell
had lived in Italy in his youth, and that he also owned copies of
Petrarch's *Triumphs* and of Machiavelli.[24]

In 1548, a certain William Patten described an acquaintance as
a man 'such . . . as Count Balthazar the Italian in his book of
Courtier doth frame'.[25] A year later, William Thomas referred to
the book in his *History of Italy*.[26] Henry Howard, later earl of
Northampton, annotated the 1541 edition with care, as we shall
see, probably in his youth, since he wrote his name but not his title
in the volume.[27]

Even after the dialogue had made its appearance in translation,
references to British readers or owners of the original text are not
difficult to find. The Thomas Wryght who wrote his name in a
copy of the 1562 edition now in Trinity College, Cambridge was
probably the college chaplain (1570–2). A Fellow of Corpus
Christi College, Cambridge, Abraham Tilman (died 1589), also

19 Picquard (1951), 206
20 Brunner (1956); Roeck (1990).
21 Dernschwam (1984); Kasparová (1990); Ötvös (1994).
22 Vincent (1964); Gabrieli (1978).
23 Hogrefe (1929–30).
24 Dickens (1959), ch. 1.
25 Patten (1548) H vii recto.
26 Thomas (1549).
27 Juel-Jensen (1956); Barker (1990).

possessed a *Courtier* in the original language.[28] Other owners include Mary Queen of Scots; the Scottish gentleman William Drummond; the avid book collector Sir Thomas Tresham; and Gabriel Harvey, Fellow of Trinity Hall and lecturer in rhetoric at the University of Cambridge, a man who seems to have been virtually obsessed by the *Courtier*, as we shall see.

For some of these readers, the text was appealing as a good example of current idiomatic Italian. Bonner, for example, wanted to learn the language before his mission to Bologna and Rome. The bilingual editions published in Lyon in 1580 and in Paris in 1585, together with the trilingual edition published in London in 1588, were clearly designed for readers who wanted to study Italian as well as good behaviour. Indeed, the 1580 edition was specifically addressed to 'those who wish to understand' either language. John Florio's reference to one who 'hath learnt a little Italian out of Castilions courtier' is likely to have hit the mark.[29] However, the book's success in translation makes it clear that the content of the dialogue was attractive as well as its form.

The Text in Translation

The importance of translations from Italian in Renaissance Europe is well known. Ariosto's *Orlando Furioso*, for instance, was translated into Spanish in 1549, into French in 1543 (and again in 1614), and into English in 1591. No fewer than eighteen editions of the Spanish translation were published between 1549 and 1588.[30] Despite widespread condemnation as an immoral book, Machiavelli's *Prince* was translated into French (twice in 1553 and again in 1571), into Latin in 1560 and into Dutch in 1615, while the French versions had been through at least nineteen editions by 1616.[31] Francesco Guicciardini's *History of Italy* was translated into Latin (1567), French (1568), English (1579), Spanish (1581) and Dutch (1599). Sebastiano Serlio's treatise on architecture was translated into German (1542), French (1545), Spanish (1552),

28 Leedham-Green (1987); cf. Jayne and Johnson (1956), 187–8.
29 Florio (1591), dedication.
30 Cioranescu (1938); Chevalier (1966), 74.
31 Gerber (1913).

Latin (1569) and English (1611) – not to mention a partial translation into Dutch. Castiglione's success was similar to that of his
four contemporaries. By 1620 it was possible to read the *Courtier*
not only in the original but also in Spanish, English, German (two
versions), French (three versions) and Latin (three, or more exactly
two and a quarter versions, the quarter being a rendering of book
1 alone).

It may be worth drawing attention to the European languages
into which the *Courtier* was not translated in the period, difficult
as it is to say whether this is to be explained by the state of society,
the state of the language (or indeed by accident). There was no
translation into Flemish or Dutch, for example, until the later
seventeenth century (although at least three of the Spanish editions
were published in Antwerp); no translation into Portuguese
(though the Portuguese would have been able to read the Spanish
version without too much trouble); no translation into the
Scandinavian languages (though some Danes and Swedes owned
the text in French, German, Italian or Spanish); or into Celtic or
Slav languages (apart from the Polish adaptation, which will be
discussed below, and anecdotes about a possible Russian version).[32] Nor was there a translation into Hungarian, despite the
receptivity of Hungary to the Renaissance – but then the book was
published two years after the battle of Mohács, when the Turks
destroyed the Hungarian army and overran most of the country,
giving potential readers other matters to think about.

The translations of the *Courtier*, or at least some of them (the
English, French and Spanish versions rather than the Latin,
German and Polish), have been studied in considerable detail,
mainly from a linguistic and literary point of view.[33] In the following account, however, the method will be comparative and the
emphasis will fall on what the different versions of the text tell us
about the cultures from which the translators came.

The Spanish translation of 1534 was the first into a foreign
language, appropriately enough, given the author's years in Spain.
The translator was Juan Boscà Almogáver (a Catalan patrician,
though writing in Castilian and better known as Juan Boscán). A

32 Benini (1778), 40, garbled in Cartwright (1908), vol. II, 440.
33 Morreale (1959); Klesczewski (1966); Nocera (1992).

leading Spanish poet in the manner of Petrarch, Boscán was aware of contemporary Italian discussions of creative imitation, which he practised in his prose as well as his poetry.[34] At least twelve and perhaps as many as sixteen editions of his translation had been published by the end of the sixteenth century (three of them in Antwerp).

Among the Spanish readers of the text in the sixteenth century were three soldier-writers. There was Garcilaso de la Vega, who brought the book to the attention of Boscán. There was Alonso Barros, who will be discussed later. Finally, there was Miguel de Cervantes, who alluded to Castiglione's dialogue in *Don Quixote* and also in his *Galatea*.[35] Spanish readers also included the diplomat Don Diego Hurtado de Mendoza (who owned three copies), and the assistant secretary of the Council of Italy, Francisco de Idiáquez (who owned two); the authors Fernando de Rojas and Garcilaso de la Vega 'the Inca'; the musician Luis Milán; and the humanists Lorencio Palmireno and Cristóbal de Villalón. The Spanish text was also read in Austria in the late sixteenth and early seventeenth centuries, a time when the influence of Spanish culture at the imperial court was still strong, and it was read in the Spanish empire, as far afield as Peru.[36] Again, the Danish nobleman and chancellor Jakob Ulfeldt owned a Spanish translation of the dialogue (despite having studied in Padua), like the French writer Jean Chapelain and the Scottish poet William Drummond of Hawthornden.

Castiglione sold even better in France. Three separate translations of the *Courtier*, one of them anonymous, appeared in twenty-three editions between 1537 and 1592. The most successful translation was the one by 'J. Colin' (perhaps the diplomat Jacques Colin), published in 1537 and revised in 1540 by the humanist printer Etienne Dolet and the poet Melin de Saint-Gelais. The interest in the book among members of their circle is revealed by the controversy of the 1540s concerning the court lady, to be discussed below (pp. 76, 112). Towards the end of the century, in 1580, the Colin translation was displaced by a new

34 Darst (1978).
35 Lopez Estrada (1948); Fucilla (1950).
36 Brunner (1956); Hampe (1993).

version by a semi-professional translator, Gabriel Chappuys, (*c*.1546–*c*.1613) who also turned Ariosto, Boccaccio and part of *Amadis* into French.

Like the Spanish translation, these versions were current not only in France but in other parts of Europe. King Erik XIV of Sweden, for example, was given a copy of a French translation by an English envoy, John Dymock, in 1561. 'About Christmas eve Ashley asked him if the King could speak Italian? He said no, and at his recommendation bought a little book in the French tongue called the *Courtisan*.' When Dymock arrived in Sweden he gave the king a pair of gloves, a dog, and 'a little gilt book called the *Courtisan*'.[37]

The German patrician Ulrich Fugger also owned a French edition, like the Surrey gentleman William More of Loseley, whose inventory of 1556 refers to 'the curtesan, in French', and also Sir Christopher Hatton, despite his knowledge of Italian. Huijch van Alckemade of Leiden owned 'Le courtisan de messire Balthasar de Castalon'. In the seventeenth century, the Danish nobles Niels Friis of Favrskov (who had studied at the university of Orléans) and Jacob Ulfeldt both owned French versions of the *Courtier*.

After the Spanish and French translations, which appeared quite soon after the original, there was something of a hiatus. An English translation was already planned in the 1550s by Sir Thomas Hoby, but it did not appear in book form until 1561. Hoby was a member of what has been called the 'Cambridge connexion' of Protestant intellectuals (among them William Cecil, Roger Ascham and John Cheke) who became influential on the accession of Queen Elizabeth in 1558.[38] Hoby's translation was reprinted three times in our period, in 1577, 1588 and 1603.

There were two separate German translations of the *Courtier*, but neither version is known to have reached a second edition. The first (1565) was the work of Laurentz Kratzer, customs officer (*Mautzahler*) of Burghausen in Bavaria, who dedicated the book to his duke; and the second (1593) was made by Johann Engelbert Noyse, another Bavarian, who dedicated his version to one of the

37 Stevenson (1867), 219, 223; cf. Andersson (1948), 167.
38 Hudson (1980).

Fuggers, in the hope, he claimed, that it would remedy the corrupt manners of actual courts.[39] There are occasional references to the circulation of these texts outside the German language area, notably the inventory of the books of Prince Christian of Denmark (eldest son of Christian IV), drawn up on his death in 1647, which mentions 'Chastilons Hoffmann quarto'.

Outside Italy, Spain and France, the *Courtier* was probably best known in its Latin versions, a reminder that Latin was the language of the international republic of letters at this time, not only among scholars but among educated men more generally. The works of Machiavelli and his friend the historian Francesco Guicciardini, for example, were probably better known in Europe in Latin than in their original Italian.[40]

A Latin translation of the *Courtier* by Johannes Turler was published in Wittenberg in 1561; a second version, by Bartholomew Clerke, in London in 1571; and a third Latin version, of book I only, was published by Johannes Ricius in 1577. They were presumably intended for the university market. At any rate Turler was professor of Roman law at the University of Marburg, while Clerke was a professor of rhetoric at Cambridge and a Fellow of King's College.

Clerke's version was criticized in the eighteenth century, in the preface to Samber's English translation, for its 'stiff Manner, and far-fetched Metaphors'. All the same, it seems to have had considerable success in its own day, when Latin culture flourished in Britain.[41] A number of copies can still be found in several Cambridge college libraries, as well as in the inventories of the books of Cambridge men (including two booksellers, John Denys and Reynold Bridge, the latter having three copies in stock at his death in 1590). It was the Latin version which Gabriel Harvey advised his pupil Arthur Capel to read. In Oxford too several students and teachers (including Robert Burton) are known to have owned the *Courtier* in Clerke's translation. Of the ten editions of the text published in England between 1561 and 1611, six were of Clerke's Latin version compared to four editions of

39 Stöttner (1888), 494–9.
40 Burke (1993), 41–2; I have a more detailed study of this topic in the press.
41 Binns (1990).

Hoby's English one. No wonder that so many people called the
author of the dialogue by his Latinized name, 'Castilio'.

The Rewriting of the Text

It is time to examine these versions more closely, to see how the
translators interpreted and presented Castiglione's text. Translations are an object of increasing scholarly interest, and they can
of course be studied from a number of points of view, such as the
conflict between 'free' and literal renderings, the predilections of
individual translators, and the compatibility or incompatibility
between different languages. Sir John Cheke, for example, who
taught Thomas Hoby at Cambridge, advised him that 'our own
tongue should be written clean and pure, unmixed and unmangled
with borrowing of other tongues'.[42] When he translated the New
Testament, for example, Cheke preferred 'crossed' to 'crucified'
and 'hundreder' to 'centurion'.

From the point of view adopted in this essay, the importance of
the translations of the *Courtier* is that they offer unusually detailed
evidence of the responses of particularly careful readers of the text.
If marginal annotations are valuable documents for reader-
response, translations are still more precious. They often reveal
enthusiasm, occasionally criticism, and they go a long way to
telling us how contemporaries, at least outside Italy, understood
key passages of the dialogue.

It is of course impossible to discuss the reception of a text in
translation without going into philological detail, as monographs
on particular versions of the *Courtier* have done.[43] Apparently
minor divergences between the original and the translation are
sometimes extremely clear indicators of cultural distance. In the
Spanish translation, for example, the terms *cittadino* and *civile*
disappear altogether, reminding us that Spain lacked the kind of
civic culture which was characteristic of Renaissance Italy.[44]

42 Letter prefixed to Hoby (1561).
43 Klesczewski (1966); Morreale (1959); Nocera (1992).
44 Morreale (1959), 110, 113.

Again, it has been pointed out that Hoby translated the Italian term *architetti* by 'carpenters', whether because he was uncomfortable with the new word 'architect' or because he was trying to adapt Castiglione to the English situation where buildings were designed by craftsmen, while wood was a more common material than stone. On the other hand, Hoby's renderings of technical terms from music have been praised by a specialist as much more 'successful' than the atttempts by his opposite numbers in France (Sir Thomas was extremely interested in music, and owned a number of Italian music books).[45]

In a relatively brief account such as this one, however, philological detail can only be presented at the price of extreme selectivity. For this reason the discussion will concentrate on the renderings of certain of Castiglione's key terms, notably *cortegianía, grazia* and *sprezzatura*. An attempt will be made to compare the way in which the different translators jumped these hurdles, not to award them points for skill but to draw conclusions about their responses to the text. It will be obvious that a task of this kind taxes a historian's linguistic resources to the limit. For this reason, the English version will be considered in the greatest detail, as a case-study of more general problems.

Cortegianía seems to have been an unusual term when Castiglione used it, and one which does not seem to have enjoyed great success in Italy, although it was used by the Lombard writer Matteo Bandello, while the author's namesake Sabba da Castiglione devoted a chapter of his book of advice to what he called 'the courtiership of our time' (*la cortegianía de' nostri tempi*).[46] Boscán translated the term into Spanish without apparent difficulty as *cortesanía*, but other translators seem to have found it a stumbling-block. In France, for example, Colin coined a new word, *courtisannie*, Chappuys used the roundabout solution *forme de courtiser*, while the anonymous French translator tried out alternative paraphrases such as *profession courtisane*,

45 Kemp (1976), 361.
46 Bandello (1554), book II, no. 57; Castiglione (1549). Cf. Sigismondi (1604), 5.

l'art du courtisan, or *façon de bon courtisan*, as if not quite happy with any one of them.[47]

Thomas Hoby also found the term rather hot to handle. In English the term 'courtesy', like 'courtier', has come into use by the thirteenth century at the latest, but courtesy in the medieval sense is not quite what Castiglione is discussing. By the end of the sixteenth century, new terms had come into existence, including 'courtliness' or even 'courtship' in a non-amorous sense, thanks perhaps to the vogue for Hoby's translation.[48] However, the terms were not available to him. Hoby had to coin a new word, 'courtiership', which he sometimes preferred to paraphrase as 'the trade and manner of courtiers'.[49] The Latin translators too found the term a difficult one. Ricius avoided it altogether, while Clerke, in his preface to the reader, waxed eloquent about the problems. 'How shall I render what the English call *courtiership* and the Italians *cortegianía*? To say *aulicalitas* is not a good idea . . . I am forced to use the term *curialitas* although it is not pure Latin because it is closer to classical Latinity.'

'Grace' (*grazia*) was another key concept which posed problems to some translators, especially in those better-known contexts where it refers not to the favour of a prince but to a style of behaviour. For instance, the first German translator, Kratzer, rendered *grazia* by *Gnade* (the traditional term for 'favour'), while the second, Noyse, preferred to import the term *Gratia*, which stands out on the page as one of the few words in Roman type in a book printed in Gothic. Hoby too wrote that 'the courtier ought to accompany all his doings, gestures, demeanours: finally all his motions with a grace.' One may be allowed to wonder what his mentor Sir John Cheke would have thought about this borrowing from Latin. Among the Latin translators, Ricius chose *venustas*, and so did Clerke on occasion. Boscán was fortunate in that Spanish resembled Italian closely enough for him to be able to employ the elegant antithesis *gracia/desgracia*.

A still greater challenge was posed, as one might have guessed, by what has become the most famous concept in the whole of

47 Klesczewski (1966).
48 Bates (1992).
49 Nocera (1992).

Castiglione's book, *sprezzatura*, a term used (as we saw in chapter 2) 'to show that what is done and said comes without effort and as if without thought' (1.26), developing the ancient Roman idea of negligence (above, p. 11). Earlier in the Renaissance, Petrarch had used the phrase 'rather negligent in behaviour' (*habitus neglectior*) while the humanist Pietro Paolo Vergerio had used 'ease' (*facilitas*).[50]

The problems of the translators are revealed by their choice of different equivalents for *sprezzatura* in different passages – or even in the same passage – as if they were less than happy with their own solutions. Boscán, for instance, sometimes translates *sprezzatura* literally by *desprecio* ('contempt'), at other times more freely by *descuido* ('carelessness'), allowing the antithesis *cuidado/descuido* to render the contrast between 'affectation' and 'negligence'. By contrast, Castiglione's synonym *disinvoltura* presented no problem. Itself a borrowing from Spanish, it could return to that language.[51]

Facing the same hurdle, Colin opted for *nonchalance*, a word which has certainly become a close analogy to the Italian term (whether or not this was already the case in his day). The anonymous French translator and Chappuys were both more cautious and sometimes doubled words up, *nonchallance et mesprison* in the first case, *mespris et nonchalance* in the second.[52] It should be noted that the French word *insouciance*, which may now seem an appropriate equivalent for *sprezzatura*, goes back no further than the early nineteenth century.

Of the two German translators, Kratzer seems to have been the freer and more confident, Noyse the more hesitant and literal. The first rendered affectation by *Begierlichkeit*, the second by *Affectation*. Kratzer translated *una certa sprezzatura* by a certain *Unachtsamkeit*, while Noyse recommended the use in all things of *ein Verachtung oder Unachtsamkeit*, doubling up once again.

Among the Latin versions, Bartholomew Clerke returned, appropriately enough, to Cicero's *non ingrata neglegentia* and so spoke of the need to behave 'in a negligent manner' (*negligenter*).

50 Loos (1955), 116.
51 Cf. Morreale (1959), 163–5.
52 Cf. Klesczewski (1966), 168ff.

He glossed the term with the phrase '*(ut vulgo dicitur) dissolutè*'. The last word now looks somewhat odd in this context, but in sixteenth-century English, 'dissolute' could mean 'negligent' or 'at ease' rather than 'loose' in the moral sense of the term. Clerke also uses the term *incuria*, which one might translate as 'deliberate lack of care'. As for Ricius, like Castiglione he invented a new term and rendered *una certa sprezzatura* by *certa quaedam veluti contemptio*. The circumlocution 'certa quaedam veluti' surely betrays a certain hesitation or discomfort with his own translation.

Like Boscán, Chappuys and others, Thomas Hoby made more than one attempt at finding the right word. In his rendering of the Italian passage quoted above, he wrote that the courtier must '(to speak a new word) . . . use in every thing a certain disgracing to cover art withal, and seem whatsoever he doth and saith, to do it without pain, and (as it were) not minding it'. The second time *sprezzatura* occurred, it was again rendered 'disgracing', but on the third occasion Hoby chose 'recklessness'. It would appear that Hoby's printers or editors were not all happy with his rendering, for the 1588 edition, published twenty-two years after the death of the translator, changed 'recklessness' into 'disgracing'.[53]

Hoby's choice of terms is precious evidence of his own reaction to Castiglione, if only we can interpret it – which is no easy task, given all the changes which have taken place in the English language in the 400-odd years which separate us from him. We can begin by asking what alternatives were open to him. He did not opt for 'nonchalance' like the French translators, whose work he probably knew since he was working on his translation in Paris, perhaps because this would have meant coining a new term (the OED's first reference to 'nonchalance' is as late as 1678).

Hoby also avoided the terms 'carelessness', 'effortlessness', and, perhaps more surprisingly, 'negligence', which had already been employed in English in Chaucer's day. The reason for this omission may be the tradition of using the term 'negligence' in moral and spiritual contexts, to mean something like 'omission of duty' or 'sloth'.[54] By the eighteenth century, however, when two new

53 Nocera (1992).
54 Kuhn and Reidy (1954–).

English translations of the *Courtier* were published in the same decade, the positive meanings of 'negligence' were dominant, and both translators fastened on this term. In Robert Samber's version of 1724, so free that it introduced references to perrukes and shoe polish, it was said that the courtier needed 'to make use of a certain kind of Negligence, and do everything easy, and, as it were, without minding it'. Elsewhere he wrote of 'an easy Carelessness'. In the more literal version of 1727, the courtier was described as needing 'to discover in every thing a certain Negligence, to conceal his Art withal, and to appear that whatsoever he saith or doth comes from him naturally and easily, and as it were without attending to it'.

What, then, were the associations of the terms which Hoby did use? 'Recklessness' is an old English word, already in use by the tenth century, and Hoby's choice may reflect Cheke's concern to use authentic English words. Whether the term was as strongly pejorative in the sixteenth century as it is today remains less certain. It is interesting to find that in Hoby's time the translator of a historical work, Sleidan's *Commentaries*, could use the phrase 'a certain negligence and recklessness' as if the terms were more or less synonymous.

We come now to 'disgracing'. Unlike *sprezzatura*, 'disgracing' was not newly coined. It corresponds closely to the term *disgrazia*, which Castiglione uses from time to time to describe behaviour of which the speaker does not approve (affectation, for example). In English too the term seems to have been strongly pejorative. 'Rude and unlearned speech defaceth and disgraceth a very good matter', wrote Robinson in his 1551 translation of More's *Utopia*. 'Filthy disgracements' wrote Norton in his 1561 translation of Calvin.[55] *Love's Labour's Lost* opens with a reference to 'the disgrace of death'. The usage closest to Hoby's is Philip Sidney's in his *Defence of Poetry*, where 'disgracefulness' seems to mean 'inelegance', but this is later than Hoby and may even allude to his solution.[56]

It is possible that Hoby simply meant to follow Castiglione's deliberate paradox and desire to surprise, but we should at least

55 OED, s.v. 'disgrace'.
56 Sidney (1973), 111.

entertain the possibility that he was, consciously or unconsciously, subverting his text. Given what is known about his life and attitudes, one might have expected Hoby to be a little ambivalent about the *Courtier*. On one hand, Hoby was an Italophil who studied for a time at the University of Padua. On the other hand, he was a Protestant who took his religion seriously enough (like his tutor John Cheke) to go into exile when Protestantism was outlawed in England by Queen Mary.[57] In Strasbourg, he lived in the house of a leading Protestant theologian, Martin Bucer. His friend Roger Ascham, whose attitudes will be discussed below (pp. 76-7, 112), is a more explicit example of the ambivalence of a Protestant humanist.

To conclude this section, it may be of interest to look at other attempts to render Cicero's *neglegentia* and Castiglione's *sprezzatura* or *grazia* into English. Gabriel Harvey's marginalia to his copy of the Hoby translation rendered *disinvoltura* as 'negligent diligence', though one might have thought 'diligent negligence' even more apt.[58] George Puttenham's *Arte of English Poesie* went back beyond Cicero to 'such as the Greeks call *charientes*, men civil and graciously behavoured and bred'.[59] Another Elizabethan writer, George Pettie, preferred a paraphrase and so referred to those who 'think it most commendable in a Gentleman, to cloak his art and skill in everything, and to seem to do all things of his own mother wit'.[60] Let Ben Jonson have the last word.

> Give me a look, give me a face
> That makes simplicity a grace;
> Robes loosely flowing, hair as free:
> Such sweet neglect more taketh me,
> Than all th'adulteries of art.
> They strike mine eyes, but not my heart.

He was echoing Horace and Ovid, but 'sweet neglect' remains an attractive equivalent for *sprezzatura*.

57 Garrett (1938), no. 204.
58 Stern (1979).
59 Puttenham (1589).
60 Pettie (1576).

The Paratext

Another way to study responses to the *Courtier* is to examine the foreign editions in the same way that the Italian editions were examined in the last chapter, paying attention to the paratextual apparatus as a set of clues to how the text was read. To discuss each edition one by one would certainly be tedious and might not be illuminating, but an analysis of a few editions is absolutely indispensable.

The early editions of the Spanish translation, for example, look very different from the Italian editions, because they are printed in black-letter. They carry additional prefatory material, notably a prologue by the translator Juan Boscán and a letter from his friend the poet Garcilaso de la Vega. Boscán described the content of the book as 'not only useful and pleasing but also necessary' (*no solamente provechosa y de mucho gusto: pero necessaria*), noted the differences between the customs of the Spanish and Italian nations, and acknowledged the encouragement of two noble ladies. For his part, Garcilaso praised the translation and its 'extremely courtier-like vocabulary' (*terminos muy cortesanos*), and attempts to anticipate and answer possible criticisms (to be discussed below, pp. 99–116).

Later Spanish editions, from 1540 onwards, added marginal notes. The Antwerp edition of 1574 divided the text into thirty-two chapters, summarized in a table at the end. The point of this division was explained in a prefatory note, presumably by the printer, Philippo Nucio, a note which is of considerable interest for historians of reading. 'The author did not divide these books into chapters; but it now seems to some people that to read a book from beginning to end without having a place to stop and rest one's mind is somewhat exhausting.'

The first French translation appeared without any index or marginal annotations, but it did contain a Latin poem addressed by Nicolas Bourbon to the reader commending Colin's version, to which the 1538 edition added a letter by Etienne Dolet to Melin de Saint-Gelais, reminding him that they were reading the book together in Lyon 'and found a number of mistakes and omissions'. Dolet thus confirms Roger Chartier's point that early modern reading was sometimes collective rather than private.[61]

Several editions of the 1540s and 1550s omitted the prefatory letters, presumably to cut costs. On the other hand, the Chappuys translation (1580) was furnished not only with a new dedication, to Nicolas de Bauffremont, but also, on the model of recent Italian editions, with an elaborate table of 'the most important contents and maxims' (*Table des principales matières et sentences*), listing 'Qualities which a prince should possess', 'Gestures required for telling a funny story', declaring that 'Honour is the bridle of women', and so on.

In Hoby's English version, printed like the early Spanish editions in black-letter, no fewer than four voices precede that of Castiglione himself. The printer, William Seres, writes to the reader explaining the delay in publication. The poet Thomas Sackville, who probably knew Hoby in their student days, produces a panegyric on both the author and the translator in the form of a sonnet, describing the *Courtier* as 'a work of worthy praise'. A letter from Sir John Cheke to 'his loving friend Master Thomas Hoby', thanks him 'for submitting your doings to my judgement' and puts forward his theory of translation (above, p. 66). Finally, Hoby himself writes to Lord Henry Hastings, expressing his satisfaction that Castiglione 'is become an Englishman' at last, instead of his book being judged at second hand or 'unperfectly received' or confined to readers 'skilful in his tongue'.

Other elements of the paratext fill out the picture, starting with the publisher's blurb, describing the book on the title-page as 'Very necessary and profitable for young Gentlemen and Gentlewomen abiding in Court, Palace or Place'. As usual by now, there are marginalia. More remarkable is the final section of the book, a 'brief rehearsal' or summary of the main qualities of the courtier and court lady (eighty-two qualities for the gentleman and forty-eight for the lady). As we have seen (above, p. 42), a list of this kind had been appended to the book by an editor, Ludovico Dolce, but Hoby amplified it in a most elaborate way. His list for males includes 'To be well born and of a good stock', 'To shun affectation or curiosity above all things in all things', 'use a reck-

---

61 Klesczewski (1966), nos 7–12, 14; Chartier (1987), 231.

ness to cover art', 'To be more than indifferently well seen in
learning, in the Latin and Greek tongues', 'To have the feat of
drawing and painting', and 'To play upon the lute, and sing to it
with the ditty'.

In Clerke's Latin version, printed in an elegant italic type, the
number of newly written prefaces rises to six, at the expense of
Castiglione's own prefatory letter to Miguel da Silva, which is
omitted. The translator dedicates his work to Queen Elizabeth and
writes to his patron Lord Buckhurst (none other than Hoby's
Thomas Sackville, now raised to the peerage), in order to introduce his book. Buckhurst writes back to Clerke. Clerke's Cambridge colleague, the physician John Caius, also writes to him,
while Edward Vere, earl of Oxford, and Clerke himself both write
to the reader. The book ends with poems addressed to Clerke by
some of his friends. There are no divisions into chapters in this
Latin translation, and there is no index, but the customary marginal notes are provided on 'the force of custom', 'affected negligence', and so on. An index also made its appearance in later
editions, taking the usual hortatory form, 'Let the courtier not be
an actor', 'Let the courtier not be envious', 'let the courtier not
despise hunting', 'the art of painting necessary to the courtier', and
so on. As in the case of the Italian editions, the French, English and
Latin paratexts all encouraged the readers to treat the dialogue as
a series of rules or recipe-book.

Readers' Responses

It is time to lift our eyes from these philological and bibliographical details in order to try to convey a more general impression of
responses to the *Courtier* outside Italy between 1528 and 1619.
The emphasis, here and in chapter 5, will be on the favourable
responses, leaving the criticisms for chapter 6.

In France, the preface to a manuscript translation of book III
declared that 'among the Italian books which are well composed
and highly esteemed by connoisseurs, we consider the *Courtier* to
be the most excellent and the last to deserve to be ignored.'[62]

62 BNP fonds français. 2335, quoted Héroet (1909).

Although it was not mentioned by name, Castiglione's dialogue
seems to have been a stimulus for a French debate on courtly love,
the so-called *querelle des amies*, a debate which included Bertrand
de La Borderie's *Amie de cour* (1541), Charles Fontaine's
Contr'amie (1541) and Antoine Héroet's *Parfaite amie* (1542).[63]
These playful examinations of the behaviour of the court lady
included remarks on grace, including *une grace assurée*, quite a
close equivalent for *sprezzatura*. It is worth noting that the books
by La Borderie and Héroet were both published by Etienne Dolet,
the humanist printer who had himself participated in one of the
French translations of the *Courtier*.

For other readers, the political aspect of the book was more
important. The poet Jean de La Taille, in his *Necessary Prince*,
wished for a courtier 'like the one Castiglione describes', in order
to teach the prince 'the art of reigning justly'. La Taille was writing
at about the time of the massacre of French Protestants in 1572, an
incident which suggested to many that the young Charles IX was
much in need of good advice and advisers.[64] Montaigne, who is
known to have read Castiglione (probably in translation, despite
his knowledge of Italian), paraphrased him at two points in his
Essays, to condemn affectation in speech and dress alike and
to declare that actions show grace if they are carried out with
nonchalance.[65] Again, Montaigne's friend Jacques-Auguste de
Thou, a lawyer who was later to become a distinguished historian,
responded warmly to the dialogue. When he arrived in Italy in
1573, de Thou visited Urbino, and at Mantua he met Camillo
Castiglione, 'son of Count Balthasar, who has made a great reputation for himself by his learning, by his poetry, and above all by
his *Courtier*, a work of imagination like Cicero's *Orator*'.[66]

In England in the mid-1560s, soon after the Hoby translation
had been published, Roger Ascham, a humanist in Hoby's circle at
Cambridge, made the following comment about it in his treatise
on the education of young gentlemen.

To join learning with comely exercises, Conte Baldesar Castiglione
in his book *Cortegiano*, doth trimly teach: which book, advisedly

63 Screech (1959).
64 La Taille (1878–82), vol. III, cxxi; Daley (1934), 218.
65 Montaigne (1580–8), book I, no. 26 and book III, no. 10.
66 Thou (1713), 24, 43.

read, and diligently followed, but one year at home in England, would do a young man more good, I wiss, than three years' travel abroad spent in Italy. And I marvel this book is no more read in the court than it is, seeing it is so well translated into English by a worthy gentleman Sir Thomas Hobbie, who was many ways well furnished with learning, and very expert in knowledge of divers tongues.

Ascham made his own the recommendation that 'a courtly gentleman' ought to be able to ride, dance, sing and play instruments, though he made no reference to painting, adding archery in its place.[67]

Other favourable testimonies soon followed. Henry Howard, later earl of Northampton, referred in 1569 to 'that most excellent work of the Count of Castiglione called the *Courtier*'.[68] In the 1570s, John Rainolds referred to it in passing in his Oxford lectures on Aristotle's rhetoric as if taking it for granted that his audience was familiar with the text.[69] Again, around 1580, Gabriel Harvey, in a letter to his friend the poet Edmund Spenser, declared Castiglione to be 'of no small reputation' in Cambridge.[70]

At much the same time, in an anonymous dialogue on *Civil and Uncivil Life*, one speaker refused 'to take upon me to frame a Courtier', preferring to 'leave that to the Earl Baldazar, whose book translated by Sir Thomas Hoby, I think you have, or ought to have read'.[71] In 1589, Thomas Nashe referred to a discussion between several gentlemen of his acquaintance which raised 'divers questions, as touching the several qualities required in Castalions *Courtier*'.[72] Three years later, Nicholas Breton, dedicating a book to the countess of Pembroke (sister to Sir Philip Sidney), compared her to the Duchess Elisabetta and her 'courtlike house' at Wilton to the palace of Urbino.[73]

In 1608, an English traveller in Italy made a pilgrimage to the tomb (in a church outside Mantua) of the 'worthy poet and orator'

---

67 Ascham (1568), 19–20. Cf. Ryan (1963).
68 Peck (1991), 150.
69 Rainolds (1986), 336.
70 Harvey (1884), 78–9.
71 Javitch (1978), 5n.; cf. Breton (1618).
72 Nashe (1589), dedication.
73 Waller (1979), 41–2.

who wrote that 'most elegant' book, the *Courtier*.[74] In 1612, the recorder of Exeter, discussing exercises, recommended to his son and other young men 'the deliberate reading and meditating upon that excellent and ever most praiseworthy work of Balthazer Castilion, who by his choice precepts, hath cast young gentlemen into a fairer mould than their fathers did'.[75] In 1615, an English knight referred to 'that most learned and judicious noble gentleman the Count Baldesser Castilio', praising his recommendations for the study 'of riding, and of painting and of portraying, and of dancing' as well as the practice of arms.[76]

References of this kind, which could easily be multiplied, and have parallels in many parts of Europe, are of course too brief and too general to give more than the vaguest impression of readers' views of the *Courtier*. There are, however, at least two possible methods for going beyond them.

In the first place, as historians of the book have pointed out, the reception of a text may be studied through the comments of its readers, scrawled in the margins, on the fly-leaf, and so on.[77] For instance, Bishop John Hacket's copy of the Latin version of the *Courtier* contains marginalia such as 'Note' (*Nota*) or 'Read carefully' (*Perlege*).[78] Even underlinings, or their sixteenth-century alternatives the cross or the 'maniculus', the pointing finger in the margin, are of some value in suggesting that parts of the text evoked more responses than others. The heroic method of studying Castiglione's reception would therefore be to examine every surviving copy of the text for annotations from the sixteenth and early seventeenth centuries. I cannot pretend to such heroism, but an analysis of even a few annotated copies of the *Courtier* may be of some interest.

One of the best-documented sixteenth-century responses to Castiglione is that of the Cambridge don Gabriel Harvey, a man who owned a number of Italian books (Aretino's plays, Guazzo's 'Conversation', Tasso's *Aminta*, and so on) and frequently annotated the books he read in a fine Italianate hand. Harvey's copy of

74 Coryate (1611), 1, 268.
75 Martyn (1612), 109.
76 Sir George Buck quoted Hale (1976), 231.
77 Chartier (1987); Darnton (1986).
78 UL, L*.15.10.

the Italian edition has been lost, but his copy of the Hoby translation, now in the Newberry Library, Chicago, contains a number of
notes. These notes are generally summaries of the text rather than
comments on it, but at least they reveal what it was in the dialogue
which most impressed one reader.

For example, Harvey's marginalia stressed the importance of
'grace, or fine comely behaviour'; and also the need to be 'skilful
and expert in letters and arms' (a significant reversal of the arms
and letters in the original text, since Harvey was a literary man).
'To do all things with a certain seemly Grace and Decorum', he
wrote at one point. And at another:

> Above all things it importeth a Courtier to be graceful and lovely
> in countenance and behaviour; fine and discreet in discourse and
> entertainment; skilful and expert in Letters and Arms; active and
> gallant in every Courtly Exercise; nimble and speedy of body and of
> mind; resolute, industrious and valorous in action; as profound and
> invincible in action as is possible; and withal ever generously bold,
> wittily pleasant and full of life in his saying and doings.[79]

Like other sixteenth-century readers, Harvey showed great interest in Castiglione's section on jokes, to which he returned in his
annotations on Quintilian's treatise on rhetoric. The closest
Harvey comes to a critical comment on the text is his suggestion
that a man needs not only to be 'urbane' but also 'pragmatic'
(*pragmaticus*), whatever he meant by that term (perhaps politically aware, perhaps legal-minded).[80]

The fullest and most systematic annotations on Castiglione
known to me come, once again, from England. They are to be
found in the copy of the Venice 1541 edition owned by Henry
Howard, later earl of Northampton. Howard went through the
first and most of the second book, not only underlining many
passages but writing summaries in the margin, generally in Italian.
These annotations suggest that he did not only read the text but
studied it closely, and also that some readers were feeling the need
for the subject index and the marginalia which later editions
provided, as we have seen (above p. 42).

Although there are few explicit comments, Howard's choice of

79 Ruutz-Rees (1910), 635; Stern (1979), 159; Jardine and Grafton (1990).
80 Moore Smith (1913), 114; Stern (1979), 160–1.

passages to annotate reveals something of his interests. In the first place, the notes reveal the preoccupations with honour and war which were characteristic of a young aristocrat of his time, and are confirmed in Howard's case by his library, which contained many military treatises. The passage declaring arms to be the main profession of the courtier is marked, like the remarks on the importance of honour and an 'unconquered mind' (*animo invitto*), on fame as the spur in battle (*il vero stimulo e la gloria*), and so on.

The owner's keen interest in the visual arts is also apparent in his notes, with MUSIC, PAINTING, SCULPTURE, PERSPEC-TIVE written in capitals at the top of the pages dealing with these subjects, and the references to Raphael and Michelangelo marked, with 'most excellent painters' written in the margin. The annotations also suggest that – unlike some of its twentieth-century readers – Howard viewed the text as a moral, or even a moralizing work, since he notes 'dishonourable matters', for example, or 'the vices of the old'. That he considered the text to have been written in the spirit of Cicero is suggested by his marginal comparisons to no fewer than four of Cicero's works.

However, Howard seems to have been most impressed by Castiglione's discussion of grace. *Sprezzatura* and *Affectatione* are among the words written in the margin, while remarks on simplicity, the concealment of art and on gracious movements in the dance are underlined, like the claim that the courtier needs to make a 'good impression'. In similar fashion, George Puttenham, adapting the art of courtiership to the art of poetry, recommended the 'courtly poet' to act so that his skill 'may not appear nor seem to proceed from him by any study or trade of rules, but to be his natural'.[81] Again, Francis Bacon, in his essay 'Of Ceremonies and Respects', criticized those who 'labour too much' to attain good forms, and so 'lose their grace; which is to be natural and unaffected'.

Puttenham and Bacon were not so much commenting on Castiglione as imitating him. Another method of discovering how contemporaries responded to the text is to examine its imitations. Some of the most famous of these will be discussed in the following chapter.

81 Puttenham (1589), 302, quoted in Javitch (1972), 881.

5

The Courtier *Imitated*

Lists of editions, translations and readers, however illuminating, are not the only ways to assess the importance of the *Courtier* in European culture. It is also necessary to consider the exemplarity of the text, the extent to which and the modes in which it inspired imitation in life or in literature, whether this took the form of simple plagiarism or the creative imitation discussed in the pages of the dialogue itself.

The Problem of Imitation

It is generally difficult to demonstrate that a particular text or person imitated another, or conversely, that a particular text or person influenced another (above, p. 3). Looking back at our own lives, we may indeed remember books or people who deeply impressed us at one time, but it is always possible that they impressed us precisely because they were nudging us in a direction in which we were already intending to travel, consciously or not.

The concept of imitation is more complex than it may look at first sight. The process was discussed, indeed debated, during the Renaissance, as one might have expected in the course of a movement whose defining characteristic was the attempt to revive classical antiquity, especially the age of Cicero and Vergil, writers who both followed Greek models and tried to adapt them to Roman values. In Rome in 1512, for example, Gianfrancesco Pico della Mirandola argued for an eclectic approach to imitation, while Castiglione's friend Bembo argued in favour, of the imitation of individual writers, emphasizing the need for the complete assimilation of the style to be imitated (Cicero for prose, and Vergil for poetry) and also for the 'emulation' of the classics.[1]

Castiglione's characters also discuss this question, which leads one of them to the conclusion that if we imitate the ancients we do not imitate them – since the ancients did not imitate others – while another points out that the Romans imitated the Greeks (1.31–2). The *Courtier* not only discusses creative imitation but also exemplifies it, especially in its relation to the three classics cited at the beginning of the dialogue – Plato's *Republic*, Xenophon's *Education of Cyrus*, and above all Cicero's *Orator*.

In turn, Castiglione's dialogue became the object of further imitation. In the case of the *Courtier*, which expresses few novel opinions, the importance of this imitation is more difficult to assess than in the case of (say) Machiavelli. An American scholar once listed no fewer than 945 treatises on the gentleman published in Europe before 1625. She later discovered another 472, not to mention 891 books offering 'doctrine for the Lady of the Renaissance'.[2] To my mind, she cast her net rather too widely, but even if the list were reduced by more than half, a thousand titles would remain. Another scholar produced a list of 2,000 'courtesy-books' in the Newberry Library in Chicago.[3] Of these texts, fifty or sixty of particular relevance are discussed here or in chapter 7. The key question for us must be, how different would all these treatises have been if the *Courtier* had never been written?

In the discussion which follows, an attempt will be made to avoid two extremes. On one side, there is the danger of seeing Castiglione everywhere, as some scholars have done, even in the most commonplace discussions of the virtues of gentlemen. I shall not be arguing that Shakespeare's heroes and heroines – Beatrice and Benedick, for example – are derived from characters in the *Courtier*, notably Lady Emilia and Gasparo Pallavicino, or even that they are incarnations of an ideal specifically derived from this

1 Santangelo (1954); cf. Greene (1982), 171–6.
2 Kelso (1929, 1956).
3 Heltzel (1942).

book.[4] In similar fashion, the argument that Alonso de Ercilla, author of a famous epic poem on the conquest of what is now Chile, was among Castiglione's imitators fails for lack of evidence.[5]

The opposite danger is that of noticing borrowings from the *Courtier* only when the author's name is mentioned. There can be little doubt, for instance, that Giovanni Della Casa, author of the famous courtesy-book the *Galateo*, or Antonio de Guevara, author of an equally famous critique of the court, made use of the *Courtier* without naming the book or its author. Again, the French soldier François de La Noue made no mention of Count Baldassare in his discourses, but he borrowed one of the most famous anecdotes in the *Courtier*, the one about the soldier who boasted of being able to speak of nothing but war, and was put in his place by the lady who told him that in time of peace he should be put away in a cupboard with the arms and armour (1.17).[6] Thirty-five examples of writers who appear to have used the text without acknowledgement will be found in appendix 2.

A particularly popular object of imitation was the final set-piece in the *Courtier*, Bembo's speech on divine love. For example, Luis Milán, discussed later in this chapter, followed it in the description of the universe, the creator and the heavenly bodies put into the mouth of Mastro Zapater at the very end of his dialogue.[7] Again, the Portuguese friar Heitor Pinto followed it in the discussion of love in his 'Dialogues on the Christian Life' (1563).[8] Francis Bacon also followed the Bembo speech in a court entertainment of 1592, 'Of Tribute'.[9]

It was of course easier to imitate Castiglione creatively by leaving the court behind and writing about another form of conduct altogether, like that of the physician (as an anonymous writer did in sixteenth-century Spain).[10] After all, this was exactly the manner in which Castiglione had imitated Plato's *Republic* and

4 Scott (1901); cf. Bhattacherje (1940), 38ff; Praz (1943), 195–6.
5 Corominas (1980), 6.
6 La Noue (1587), 235.
7 Milán (1561), 362ff.
8 Deswarte (1991).
9 Martin (1992), 64–6.
10 Bataillon (1939), vol. II, 266.

Cicero's *Orator*. A natural subject for humanists to choose was that of the ideal teacher or student – indeed, in the text itself, Ottaviano Fregoso had been criticized by one of his listeners, Cesare Gonzaga, for advising the prince in the manner of 'a good schoolmaster rather than a good courtier' (4.36).

One English humanist, whose praise of Castiglione's book has already been quoted, appears to have been tempted in a similar direction. The preface to Roger Ascham's *Schoolmaster* (posthumously published in 1568), represents a dialogue in a circle of friends, including Sir William Cecil, Sir Richard Sackville and Sir Walter Mildmay, whose interest in education would lead him to found Emmanuel College. The dialogue takes place in Cecil's chamber at Windsor Castle, to which they had retired, like the characters in Boccaccio's *Decameron*, to escape the plague (then raging in London). At dinner they learned of the flight of some pupils from Eton for fear of beating, and began to speak about methods of education, Ascham himself arguing that 'young children were sooner allured by love, than driven by beating, to attain good learning'.

This dialogue led to a second conversation, between Sackville and Ascham alone, discussing, among other matters, 'the common going of Englishmen into Italy', and culminating in Sackville's request to Ascham to write a book about 'the bringing up of youth'. The book which follows includes reflections about courts, grace, the importance of learning for nobles, François I of France, the dangers of travel in Italy, and the value of Castiglione's book. However, the *Schoolmaster* itself took the impersonal form of a treatise. Perhaps Ascham, a Protestant of the more severe kind, rejected the dialogue form as too playful.[11]

In fact a similar adaptation of the *Courtier* to an academic environment had already been attempted in Spain, though Ascham could hardly have known this. It was probably in the 1550s that the humanist Cristóbal de Villalón wrote a dialogue on education which remained unpublished until our own century.[12] *El scholástico*, as it is called, is concerned to paint a picture of an

11 Ascham (1568).
12 Villalón (1911, 1967); cf. Bataillon (1939), vol. II, 266–71; Kerr (1955); Kincaid (1973).

1 Raphael's image of Castiglione

2 Rubens's image of Raphael's image

3 Rembrandt's free version of Raphael's image

BALDASAR CONTE DE CASTILLION DETTO IL CORTEGGIANO

Qui vedi il Balthasaro Castiglione,   Ritratto se del suo Paësano,   Reg.-Persinius
Che l'arte di corte rese si fino;   Per l'haver intero dopò la morte;   sculptor fecit
ch' al mondo visse senza paragone;   Lo spirito, da lui nel corteggiano;
pero quel grand' Raphaelo d'Vrbino   La vista al vivo, di questa altra sorte.

ILLVSTRISSIMO DÑO ALPHONSO DE LOPEZ REGI CHRISTIANISSIMO A CONSILYS EQVITI
ORDINIS SANCTI MICHAELIS, AC REGII PALATII MAGISTRO L.M.Q.D.D. Ioachimus Sandrart.
Ioachimus Sandrart del: et exc. Amsterd: RAPHAEL VRBINAS Pinx.   in ædibus Alph. Lopez.

4 Castiglione at third hand: a copy of a copy of the Raphael

COMES

BALTHASSAR CASTILIONIUS

E TABULA RAPHAEL. URBINATIS
IN ROMANO INSIGNI MUSEO
CARDINALIS VALENTI.

alt.p. 2. unc. 4 ½.   *lat. p. 1. unc. 10.*

Jo: a Plano del.   Venetiis   Jos: Daniotto sculps.

5 Anonymous engraving after Raphael's portrait

BALDASSAR CASTIGLIONE
Conte di Castiglione & Nuvolara &c.

6 Castiglione as an eighteenth-century gentleman

7 Drawing of the court of Urbino

8 Engraving of the court of Urbino

'academic republic', in other words to describe the ideal student and the ideal teacher at the university. The dialogue is set at the University of Salamanca and in a garden nearby belonging to the duke of Alba, and it takes the form of a discussion between the rector of the university and nine of the teachers there, including the celebrated scholar Hernán Pérez de Oliva. As in the case of the *Courtier*, the discussion takes four days, described in four books and it is placed, somewhat nostalgically, in the past (in 1528, a date presumably chosen in homage to Castiglione).

The main subject of *El scholástico* is the university curriculum, including topical, controversial issues such as the place of magic and the role of the pagan classics, but the speakers gradually go beyond academic concerns and so move closer to the discussions at Urbino. The themes of the fourth book include the virtues and failings of women and their place, like that of love, in the life of a scholar; the relevance of music, painting, architecture and other arts (stressing their prestige in antiquity); and the ways to speak and act in different social situations, combining gravity with grace. The book ends with the speakers telling funny stories.

Villalón felt the need to rebut the charge of plagiarism. 'Some people who have already seen our book', he wrote in his prologue, 'have criticized it by saying that I followed Count Baldassare Castiglione's *Courtier* so closely that I virtually translated it.' He defended himself by pointing to the similarity of their aims and to their use of the same classical sources (especially Plato and Cicero). 'However, if anyone who has seen the works of these wise men still thinks that I preferred to imitate Count Baldassare Castiglione, I have no objection, since . . . he is one of the wisest men of whom learned Italy may worthily be proud.'[13]

El scholástico is not a great work of literature, and it lacks Castiglione's lightness of touch, but the dialogue does have a certain charm and it was a loss to sixteenth-century readers that it was not published in their day, doubtless because of the Erasmian opinions expressed by some of the characters, the description of Plato as 'divine' and Seneca as 'religious', and above all the criticism of Christians who are 'so delicate in their faith' that they

---

13 Villalón (1911). This passage is missing from the manuscript used as the basis for the 1967 edition; cf. Kerr (1955).

reject Greek and Latin literature as pagan.[14] As the fate of the *Decameron* during the Counter-Reformation demonstrated (below, pp. 102–3), the Inquisition was always peculiarly sensitive to reflections on itself. Readers in Renaissance Spain had to make do with Lorencio Palmireno's *El estudioso cortesano* (1573), which includes aphorisms summing up the qualities of a good teacher and hints for readers to shine in conversation, but cannot rival Villalón, let alone Castiglione, in either its form or its content.

Portraits of the Court

Since one of the aims of this essay is to explore the changing values of the nobility of early modern Europe, attention should be focused on a number of attempts to describe the ideal member of the ruling class, descriptions produced outside Italy by authors who are extremely likely to have been familiar with Castiglione's work. Sir Thomas Elyot's *Book of the Governor* (1531) is one well-known example of this genre. Another is 'The Ideal Senator' (1568), by Wawrzyniec Goślicki, or – as he described himself in Latin – Laurentius Grimalius Goslicius.

In Poland as in England the monarchy was a constitutional one, and the nobility and gentry were proud of their independence. This gave to both treatises a bias very different from Renaissance works on courts and courtiers. Thus Elyot chose to describe the education of a member of the class of 'inferior governors' or 'magistrates', in other words of 'a gentleman, which is to have authority in a public weal', whether as a Justice of the Peace or a Member of Parliament. His emphasis on the need to study history and law follows from this choice.[15] In similar fashion, Gabriel Harvey added 'civil law' to Hoby's summary of the chief qualities of the courtier.[16] Goślicki too stressed the study of history and law, and the need to speak persuasively in the Polish 'senate'. He claimed to be practical, unlike Cicero, Plato and Xenophon – an indirect way of declaring his distance from the *Courtier*, since

14 Villalón (1967), 145, 152.
15 Elyot (1531), book I, chs 3–4.
16 Ruutz-Rees (1910), 628.

these were the very classical authors whom Castiglione had claimed to follow.

In the case of Elyot, who knew Thomas Cromwell and may well have learned of the *Courtier* through him as early as 1530, the most striking parallel between the two texts is Elyot's suggestion that a young nobleman should study not only music but also the visual arts, 'if nature do thereto induce him', though without turning into 'a common painter or carver'.[17] Elyot's defensiveness underlines the fact that this suggestion was unusual in Henry VIII's England.

As for Goślicki, he was one of a substantial number of Polish nobles who had completed their education at the university of Padua before embarking on a career in public life (in his case, like that of Castiglione, as a diplomat and a bishop). His treatise had nothing to say about the visual arts. Indeed his remarks on the study of music and gymnastics and on the physical beauty of his ideal senator stand out as exceptions in a treatise which generally preferred gravity to grace and the virtues of the Venetian republic to those of princely courts. In a country where magnates still maintained private armies and where life on the frontier of Christendom encouraged the more bellicose virtues, the author's enthusiasm for Venice must have come as something of a surprise to his noble readers. In fact, Goślicki appears to have been the spokesman for a group of Polish nobles who believed that more power should be given to the senate.[18]

Turning to the books concerned with life at court, we are confronted with such an embarrassment of riches that it is difficult to know which texts to choose. They do not always take the form of treatises or dialogues. For example, 'The Perfect Gentleman' (1620) by Alonso Jerónimo de Salas Barbadillo is a novel in which the hero is characterized by his 'careful negligence' (*descuido cuidadoso*).[19] Again, following the tradition of the Italian parlour-game (above, pp. 45–6), the 'Philosophy of the Court' (1587) by the Spaniard Alonso Barros tells its readers how to play a board game played with dice – rather like the twentieth-century game of

17 Elyot (1531), book I, ch. 8. Cf. Woodward (1906), 292; Major (1964), 60–76; Hogrefe (1967), 118, 129, 138–9, 149–50, 152.
18 Goślicki (1568), 28, 75; Bałuk-Ulewiczowa (1988).
19 Salas (1620); cf. Brownstein (1974), ch. 3.

snakes and ladders – in which the sixty-three squares represent the stages in the career of a courtier, who enters by the gate of reputation, labours, climbs, returns to zero on the death of his patron, and so on.[20]

Barros includes an inventory of the means to succeed (liberality, adulation, diligence and work) as well as of the dangers ('false friendship', poverty, 'the well of forgetfulness', and so on). There is nothing in this game which could not have been derived from a hundred books on courts. All the same, Barros is known to have owned the *Courtier*, and one might say that he simply makes explicit and formal the idea of the 'rules' of the 'game' which was more or less implicit in Castiglione's dialogue.[21]

The texts to be discussed in more detail below have been chosen because they engage explicitly with Castiglione in a way that Barros does not. Even this criterion gives us a considerable range of texts to choose from. For example, 'The Prince, Counsellor, Courtier' (1599), by the German writer Hippolytus a Collibus, drew on Castiglione in his discussion of nobility, costume and other topics.[22] Again, an essay by a French nobleman Louis Guyon 'Of the Courtier, and how he should behave' (1604) offered little more than a ten-page summary of the first book of the *Courtier* (noble birth, skill in arms, dancing, playing and singing, wearing black or dark clothes and so on) finally paying his debt with a reference to 'Baltazar Castillonnois'.[23] By contrast another French nobleman, Thomas Pelletier, writing ten years earlier, stressed the differences between the Italian and the French styles of behaviour, taking his distance from the court and the city and placing more stress on manliness and on practical matters, rejecting lute-playing for instance, and recommending drawing only for military reasons.[24]

Still closer to Castiglione was the Cambridge don Gabriel Harvey. Harvey published two Latin poems in 1578, one concerned with the ideal courtier and the other with the court lady, introducing them with the bold claim:

20 After a 400-year interval, Dr Trevor Dadson is preparing to launch this game again.
21 Barros (1587); cf. Wilson (1964–8); Dadson (1987), nos 98, 130.
22 Collibus (1599), 310, 345, 346.
23 Guyon (1604), 192–202.
24 Pelletier (1594), 62, 64, 88–9, 96.

Let Castiglione claim the first place; Casa the second
The third place is Guazzo's; the fourth is about to be mine.[25]

As might have been expected from the comments quoted in the previous chapter, Harvey followed his model's recommendations closely, from painting and music to grace (*gratia*) and the impression of effortlessness (*Ars casus videatur*). He made only minimal attempts to adapt the ideal to English realities (notably in the case of ladies, who are told to read Chaucer, Surrey and Gascoigne as well as Petrarch and Bembo). Indeed, Harvey described his ideal precisely as 'Castiglione's Courtier' (*Castilionaeus Aulicus*).

At this point it may be useful to concentrate attention on four texts, each from a different culture, respectively Spanish, Polish, Portuguese and French, which not only take Castiglione as a model but adapt him to local circumstances. These texts are, in chronological order, *El cortesano* (1561), *Dworzanin polski* (1566), *Côrte na aldeia* (1619), and *L'honnête homme* (1630).

Luis Milán (*c.*1500–*c.*1561) is probably best known today for his music for the *vihuela de mano* (the ancestor of the guitar), but he also deserves to be remembered for his dialogue *El cortesano*, set in Valencia among the ladies and gentlemen of the court of Queen Germana and her husband the duke of Calabria, including the author himself and his friend the poet Juan Fernández de Heredia, the court jester 'Gilot' and a number of ladies – Doña Francisca, Doña Mencía, and the long-suffering wife of Juan Fernández, Doña Hierónima.[26]

As in the *Courtier*, the dialogue is set in the recent past, in this case in the 1530s. The conversations, which are spread over six days, form the framework for an anthology of anecdotes, jokes, songs, proverbs, and descriptions of clothes, festivals and *imprese*.

Luis Milán reveals himself to be a disciple of 'Count Baldasar Castellon', as he calls him. In his prologue, he explains that the idea of writing the book was suggested to him by 'certain ladies of Valencia', whom he saw with Castiglione's book 'in their hands'. On the first day of the dialogue, the duke and his knights discuss the rules for courtly behaviour (like Boscán, they use the word *cortesanía*). These rules include 'knowing how to speak and be

25 Harvey (1578), book IV, 17; translation in Barnett (1945), 148.
26 Milán (1561); Trend (1925).

silent' in the appropriate places and times, for example, or how to combine gravity with graceful wit (*agudeza muy graciosa*).

However, Milán's book lacks a central story or argument of the kind which gives unity to Castiglione's work. What is more, *El cortesano* has virtually nothing to do with classical antiquity. The references to Achilles, Hector, Andromache, Hecuba and others present them as knights and ladies in a romance about 'the matter of Troy'. Achilles, for example, guards a spring against all comers. The text draws on, exemplifies and celebrates medieval traditions, notably those of knights errant, heralds, hunting, tournaments and courtly love. There can be no doubt that the author was writing with Castiglione in mind, yet what he produced was very different from the *Courtier*. Generally speaking, Milán is attracted to precisely what was most traditional in his model. What he exemplifies more clearly than usual is a view of Castiglione through late medieval spectacles.

A less traditional reading of the text, but also one which vividly illustrates the cultural differences between different parts of Renaissance Europe, is that offered by Łukasz Górnicki in his 'Polish Courtier' (*Dworzanin polski*), published five years later, in 1566. Górnicki, like Goślicki, had studied at the University of Padua before returning to serve the king, Zygmunt II August, to whom his book was dedicated.[27] The king, whose mother was an Italian princess, Bona Sforza, was well known for his interest in the arts.

The 'Polish Courtier' both is and is not a translation of the book which Castiglione, as Górnicki puts it, 'wrote with wisdom, learning and great eloquence'. It might be better to describe it as a 'transposition' of the original text. The dialogue was literally transposed in the sense that the scene was transferred from Urbino to Pradnik, a villa near Cracow which had belonged to Górnicki's former patron, Samuel Maciejowski, bishop of Cracow and chancellor of Poland, who had died in 1550 (like the dialogues of Villalón and Milán, as well as Castiglione himself, the 'Polish Courtier' was set in the past). The speakers are nine Polish nobles, including several who had studied at the University of Padua – Jan Dersniak, Andrzej Kostka, and Wojciech Kryski, who was

27 Górnicki (1566), i–cxxvi; cf. Löwenfeld (1884); Welsh (1963).

described by a contemporary as 'an extremely urbane and extremely erudite man' (*homo perurbanus et pereruditus*).[28]

This kind of transposition is not uncommon in the Renaissance. For example, when Gianbattista Giraldi's dialogues on civil life were adapted into English by the poet Ludovick Bryskett, the scene was shifted from Italy to the author's 'cottage' near Dublin, and the characters metamorphosed into a circle of Bryskett's friends (including Edmund Spenser).[29]

In the case of Górnicki, it was not only the setting of Castiglione's dialogue which was naturalized in this way, but its content as well. The book is of particular relevance to a study of the reception of the Renaissance because its author was so well aware of the problems of adapting to the Polish environment a book so rooted in its Italian milieu. Indeed, he began his book with the observation that 'Groph Balcer Kastiglio', as he calls him, wrote for people 'whose customs are far removed from ours'.[30]

Thus Górnicki declared his intention of leaving out Castiglione's discussion of painting and sculpture (though Apelles does make an appearance later in the book), explaining the omission with the disarming remark that 'we don't know about this here' (*u nas nie znają*).[31] Again, the discussion of music was rejected because Polish nobles did not play musical instruments (there is a reference to lute-playing later in the text, but in Hungary).[32] Górnicki also pointed out that masks were not worn in Poland and that gentlemen did not serve married ladies, as was the Italian custom, so further changes in the text were required.

Still more significant was the omission of the female characters, who had, as we have seen, a significant if unobtrusive role to play in the original text. They disappeared from the 'Polish Courtier' because in Poland, again according to Górnicki, ladies were not learned enough to take part in this kind of discussion. In any case, their presence might well have been considered inappropriate at the court of a bishop of the Counter-Reformation – for the Council of Trent was in session in 1550 and concluded its deliberations

28 Górnicki (1566), lxxix–xciv; cf. Damiani (1929).
29 Bryskett (1606).
30 Górnicki (1566), 8.
31 Górnicki (1566), 8, 74.
32 Górnicki (1566), 198.

in 1563, three years before Górnicki published his book. In similar fashion, the 'Polish Courtier' omitted some of the jokes at the expense of the clergy to be found in the Italian original.

The departure of the ladies naturally led to other changes in the dialogue. The place of the duchess and her lieutenant Lady Emilia as *animatrices* was taken by the bishop himself. Their absence did not prevent Kostka and Myszkowski from introducing the subject of the 'court lady' (*dworna pani*) in book III, although, unlike her Italian model, the Polish lady was discouraged from dancing and recommended to be humble. On the other hand, the misogyny of Count Gasparo Pallavicino naturally became superfluous. Into his place stepped Stanislaw Lupa Podlodowski, an unashamed defender of the good old days when Poles were more concerned with fighting than with writing, and a sharp critic of people like Kryski who praise everything that is Italian. Podlodowski's interventions offer comic relief, while giving Górnicki another opportunity to express views about the process of imitation and reception.[33]

In order to add local colour, the frequent references to the Spaniards and the French in Castiglione's book were replaced by allusions to Hungarians, Cossacks, Muscovites and Tartars. The language question, which was, as we have seen, so important as well as so topical a theme in the *Courtier*, was transformed from a debate on the best form of Italian into a discussion of the various languages from which writers in Polish might borrow, notably Latin, Czech, Croat and Old Church Slavonic (though Bulgarian and Turkish were also considered).[34]

Among the elements which survived the transposition, it may be worth mentioning Bembo's speech on creation and the cosmos (which is given to Kryski), the discussion of wit (*dowcip*), and the definition of grace (*gracyja*, a term borrowed from Italian), and *sprezzatura* (rendered as *niecudna*, literally 'not wonderful'). Given Castiglione's own views on the subject of imitation, we may perhaps be allowed to conclude that Górnicki was more faithful to his original than mere translators like Hoby and Clerke precisely because he was less faithful to the letter of the text. All the same,

33 Górnicki (1566), 25ff, 97–8.
34 Górnicki (1566), 80ff.

the differences between the two texts do reveal a great deal about the cultural distance between Poland and Italy in the sixteenth century. So does the reception of the Polish text; it is a classic today, but it had no second edition in the sixteenth century. Perhaps the Podlodowskis of this world were in the majority.

It may be illuminating to juxtapose this effectively original work which claims to be a translation to an example of the reverse. Nicolas Faret's *Honnête homme* first appeared in print in 1630. It was not a dialogue but a treatise on 'the art of pleasing at court'. It made no reference to the *Courtier*, but stole from it with both hands. Faret was clearly a master of the art of scissors and paste.[35] The discussion of grace shows Faret's dependence on his source with particular clarity. The ideal recommended to his readers was 'a certain natural grace . . . beyond the reach of art' (*une certaine grace naturelle . . . au dessus des preceptes de l'art*), rejecting 'the affectation of negligence' (*la negligence affectée*) but praising *nonchalance* – in other words, *sprezzatura*.[36]

It is not easy to reach a balanced verdict on this book. It is a literary equivalent of Ludwig Wittgenstein's famous image of the 'duck-rabbit', in other words an image which can be perceived in two very different ways. As the reception theorists say, what matters is the 'horizon of expectation'. If one approaches the *Honnête homme* expecting an original work, it immediately looks like pure plagiarism. On the other hand, if one treats it as a translation, then its freedom quickly becomes apparent. In the first place, unlike Milán and Górnicki, Faret suppresses the dialogic element in his model, thus flattening the text. In the second place, he takes something from later writers on good behaviour, notably Della Casa, Guazzo on conversation, and Montaigne on the education of children – the critique of pedantry, for example.[37]

Faret passed quickly over some sections of the *Courtier*, including those dealing with music and painting, as if in France, like Elyot's England a century earlier, this interest was considered inappropriate for a gentleman.[38] In compensation, he amplified other sections, including the discussion of poetry, of boasters, of

35 Quondam (1980), 29.
36 Faret (1630), 18–20.
37 Faret (1630), 24, 66n., 67n.
38 Faret (1630), 31.

princes and of religion, presumably in response to what he perceived as the deficiencies of the original text. Faret presented the prince as the 'heart and soul' of the 'state' (a term not to be found in the *Courtier*), and he appears to have shared the French moral panic of the 1630s in which orthodox writers denounced what he calls the 'abominable', 'new' and 'arrogant sect' of atheists.[39]

As in the case of Górnicki, a comparison between the disciple and the master reveals something of the cultural distance between Italy and other parts of Europe, as well as something of the cultural changes which took place after 1528; notably the Counter-Reformation and the rise of absolute monarchy. Faret was writing in the age of Louis XIII and Richelieu, when nobles were increasingly expected to serve the state as well as ornament the court (below, pp. 119–20).

Further from the letter of the *Courtier* but closer to the spirit of Castiglione is the last of our four cases, 'Court in the Village and Winter Nights' (*Côrte na aldeia e noites de inverno*) published in 1619 by Francisco Rodrigues Lôbo, a nobleman in the circle of the duke of Bragança, later King João IV of Portugal.[40] The reason for the title was a political one, the court being imagined as in rural retirement after the king of Spain had taken over Portugal. In sixteen nights the five main characters discuss a variety of literary and social topics, beginning with the value and the dangers of romances of chivalry, and moving on to the etiquette of visiting, correct forms of speech, the twin arts of love and letter-writing, the composition of *imprese* (especially their mottoes), the nature of courtesy, different ways of responding wittily when the occasion requires it, and even the art of dialogue itself.

The conception and some of the themes were clearly inspired by the *Courtier*; *cortesanía*, for instance, grace, and also the language question, in which Portuguese is described as possessing the best qualities of Latin, Greek, Spanish, French and Italian. Like Faret, however, Rodrigues Lôbo also drew on more recent writers on behaviour, such as Della Casa and Guazzo. He also returned to Castiglione's own classical models, not only Plato, Xenophon and

39 Faret (1630), 32, 36.
40 Rodrigues Lôbo (1618); cf. Schnerr (1961) and Preto-Rodas (1971).

Cicero, who were cited together in the first dialogue, but also Horace, Quintilian and Seneca. Indeed, his discussion of grace and urbanity (*graça, urbanidade*) is closer to Cicero, Quintilian and their rhetorical context than it is to Castiglione himself.

In certain respects, 'The Court in the Village' appears to reflect the preoccupations of the author's place and time more than those of its 'original'. The value of romances of chivalry was debated all over Europe, but the debate seems to have been particularly intense in the Iberian peninsula, as the example of Luis Milán – not to mention Cervantes – may remind us. Again, the formalities of visiting and letter-writing seem to have been taken more seriously in the early seventeenth century than they were in Castiglione's own time, 100 years earlier.

What Rodrigues Lôbo imitated with considerable success was not so much specific details in the *Courtier* as its manner, its lightness of touch and especially its art of presenting a case in the form of an argument between two contrasted characters who impress the reader as individuals – Leonardo, the host and moderator; Lívio, the scholar; the humorous and critical Solino, and so on. Castiglione would surely have appreciated this dialogue as a creative and graceful imitation in the manner of his own dealings with Cicero.

Exemplary Lives

It would be odd to confine our discussion of the imitation of the *Courtier* to texts alone. Difficult as it must be for a historian to answer such a question, we must at least ask whether Castiglione's dialogue had any effects on social behaviour in his century. One way to approach the problem a little more closely might be to examine the lives of a few individuals who were described as exemplary by their friends or acquaintances – as Castiglione had himself been described in his day or soon afterwards. I shall not be arguing that these individuals were inspired to change their behaviour by reading Castiglione's text. The point is rather to suggest that they were perceived as exemplary because there was some kind of fit between their public behaviour and the recommendations made by characters in the dialogue. Hence these individuals can tell us something of value about the responses of other readers as well as their own.

To begin with the *donna di palazzo*. In the two volumes of verses published to commemorate her early death, a young noble-woman from Friuli, Irene di Spilimbergo, was presented by her admirers not only as a constant reader of the *Courtier* but also as someone who took its advice to heart and was actively interested in poetry, painting and music.[41] In England, on the other hand, learned ladies were encouraged to have rather different interests. The daughters of Sir Thomas More were taught Latin, Greek, mathematics and astronomy. The daughters of Sir Anthony Cooke learned Latin, Greek and Hebrew.[42] So did Lady Jane Grey, who knew the ancient languages well enough to read Plato's *Phaedo* in Greek and to scratch a Latin verse on her prison wall. All these examples give the impression of a certain cultural distance be-tween Tudor England and Castiglione's Italy, an impression con-firmed, as we have seen, by men such as Ascham and Hoby. English high culture appears to have been more serious, more pragmatic and more pious.

Let us turn to male exemplars of virtue. In the Iberian pensinsula, for example, Garcilaso de la Vega combined, and was seen to combine, distinction in letters with distinction in arms in the way recommended by Count Lodovico da Canossa in the first book of Castiglione's dialogue. In Tudor and Stuart England, at least four gentlemen were described by their contemporaries as incarnations of Castiglione's ideal.

Sir John Luttrell of Dunster in Somerset was described in a passage already quoted, as a man 'such . . . as Count Balthazar the Italian in his book of Courtier doth frame'.[43] Knighted in 1544, Luttrell served as a soldier in France and Scotland before his early death from the sweating-sickness. Little is known about him apart from the fact that he was a client of Thomas Cromwell (who owned a copy of the *Courtier*), and that he was portrayed waist-deep in water to illustrate the stoic maxim that 'Like as a rock amidst the raging seas/The constant heart no danger knows nor

41 Atanagi (1561), preface; cf. Schutte (1991).
42 Warnicke (1988), 46-7.
43 Patten (1548), H vii recto.

fears.' What Luttrell did to deserve the comparison with the ideal courtier remains unclear.[44]

A few years later, it was the turn of John Astley to be described in a poem, by the Italian exile Pietro Bizzarri, as 'the only courtier on Castiglione's model' (*solus est ille Aulicus . . . qualem Castilio praecepit*). Gabriel Harvey echoed this verdict, writing that he was not surprised that 'Pietro Bizzaro, a learned Italian, proposeth him for a perfect pattern of Castilio's *Courtier*.' As in the case of Luttrell, posterity is in no position to judge. Virtually all that is known of Astley is that he was Master of the Queen's Jewel House and the author of a book on the art of riding, published in 1584. His example reinforces the underlining by some readers of the remarks in the *Courtier* on riding. Astley must have demonstrated *sprezzatura* in the saddle.[45]

There is no such difficulty in the case of Sir Philip Sidney, who has been described as 'a thorough disciple of Castiglione' or even 'Castiglione's courtier made flesh'.[46] The parallel goes back to Gabriel Harvey, whose Latin praises of Sidney as a courtier were printed with his poem *Castilio*. It was reinforced by Thomas Nashe, who reported a conversation about Castiglione's ideal culminating in the statement that 'England afforded many mediocrities, but never saw anything more singular than worthy Sir Philip Sidney, of whom it might truly be said, *Arma virumque cano*.'[47] Again, the biography of Sir Philip by his friend Fulke Greville presented him as 'a true model of worth' and stressed his 'native courtesy'.[48]

Thomas Howard (1585–1646), fourteenth earl of Arundel, was once described by his librarian, the Dutch scholar Franciscus Junius, as the 'epitome' of Castiglione's *Courtier*.[49] Arundel was a *virtuoso* who travelled in Italy and collected classical statues and Renaissance paintings (including thirteen attributed to Raphael). As tutor to his sons he engaged Henry Peacham, the future author of *The English Gentleman*.

---

44 Maxwell Lyte (1909), 141–65; cf. DNB, s.v. 'Luttrell'.
45 Ruutz-Rees (1910), 614, 616; Firpo (1971), 39. Cf. DNB, s.v. 'Astley'.
46 Myrick (1935), 26; Buxton (1954), 37.
47 Harvey (1578), book IV, 17; Nashe (1589).
48 Greville (1907), 33, 35, 154.
49 Taylor (1948), 225, with an incorrect reference.

To these four examples it is worth adding that of Sir Henry Killigrew, who died in 1603. Killigrew, a Cornish gentleman, made the acquaintance of Thomas Hoby in Italy in his youth.[50] Like Hoby, he married into the Cooke family of learned ladies, and like him, served as a diplomat, which gave him occasion to present a copy of the *Courtier*, in Hoby's translation, to Mary Queen of Scots. Killigrew was remembered in the seventeenth century as an example of the 'complete gentleman', a student of history, geography, fortification, and a man skilled in riding, shooting, music and painting. In the case of painting, he was 'a Dürer for proportion, a Goltzius for a bold touch, an Angelo for his happy fancy, and an Holbein for oil works'.[51] If contemporaries did not compare him to Castiglione's ideal courtier, they surely should have done so.

It should not be assumed, however, that all readers of the *Courtier* led exemplary lives. Several of the people listed in appendix 2 came to an abrupt end. Giovanni Francesco Valier and William Thomas were both executed for treason, while Thomas had earlier been forced to flee the country on an embezzlement charge.

So much for various forms of enthusiasm. It is time to turn to some cooler responses to Castiglione and his book.

50 Hoby (1902); cf. Miller (1963), 13–14.
51 Lloyd (1665), 585–6.

6

The Courtier *Criticized*

————————◦◦◦◦◦◦◦◦◦◆◦◦◦◦◦◦◦◦◦————————

H istorians are becoming increasingly aware of the danger of presenting past cultures as homogeneous, and consequently of the need to tell their stories from multiple viewpoints. In the case of Castiglione, we need to remember that his reception was not always a warm one. Indeed, on occasion it was positively frosty. The purpose of this chapter is therefore to describe the cool reception and to try to explain why a book which evoked such enthusiasm in some of its readers should have irritated and provoked others. As in the case of the imitations, it is difficult to know where to stop and to decide whom to exclude. Many writers may or may not be alluding to Castiglione's dialogue in the course of more general attacks on the court, but only a hard core of denunciations focus on his text or mention the author by name.

The *Courtier* Censored

One might reasonably begin this account with Castiglione's self-censorship. Comparisons between the different drafts of the text show the author modifying passages which might give offence in the spiritual climate of the 1520s, when the Luther affair gave a different meaning to mockery of the clergy.[1] Some of Castiglione's

1 Guidi (1982), 111.

friends went further. When Jacopo Sadoleto, for instance, came to publish his treatise on education in 1533, he felt the need to criticize 'simulation' and to insist on moderation in music and dancing, as if he thought that the *Courtier* had gone too far in these directions.[2]

Criticism was followed by censorship. The years which followed 1528 were not exactly a placid time for booksellers and publishers in Italy or elsewhere. The Protestant reformers relied on print to spread their message, and the Catholic Church riposted by attempting to control printing by means of the Inquisition and *Indices of Prohibited Books*: catalogues – or should one say 'anti-catalogues'? – of works and authors which the faithful were forbidden to read. The Council of Trent approved a general *Index* of this kind which was issued in 1564 and was binding on the whole Church. Three kinds of book were prohibited – heretical books, like the works of Luther; immoral books, like the works of Machiavelli and Aretino; and works dealing with magic. The Tridentine Index, which was regularly revised and brought up to date, also distinguished between authors and works which were prohibited altogether and works banned only 'until they were corrected', in other words expurgated.[3]

In Venice, for example, booksellers began to be interrogated by inquisitors on charges of smuggling heretical books from abroad. Printers such as Gabriel Giolito, who had profited from Castiglione in the past, now began to shift their investments from secular to religious works. The *Courtier* and books like it could not escape these developments. Take the case of the professional writer Ludovico Domenichi, who worked for Giolito. In 1549, as we have seen (p. 50), he published a book on the 'Nobility of Ladies', which paraphrased the arguments put forward in the third book of the *Courtier*. In 1564, however, in a book entitled the 'Court Lady', Domenichi changed his mind in certain important respects. Although he still agreed with Castiglione that a court lady needs to be affable, the main point he now made was that 'the virtues of courtiers are not suitable for ladies'. He also condemned discussions of love between ladies and gentlemen.[4]

2 Sadoleto (1737).
3 Rotondò (1973).
4 Domenichi (1564), 3, 9.

In similar fashion the Polish adaptation of the *Courtier*, discussed in the previous chapter, published in 1566 and set at the court of a bishop, announced at the start that 'lascivious' matters would be omitted.[5] In these two books, published shortly after the conclusion of the Council of Trent in 1563, we can sense the chillier atmosphere of the Counter-Reformation. Censorship of the original text could not be far away.

Curiously enough, the story of this censorship of the *Courtier* begins in England. In the first edition of the Hoby translation, in 1561, the printer, William Seres, informed readers that the book should have been published much earlier. However, 'there were certain places in it which of late years being misliked by some, that had the perusing of it (with what reason judge thou), the author thought it much better to keep it in darkness a while, than to put it in light unperfect and in piecemeal to serve the time.' These somewhat cryptic remarks have been decoded as references to the censors of the press in the reign of Queen Mary, who if she was not more Catholic than the pope, at least anticipated papal policy in this respect by several decades.[6]

For it was only in 1576 that Count Camillo Castiglione, Baldassare's son, was warned by the Roman censors of the need to expurgate the book. The duke of Urbino, who was honour-bound to defend a book which glorified his predecessors, wrote to Rome in its favour, but he was unable to prevent the preparation of an emended edition, which was first published in 1584.[7] Meanwhile, the authorities in Parma had banned the *Courtier* in 1580.[8]

It is not easy to interpret the text as heretical, immoral or magical. So why should good Catholics have been forbidden to read it? The prohibition becomes a little easier to understand when we discover that a leading Jesuit intellectual, Antonio Possevino, discussing the 'stratagems of Satan', included among them Ariosto's *Orlando Furioso*, Boccaccio's *Decameron* and Montalvo's *Amadís de Gaula*.[9] What disturbed the authorities becomes still more clear if we look at the edition of 1584, 'revised

5 Górnicki (1566), 12.
6 Raleigh (1900), xxxvi.
7 Cian (1887); Guidi (1983), 162–82. Coseriu (1987) adds little to its predecessors.
8 Reusch (1886), 581.
9 Possevino (1593), 113.

and corrected' by the theologian Antonio Ciccarelli, best known for the publication of discourses on Livy in reply to those of Machiavelli.[10] His dedication – to the duke of Urbino, doubtless to mollify him – stressed the fact that Castiglione, 'that most virtuous gentleman', did not mean to write anything scandalous, but went on to suggest that 'contrary to the intention' of the author, the text may have given occasion to others to be disrespectful of the Church, so that anything 'which might stain its purity' had been emended.

Most of the changes made by Ciccarelli were small but revealing. The word 'fortune', for example, was deleted (Montaigne too was criticized by a Roman censor in the 1580s for his use of that pagan term). Theological metaphors used in secular contexts were replaced. In the dedication, for example, the reference to the 'divine' virtue of Vittoria Colonna was turned into 'lofty and rare'. The astrological term 'influence' was deleted. References to the clergy were removed from the funny stories in book II. In the story of a practical joke played on a man who vowed a pair of silver eyes to the Virgin of Loreto if he was cured from his – imaginary – blindness, the word 'vow' was deleted, like references to confession and sacrilege elsewhere.

Among the longer passages of the *Courtier* to be blue-pencilled was a joke reflecting on Pope Alexander VI (2.48); a joke which implied that cardinals are heretics (2.62); and a section denouncing the hypocrisy of friars (3.20). Bembo's speech about spiritual love also worried the censor. Apart from deleting a section equating beauty and goodness (4.57), and changing a reference to 'the most holy mysteries of love' into 'secrets of love', Ciccarelli added a marginal note declaring that 'the author was not expressing his own opinion but that of the Platonic school'. That the Church was becoming increasingly hostile to neoplatonism in the late sixteenth century, is suggested by the censorship of the work of the humanists Francesco Giorgi and Francesco Patrizzi in the 1570s and the 1590s respectively.[11]

The parallel to the expurgation of Boccaccio's *Decameron* is also a close one – and Ciccarelli did indeed excise from the

10 Cian (1887); Mattei (1967).
11 Rotondò (1982).

Courtier one remark about the *Decameron* (2.49). Boccaccio's stories might have been prohibited altogether by the Council of Trent if the duke of Florence, Cosimo de' Medici (honour-bound to protect one of 'his' writers, like the duke of Urbino in the case of Castiglione), had not sent an ambassador to the Council to beg for a reprieve. The stories reappeared in expurgated form only two years before Ciccarelli's *Courtier*, in 1582. One story, concerning the hypocrisy of an inquisitor, had disappeared entirely from the collection, while other stories which mocked the clergy suffered drastic revision. Terms like 'friar' and 'archangel' were removed, at the price of making one story completely meaningless – that of friar Alberto, who pretended to be the archangel Gabriel in order to seduce a pious Venetian lady. In short, the changes made to the *Decameron*, like those made to the *Courtier*, suggest a certain literal-mindedness on the part of the censors, together with a hypersensitivity to criticisms of the clergy.[12]

Four expurgated Italian editions of the dialogue were published between 1584 and 1606. The reader may be wondering about the many unexpurgated editions of the *Courtier* which were already in circulation in Italy in 1584. Officially, owners of such editions were supposed to take a pen and cross out or alter the offending passages. Some editions of the *Index* give instructions for do-it-yourself censorship of this kind, and copies of the *Courtier* survive which have been treated in this way. The British Library, for example, contains such a copy of the Florence 1531 edition, which belonged to a certain Rosati, Revisor to the Inquisition in Florence.[13] However, my inspection of sixty to seventy surviving copies of Italian editions of the *Courtier* suggests that the majority of owners were less diligent. The risk of discovery was probably not very high.

Somewhat more remarkable was the action of a Venetian printer, Domenico Giglio, in 1587. In that year he printed the *Courtier* unexpurgated, with a letter to the reader complaining about the text having been 'lacerated and spoiled' by men who were 'too delicate' or 'too scrupulous', and announcing his inten-

12 Cian (1887), 713; Sorrentino (1935); Brown (1967); Richardson (1994), 140–88.
13 BL, C.28.a.4.

tion to print an unexpurgated *Decameron* as well. Two years later, another Venetian printer, Tortis, published another unexpurgated version of the text, though without drawing as much attention to the fact as his colleague had done. If these printers were able to ignore Ciccarelli's revisions with impunity, it was probably because the *Courtier* was placed on the international Catholic *Index* only in 1590, in the reign of Sixtus V, 'with the exception of the emended edition, Venice 1584'.[14]

The dialogue was removed from the *Index* a few years later under Clement VIII, but returned in 1623, under Gregory XV, to remain officially prohibited for more than three hundred years – for the *Index* of 1948, which remained in force till 1966, still forbade the faithful to read any version but that of 1584.[15] By the eighteenth century, however, new editions were being produced in Italy which replaced what Ciccarelli had removed. This is the case for the edition of 1771, for instance, which, despite advertising its piety by printing DIO and CRISTO in capital letters, restored the jokes at the expense of cardinals and popes. The edition of 1822 did the same. In the school edition of 1842, the publisher criticized 'sacrilegious' expurgations of a classical text, and 'ridiculous' suppressions of such words as *divino* and *influsso*.

On the other hand, even the Italians were 'Victorian' enough in the nineteenth century to object to certain passages in the *Courtier* which appear not to have disturbed Ciccarelli. The 1831 edition, for instance, removed the quip about the sexual proclivities of the young men of Rome: 'Rome has as many catamites as a field has lambs' (2.61), while the 1842 edition rewrote the joke so as to make it anodyne. A theological-clerical censorship had been replaced by a moral one. The 1889 edition, describing itself as 'revised, expurgated and annotated for the use of schools', followed similar lines.

Sixteenth-century Spaniards was notoriously stricter than the pope where forbidden books were concerned. As early as 1534, Garcilaso de la Vega, in a letter prefaced to the Spanish translation, spoke of people with ears so 'tender' and 'delicate' that they would take offence at 'one or two' things in the book. He was

14 Reusch (1886), 471.
15 Reusch (1883–5), vol. I, 529.

absolutely right, though it took the critics some time to organize themselves. From 1573 till 1873, no edition of the *Courtier* was published in Spain.[16] In Lima in 1582, Fray Juan de Almaraz appeared before the tribunal of the Inquisition, *Courtier* in hand, to complain that the book contained 'many scandalous propositions' directed against cardinals and that it 'taught much liberty' (*enseña mucha libertad*), in other words, free-thinking.[17] The Grand Inquisitor Bernardo de Sandoval's *Index* of 1612 allowed only expurgated editions of Castiglione, whether in Spanish or Italian (thus offering additional evidence for the circulation of the Italian text abroad).[18]

Owners of earlier editions were supposed to correct them by hand, and detailed instructions for this purpose were printed in various editions of the *Index*. Notes written in individual copies tell the same story. For instance, a copy of the Antwerp edition of 1544 now in the Biblioteca Nacional of Madrid contains a note declaring that this copy was expurgated in 1613, while the Salamanca edition of 1540 is described as 'corrected and expurgated according to the new instructions' in 1614, and the 1542 edition as 'expurgated according to the catalogue of 1623'.[19] However, in the case of a copy of the Antwerp 1561 edition, ink lines were drawn around the passages which should have been expurgated, leaving them completely legible, like some of the jokes in a copy of the Valladolid edition of 1569.[20]

Górnicki's adaptation of 1566 was also a kind of expurgation (above, pp. 90–3), while the Boscán translation was revised in similar manner in 1569. An intriguing example of attempted censorship comes from the Netherlands at the time of the revolt against Spain. Huijch van Alckemade was a Protestant who was involved in the revolt of Leiden against Spanish domination, and went into exile. His goods were confiscated, including his books, of which an inventory was made in 1568. Some of these books

16 Darst (1978), 27.
17 Guibovich Pérez (1989), 41–2.
18 Reusch (1883–5), vol. I, 529; Cartwright (1908), vol. II, 443, claims that the book was already on the Spanish *Index* by 1576.
19 BNM, R.1092, R.10, 672, U.6575.
20 BNM, R.4267, R.7909. Opdycke calls the edition 'expurgated' as if the deletions had been made by the printer.

were burned, presumably the works of Protestant theology, while his copy of the *Courtier*, in French, was subject to 'expurgation' (*repurgatie*) by a Catholic, although the Church had not yet taken any action against the book.[21] However, the second German translation of 1593, published three years after the original version had been placed on the *Index*, still included the anticlerical and antipapal jokes.

From these corrections and attempts at correction there emerges an image of the *Courtier* as the devout perceived it in the sixteenth century, as a book which was fundamentally sound although it was marred by anticlerical remarks, stories in doubtful taste, and references to paganism which unsophisticated readers might interpret literally.

The Attack on the Court

Not all objections to the *Courtier* were made on religious grounds. Paolo Giovio's malicious observation that the middle-aged Castiglione dyed his hair in order to look young might be read as a critique of the art of self-presentation recommended in the text.[22] However, the most explicit secular critique of the book in the years immediately following its publication was surely that of Pietro Aretino.

Aretino was a cobbler's son from Arezzo who became famous as a writer of comic and satirical poems, plays, letters and dialogues. One of his plays, the *Courtesan*, published in 1534, presented a young man from the provinces who came to Rome to make his career as a courtier. His instructor gave him a book, and told him that a courtier needs to know how to blaspheme, to be a gambler, a frequenter of whores, a heretic, a flatterer, a brawler and a homosexual, as well as malicious, ignorant and envious of others' success (Act I, scene 22). Aretino was doing little more than utilize the anti-court tradition already discussed (p. 55), but the reference to an instruction-book raises the suspicion that Castiglione was among his targets.

21 Information from Frieda Heijkoop.
22 Giovio (1546), 47–8.

Suspicion becomes virtual certainty if we turn to Aretino's dialogues between courtesans, published in 1534 and 1536, which have been called 'a systematic demystification of the virtues praised and codified in the *Courtier*'.[23] When the experienced Nanna instructs her daughter Pippa in the tricks of her trade, she speaks at times like a conduct-book, giving instructions about table manners and about gestures such as extending the hand 'elegantly' (*galantamente*). She is even more explicit than Castiglione's speakers about the need to play a role. With some customers, it is necessary to praise the music 'even if you don't like it and don't understand it'. With others, it is always better to play dumb (*fa sempre la semplice e la babiona*).[24]

If the reader is not yet convinced that it was the *Courtier* (together with the writings of Castiglione's friend Bembo) which Aretino was parodying, he or she should turn to the dedication of the dialogue to Bernardo Valdaua, 'a royal example of courtesy'. In this dedication Aretino claimed to portray nature in writing as Titian does in paint – a passage maliciously echoing Castiglione's description of his book as a portrait of the court of Urbino in the style of Raphael or Titian.[25]

Alternatively, one may turn to the first dialogue, in which one courtesan described another as mocking everyone 'who does not speak according to rule' (*che non favella alla usanza*), who says *finestra* for 'window' instead of using the more elegant term *balcone*, and so on.[26] Today, this passage may well sound like an uncanny anticipation of the teacup-storm about 'U' and 'non-U' which disturbed certain circles in Britain in the 1950s. Its context in the 1530s, however, was the movement to reform spoken and written Italian. Here and elsewhere Aretino was mocking rules and models, whether they came from Plato or Cicero, from Petrarch or Bembo. His dialogues may be seen as a kind of anti-*Courtier*, echoing Castiglione only in order to send up his ideas.

In other quarters, especially Protestant ones, hostility to the neoplatonic elements in the *Courtier* was even stronger. There was no essential incompatibility between the book and some forms of

---

23 Larivaille (1980), 212; cf. Guidi (1985); Paternoster (1993).
24 Aretino (1534–6), 154, 163, 173.
25 Aretino (1534–6), 145–6.
26 Aretino (1534–6), 82.

Protestantism at least. Hoby translated it without qualms, and the Latin version was printed twice or three times at Wittenberg, the metropolis of the Lutheran Reformation. In Protestant cultures, however, especially Calvinist ones, Castiglione's book became increasingly vulnerable to moral criticism in the course of the century.

The rise of what might be called a 'culture of sincerity' is generally dated to the Romantic Movement, and there can be little doubt that in the early nineteenth century certain English poets, for instance, placed an unparalleled stress on what one of them, John Keats, called 'the true voice of feeling'. All the same, as the American critic Lionel Trilling showed a generation ago, the development of the ideal of sincerity goes back a good deal earlier, to the later sixteenth century if not before. According to the OED, the term 'sincerity' was in use by 1557 to describe speech, and by 1611 to describe feelings. Trilling was thinking of England, but his point might be extended to north-western Europe in general, to France, the Netherlands, Scandinavia and Protestant Germany.

The new ideal, which was both expressed and encouraged by the Reformation, placed increasing emphasis on inward feelings at the expense of 'mere' outward forms, rituals or performances, whether they took place in the theatre or on the stage of everyday life. Such a rejection of a 'culture of performance' is implicit – and occasionally explicit – in a number of Castiglione's Protestant critics.[27] Like some more enthusiastic readers, they interpreted the dialogue in a literal-minded way as a series of recommendations.

For example, the 'Courtier in Retirement', a poem by a French Calvinist nobleman, Jean de La Taille, published in 1573, made the speaker, an old and disillusioned man who has abandoned the court for the countryside, declare that he knows how to dissimulate and practise all that 'Chastillon' preaches in his 'feigned' *Courtier*, playing on the ambiguity between the ideas of a fictional text and a deceitful person.

> Je sais dissimuler, et sais bien mettre en oeuvre
> Tout ce que Baltazar Chastillon descoeuvre
> En son *Courtisan* feint.[28]

27 Trilling (1972), ch. 1.
28 La Taille (1878–82), vol. III, xxvii–xxviii. Cf. Daley (1934); Smith (1966), 164ff, 203ff.

The moral critique of dissimulation or hypocrisy sometimes fastened on the idea of *sprezzatura* in particular. George Pettie, for example, an Elizabethan writer who translated Guazzo on conversation, was careful to distance himself from those who 'think it most commendable in a gentleman, to cloak his art and skill in every thing and to seem to do all things of his own mother wit'. This was 'curiosity', in the sense of affectation.[29] In similar fashion, Philip Sidney's friend Fulke Greville rejected what he called 'that hypocritical figure Ironia', according to which men 'seem to make toys of the utmost they can do'.[30]

The poet Everard Guilpin, who had studied at Emmanuel College, Cambridge at a time when the college had a reputation as a nest of Puritans, took the *Courtier* as one of his targets in a collection of satires called *Skialetheia* (1598). He mocked a 'cavalier' in Spanish attire as 'The exact pattern which Castilio/Took for's accomplished Courtier'. Spain had of course a rather more sinister meaning for an Elizabethan Englishman than for an Italian of Castiglione's generation. Guilpin associated 'courtesy' with hypocrisy, with 'Signor Machiavell', with 'motley faced dissimulation', and in particular with empty promises. The precise reference to the recommendation of Spanish costume suggests that he had indeed examined the text rather than condemning it at second hand. However, the dark clouds of Protestant stereotypes are clearly visible on Guilpin's horizon of expectations.

> Come to the Court, and Baltazer affords
> Fountains of holy and rose-water words:
> Hast thou need of him? And wouldst find him kind?
> Nay then go by, the gentleman is blind.[31]

In similar fashion, and at much the same time, Guilpin's cousin, the poet and playwright John Marston took 'the absolute Castilio', as he called him, as a symbol of an empty-headed fop, all show and no substance.

> But oh! the absolute Castilio,
> He that can all the points of courtship show

29 Pettie (1576), preface.
30 Greville (1907), 154.
31 Guilpin (1598), 65, 86.

> He that can trot a courser . . .
> He that can purpose it in dainty rhymes . . .
> Tut, he is famous for his revelling,
> For fine set speeches, and for sonetting . . .
> Take ceremonious compliment from thee,
> Alas, I see Castilios beggary.[32]

Marston also included a courtier with the name of 'Castilio' in his play *Antonio and Mellida*.

The English stage was indeed invaded by fops at this time. Think for example of 'Baltasar', the attendant of Don Pedro in *Much Ado about Nothing*, and of the exaggerated modesty with which he declines to sing: 'Note this before my notes/There's not a note of mine that's worth the noting.' Baltasar's name is unlikely to have been chosen at random. Or think of 'Osric', the courtier who refuses to cover his head when speaking to a social superior, even when requested to do so, and is criticized by Prince Hamlet for his concern with the 'outward habit of encounter'. Again, think of 'Fastidious Brisk' in Ben Jonson's *Every Man out of his Humour* (published in 1600), a character described as 'A neat, spruce, affecting courtier' who 'practiseth by his glass how to salute'. The reference to a certain 'Count Gratiato' was another thrust at Count Baldassare.

It was of course quite unjust to identify the author of the *Courtier* with the affected behaviour which one of his main characters specifically rejected when describing *sprezzatura*. It has already been suggested (above, p. 38) that Castiglione made skilful use of the medium of dialogue in order to anticipate his critics. For the historian of reception, however, the point is not to reject this sixteenth-century reading of his text but to try to understand it. On this matter, two observations are necessary. The first is that rejecting the *Courtier* was a means of rejecting the court. The second is that the critique of courts became increasingly closely associated with a northern critique of Italy.

Satires on the court were a European tradition from John of Salisbury in the twelfth century and Pope Pius II in the fifteenth to writers of Castiglione's own time, such as the German humanist

32 Marston (1961), 68; Marston (1934–9), vol. I, 1–62.

Ulrich Hutten and the Spanish Bishop Antonio de Guevara.
Hutten, who had been in the service of the archbishop of Mainz,
published his satirical dialogue 'The Court' in 1518, describing
with vivid distaste the extravagantly absurd dress of courtiers, the
appalling food and other discomforts of court life.[33]

Guevara is best known for his 'Contempt for the Court and
Praise of the Countryside' (1539), a treatise which rivalled the
Courtier itself in the number of its editions, translations and
imitations.[34] The author, who had spent much of his life as a
preacher at the court of Charles V, contrasted the anxieties, discomforts and expenses of courtiers with the contented, leisurely
and carefree life which a nobleman could live on his country
estate. Guevara did not reject the court altogether, but suggested
that a courtier needed to retire from it at some point to prepare for
death. He also observed that in court 'everything is permitted' and
'everything is disguised' (*todo se dissimula*), so that words change
their meaning there. Thus extravagance is called 'magnificence',
malice, 'wit', and so on.[35]

Whether Guevara had Castiglione in his sights it is difficult to
say. He is likely to have met the count at the court of Charles V,
but he hardly needed to have read his book to produce this
collection of classical and medieval commonplaces. Only occasionally did he refute a point which had been made by someone
in the *Courtier*, notably in the section which discusses advice to
princes. For example, when the prince is determined to do something which may harm the commonwealth, the good courtier,
according to Guevara, should not speak out in public, as
Ottaviano Fregoso seemed to suggest (1.9), but should wait till he
can offer advice in private.[36]

Later critics placed even more stress than Guevara had done on
the idea that the court encouraged moral corruption – flattery,
hypocrisy, vanity and so on. In England, for instance, one of
Henry VIII's courtiers, Sir Thomas Wyatt, wrote a satire addressed
to a colleague, Sir Francis Bryant, who was later to publish a
translation of Guevara into English, *A Dispraise of the Life of the*

33 Uhlig (1973); Kiesel (1979), esp. 31ff on Pius II and 67ff on Hutten.
34 On Guevara, Uhlig (1973), 235–56; Jones (1975); Redondo (1976).
35 Guevara (1539b), chs 8, 9.
36 Guevara (1539a), ch. 5.

Courtier (1548). The poem advised Bryant to 'flee truth', to avoid
keeping his promises, but 'in word alone to make thy language
sweet'.[37] This satire on insincerity has been called 'the weighti-
est . . . contemporary English critique of the *Courtier*'.[38]

I see no reference to anything specific to the *Courtier* in Wyatt's
text, although his circle (which included Thomas Cromwell,
Edmund Bonner and Thomas Hoby's brother Philip), was certainly one in which Castiglione's book was known. Like Guevara,
Wyatt was reiterating the commonplaces of anti-court literature,
in his case with a bitterness born of unfortunate personal experi-
ences. In the course of the ups and downs of court life, the poet
had twice been imprisoned in the Tower of London.

Similar attitudes were expressed by Roger Ascham, who, in
terms reminiscent of Guevara, lamented the change in the meaning
of words at court, where grace consists in flattering, mocking and
'to bear a brave look'. If a youth 'be innocent and ignorant of ill,
they say, he is rude and hath no grace, so ungraciously do some
graceless men misuse the fair and godly word grace'.[39] Ascham's
idea of grace was obviously closer to Calvin's than to
Castiglione's. The same point, directed against the courtesy tradition rather than against Castiglione in particular, was made again
in the next century by the puritan preacher William Gouge.
'Religion and Grace consisteth not in Good Manners . . . Good
manners are a hindrance to Grace.'[40]

In France in the 1540s, criticisms of the *Courtier* were offered or
implied in the course of a literary debate about court morality, the
so-called 'controversy over lady-friends' or *querelle des amies*,
conducted by poets in the circle of Marguerite de Navarre.
Bertrand de La Borderie's 'Court Friend' (1541), for instance,
depicted the court lady as a creation of artifice and as someone
who cultivates 'grace and beauty' in order to be loved by many
suitors without loving anyone in return.[41] Later in the decade, a
lawyer, Philibert de Vienne, in his 'Court Philosopher' (1547)
wrote satirically of fashion as the court's philosophy and of 'living

37 Wyatt (1975), 110; cf. Uhlig (1973), 317–19.
38 Starkey (1982), 234.
39 Ascham (1568), 14 verso.
40 Gouge (1622), 539.
41 La Borderie (1541); cf. Screech (1959), 106, 113, 116; Smith (1966), 125–34.

in the court manner' as its definition of virtue.[42] Neither of these writers mentioned Castiglione by name, but both rejected ideas which had been discussed at length and in a positive way in his dialogue, notably grace and neoplatonic love.

Castiglione was of course far from the only writer of his time to write in favour of courts, but his book, like late medieval courtesy literature, made courts the centre of a moral universe. As a historian of the English aristocracy has remarked, 'The Court was as essential to the good life as conceived by Castiglione as the City State to Aristotle.'[43] Such a classic formulation of a courtly ideal made Castiglione an obvious target for critics.

What made the traditional critique of courts particularly sharp in the mid-sixteenth century was its association with anti-Italian sentiments, an Italophobia in reaction to the Italophilia associated with the Renaissance, a backlash against what the critics called the 'aping' of foreign ways. This was a very different discussion of imitation from the literary debate discussed in an earlier chapter (above, pp. 80–2). Thus a Frenchman denounced 'les singeries des Italiens', while an Englishman vilified 'The English Ape, the Italian Imitation, the Footsteps of France'.[44] In the case of Poland, too, it has been shown that the anti-Italian attitudes expressed by Stanislaw Podlodowski in 'The Polish Courtier' (above, p. 92) had their counterpart in real life. Similar views were expressed by some Hungarian nobles.[45]

This anti-Italian backlash seems to be linked to the rise of the culture of sincerity described a few pages back, with the northern Europeans rejecting the culture of performance they associated with the south. In France, the poet Pierre Gringore said in the early sixteenth century that 'there is nothing worse than an Italianized Frenchman' (*Il n'est rien pire . . . qu'est un français italiqué*).[46] In Germany at much the same time, the humanist Jacob Wimpheling issued the warning 'Beware of a bald red-headed man and an Italianized German' (*A rufo calvo et Germano italicato cavendum est*), as if the latter too was a contradiction in

42 Philibert (1547); cf. Mayer (1951), Smith (1966), 138–49.
43 Stone (1965), 400.
44 Aneau (1552); Rankins (1588). Cf. Sozzi (1972).
45 Barycz (1967); Klaniczay (1990).
46 Quoted Smith (1966), 95n.

terms.[47] Alternatively, 'An Italianized German is a devil incarnate' (*Tudesco italianato è un Diabulo incarnato*).[48] It was an adaptation of this last version, *Inglese italianato è diavolo incarnato*, which became proverbial in Elizabethan England (it was quoted by Roger Ascham in the 1560s, by John Lyly in 1580 and by Robert Greene in 1591).[49]

According to one English writer, William Rankins, whose stereotypes were close to those of Guilpin (above, p. 109), Italy was full of 'Machavillians' who 'undermine by policy, practice covertly, cloak cunningly'. Again, Greene, in his *Quip for an Upstart Courtier* (directed against Gabriel Harvey, and perhaps, via Harvey, at Castiglione), described Italy as the home of 'a multitude of abominable vices', including 'vainglory, self-love, sodomy and strange poisonings'. This was the world of John Webster's *Duchess of Malfi* and other revenge tragedies which were often set in Italy and generally ended with a heap of corpses on the stage.[50]

The vices of Italy, as foreigners perceived them, were often associated with courts in particular. Thus the Calvinist printer Henri Estienne, denouncing what he called the 'italianization' of the French language, put the blame on the court, the courtiers and their 'courtisanismes'.[51] Ascham went so far as to describe Italy as 'Circe's court', where the companions of Odysseus were turned into swine.[52] The association of courts with Italy was underlined by the visibility of Italian princesses abroad, notably Bona Sforza, wife of Zygmunt I of Poland, and Catherine de' Medici, wife of Henri II of France. After the massacre of French Protestants in 1572, for which they held Catherine to be responsible, the association between Catholicism, Italy, courts and murder seemed self-evident.

Castiglione's dialogue was viewed through spectacles coloured by these debates. The author seems to have become a convenient scapegoat for critics – especially Protestant critics – who had their

47 Quoted Baxandall (1980), 141.
48 Sastrow (1823), vol. I, 400.
49 Wilson (1970), 224.
50 Rankins (1588), 5; Greene (1592), sig. Ci recto.
51 Estienne (1578); on him, Smith (1966), 206–16.
52 Ascham (1568), 26 recto, 30 recto.

own reasons for rejecting Italy or rejecting courts. Yet this very unpopularity may be regarded as an unwilling tribute to the *Courtier*'s wide appeal.

Ambiguity and Ambivalence

Readers will have noticed the curious fact that some of the same writers – notably Roger Ascham and Jean de La Taille – have been quoted as witnesses for Castiglione's cool reception as well as for his warm one. The aim of this section is to argue that this is no mere accident or eccentricity. On the contrary, it is a valuable clue to the ways in which the *Courtier* – like other texts – was read in the sixteenth century.

Ascham, who recommended the *Courtier* while criticizing the courtly definition of grace, and La Taille, who recommended his prince to take a counsellor like Castiglione while allowing his retired courtier to condemn him, are not isolated instances of mixed or ambiguous reactions. Another example is that of Gabriel Chappuys, who translated Hutten's attack on the court as well as the *Courtier*. Again, the humanist printer Etienne Dolet not only revised the earlier French translation of the *Courtier*, but also published his own critiques of the court. His Lyon colleague Guillaume Rouillé published both Castiglione and Guevara. Two printers, Adams of London and Zetzner of Strasbourg, even published a volume combining Castiglione in Latin translation with a dialogue by the German humanist Gulielmus Insulanus Menapius arguing the case for and against the court.[53] Another humanist, Henricus Petreus Herdesianus, who taught in a German grammar school, edited a two-volume anthology contrasting the life of the court with that of the country, reprinting texts by Erasmus, Guevara and Hutten among others.[54]

These printers, editors and translators may have been concerned only with their sales, like the Protestant printers who published Catholic books for export, but another possibility is worth bearing in mind. In the sixteenth century, rhetoric and law formed an

53 Uhlig (1973), 210ff.
54 Petreus (1578); cf. Uhlig (1973), 219ff, and Kiesel (1979), 107.

important part of the education of elites, and the study of both subjects included learning how to argue *pro et contra*, both for and against a given individual or course of action. The learning process generally included the collection of commonplaces for and against some topic, such as the dignity or misery of man. Students would have been looking out for such commonplaces in the texts they read.

The dialectical method was all the more useful in this case because the court evoked ambivalent reactions, a simultaneous attraction and repulsion. Ambivalence was natural for Protestant humanists like Ascham and even Hoby, but it can be found in Catholics too. Guevara, for instance, was no simple critic of the court in which he had spent much of his adult life. In the same year in which he published his 'Contempt for the Court', 1539, he also published 'Advice for Favourites and Doctrine for Courtiers', a book which was primarily concerned with instructing its readers how to behave with dignity in the presence of the prince. If one treatise looks like a response to Castiglione, the other appears to follow in his footsteps. Together they offer a thorough exploration of the dignity and misery of courts. As for the French critic Philibert de Vienne, his ambivalence drove him to irony, which made it easier for him to be misread by his English translator, whose own attitudes seem to have been mixed in any case.[55]

Come to that, Castiglione himself gave voice to a whole series of different reactions to court life, ranging from nostalgia to bitterness (above, p. 35). His choice of the dialogue form expressed his consciousness that the moral issues were not simple, while the contradictory responses of some readers may be interpreted as a less sophisticated expression of the same awareness. His successors had to wrestle with the same problems, as we shall see in the following chapter.

55 Javitch (1971).

7

The Courtier *Revived*

————————— ❖ —————————

An Italian scholar has claimed that the *Courtier* remained 'the fundamental grammar of court society' until the French Revolution.[1] I disagree. In the ninety-two years following its publication, the text averaged well over an edition a year in one language or another in some part of Europe. After 1619, however, this never happened again, although the decline of interest in the dialogue has been followed by a number of small revivals. Hence my concentration on European responses to Castiglione's book in the sixteenth and early seventeenth centuries. The present chapter should be regarded as no more than a coda, a brief guide to the subsequent fortunes of the text.

For the remaining nine years of the seventeenth century, there is evidence of only eight editions or translations of the *Courtier* in the whole of Europe. We have of course to allow for a lag of at least some decades between a decline in editions and a major change in the attitudes of readers. Books did not go out of date quickly in early modern Europe, and a London bookseller's catalogue of books imported from Italy, published in 1633, included a 1573 edition of the *Courtier*.[2]

In order to date the decline of interest in the book, it might therefore be useful to turn from editions to recorded seventeenth-century readers, let us say those born between 1575 and 1675. In

1 Quondam (1980), 19.
2 Lievsay (1969), 43–4.

forty-eight cases the approximate date of birth of these readers is known; five in the late 1570s, ten in the 1580s, five in the 1590s, eight in the 1600s, seven in the 1610s, and five in the 1620s, falling to three in the 1630s, none in the 1640s, two in the 1650s, two in the 1660s, and one in the 1670s. If we assume that people read the *Courtier* when they were young, at the age of twenty or thereabouts, then the decline of interest in the text took place about 1650 or a little before, in other words a generation later than the decline of its editions. Indeed, it has been argued that the apogee of Castiglione's influence in France was not in the sixteenth century at all, but in the period 1600–60.[3]

Around the middle of the century, then, if not before, Castiglione's *Courtier* finally became obsolete. Why should this have been the case?

There was certainly no decline in courts, which were to remain centres of power and prestige for centuries to come. However, three kinds of cultural change all discouraged demand for Castiglione's dialogue.

In the first place, as the previous chapter showed, both the Reformation and the Counter-Reformation were bad for Castiglione's reputation. His book was viewed as insufficiently Christian. Alternative guides to courts generally had more to say about religion. Some of them, like Michele Timotei's 'Courtier' (1614), or the Jesuit Bernardino Castori's 'Civil and Christian Institution' (1622) – dedicated to yet another duke of Urbino, to underline the attempt to replace Castiglione – were specifically addressed to the 'Christian courtier' or the 'Christian prince'. Some, like Sigismondi's 'Practice of Courtiers' (1604), or Timotei's treatise, were concerned with the courts of churchmen. In the second place, there was a decline in the influence of Italian cultural models. By the seventeenth century, Spain and France – or should we say Madrid and Versailles? – had become the European exemplars of stylish behaviour. By the 1670s, Jesuit colleges in Italy had begun to teach their noble pupils French.[4] In the third place, most important of all, the basic assumption on which the *Courtier* depended, the assumption that the avenue to success at

3 Magendie (1925), 305–39.
4 Brizzi (1976), 239–40.

court was to behave in a graceful manner, rather than to do what the prince wanted, was now challenged more frequently and more forcibly than before.

A split therefore developed between the two debates – one concerning courts and the other concerning the good life – which Castiglione had combined with such skill. Books on courtiers, like the works of Etienne Du Refuge and Baltasar Gracián, now emphasized prudence rather than grace, while books on 'civility', like Courtin and Chesterfield, discussed a wider world than that of the court. The ideal was not so much the courtier as the man of fashion, *l'homme à la mode*, or the man of the world, *l'homme du monde*.[5] One might say that the salon became the central locale for the display of civility, replacing the court in the same way that the court (as chapter 1 suggested), had itself replaced the monastery and the battlefield as the milieu in which a new value-system was formed and spread. None of the later treatises rivalled Castiglione's 100-odd editions, though some of them, Gracián in particular, had a decent degree of success, thus confirming the continuing demand for instruction in the ways of both courts and 'Society', with a capital S.

The Art of Survival at Court

How would Castiglione's courtier have fared at the court of Machiavelli's prince? Not very well, one suspects. The courtier portrayed in the urbane dialogues of Urbino was too outspoken and too much concerned with self-cultivation to have suited the needs of a prince whose chief thought was maintaining or extending his power. This discrepancy may suggest that Castiglione's portrait was unrealistic, or that it was a true likeness only of small courts, or even of courts effectively ruled by women.

In any case, in the sixteenth and seventeenth centuries, European political theory and practice alike moved in Machiavelli's direction. In the age of 'absolute power', it was increasingly assumed that a prince should rule his state alone, without the aid and advice of his nobility, just as the Roman emperors had ruled

5 Ossola (1987).

without the senate. To make a career at court in these circumstances, a different style of behaviour was required, and a new
kind of treatise came into existence to teach it.

The poet Torquato Tasso, who was partly educated at the court
of Urbino and himself played the courtier in Ferrara, once planned
a dialogue in imitation of Castiglione's, set at the court of Urbino
and including in its cast of characters Baldassare's soldier son
Camillo.[6] What Tasso in fact published, however, was a dialogue 'concerning the court' which he called *Malpighi* (1583).
In this dialogue the participants discuss the question whether
Castiglione's book was one for his own time alone or whether it
would be appreciated as long as courts and courtesy survive. One
speaker, Giovanlorenzo Malpighi, 'has it almost by heart' and
knows it better than Cicero, so much does he admire it, but in the
course of the dialogue he is persuaded to take a more critical
attitude. The clinching argument is that the *Courtier* is out of date
'in these times in which simulation is one of the great virtues' (*in
questi tempi in cui l'infinger è una delle maggior virtù*).[7] One might
say that Tasso had found an elegant way of praising Castiglione by
not praising him, and also that he was a critic of his own day
rather than a critic of the *Courtier*. All the same, Tasso bears
witness to changing attitudes.

To illustrate these changes, let us look for a moment at two
Italian treatises on courts, which put forward arguments which
few if any participants in Castiglione's *Courtier* would have been
prepared to defend.

The 'Discourse on what Befits a Young Nobleman' (1565)
already implied a political critique of Castiglione's text. The 'Discourse' was the work of Gianbattista Giraldi Cinzio, a nobleman
of Ferrara better known for his tragedies, stories and literary
criticism. When it recommends the reader to cultivate elegance of
movement, to practise ball-games, to write poems, and to make
music, the treatise sounds like an echo of the *Courtier*.[8] Elsewhere
it implies a mild criticism of Castiglione, expressing fears that 'in
our times' dancing has become 'plebeian', for instance, or advising
the young nobleman against learning how to paint.[9]

6 Cox (1992), 190.
7 Tasso (1583).
8 Giraldi (1565), 23, 28, 29; cf. Woodhouse (1991).
9 Giraldi (1565), 25, 31.

More important, however, are major differences of emphasis and tone between the two books. Castiglione's courtier was an autonomous individual who was advised to speak frankly to his prince. In Giraldi's monologue, on the other hand, the keywords are 'accommodation', 'simulation' and 'dissimulation', whether the motive for these disguises is self-defence in a hostile environment, or the manipulation of the prince to fit in with one's own desires (*ridurre il Signore al suo desiderio*).[10]

Even more revealing, perhaps, is the change in meaning of another keyword, 'grace'. In the *Courtier, grazia* was generally, though certainly not always, an aesthetic quality, a way of presenting oneself in public. In Giraldi, on the other hand, the term has come to refer almost exclusively to the favour of the prince, which is assumed to be the principal object of the courtier's endeavours.[11]

Similar points might be made about Lorenzo Ducci's 'Art of the Court' (1601) concerned as it is with techniques for courting princes. Simulation and dissimulation are recommended as the means to acquire their grace and favour. 'The courtier should hide self-interest (*l'appetito del proprio interesse*) under the appearance of the desire to serve the prince.'[12] To learn how to do this, we are told, it is necessary to study 'the supreme master of courtiers', Cornelius Tacitus, whose history of imperial Rome focuses on the art of dissimulation. Ducci's treatise was liberally sprinkled with aphorisms from Tacitus, an author who was being read with increasing enthusiasm all over Europe from the late sixteenth century onwards.[13]

Three years after Ducci, Bernardino Pino published his 'Gentleman' (1604), a treatise which gave its approach away in the subtitle, 'the prudent and discreet man'. Guides of this kind proliferated in the seventeenth century. As the intellectual historian Friedrich Meinecke once remarked in the course of his survey of the parallel literature on 'reason of state', 'here are catacombs of forgotten literature by mediocrities.'[14] Collectively, these mediocre

10 Giraldi (1565), 37, 52.
11 Giraldi (1565), 12.
12 Ducci (1601), chs 4, 28; cf. Uhlig (1975), 42–4; Anglo (1977, 1983); Donati (1988), 165–6; Hinz (1992), 367–85; Hinz (1993).
13 Stackelberg (1960); Etter (1966); Burke (1969).
14 Meinecke (1924).

works are of interest to cultural historians as witnesses to a significant change of tone or mood. By the seventeenth century it was no
longer shocking, as it would have been in Castiglione's day, to
advise the courtier, as Nicolas Faret did, to 'conform himself' to
the inclinations of the prince at all times, or, like Niccolò Strozzi,
not only to disguise the fact that he knows more about literature
than his prince, but even 'to pretend the contrary of what is the
case'. One Italian writer even published a whole treatise devoted
to what he called 'honourable dissimulation'.[15]

One of the most popular seventeenth-century books of this type
was Etienne Du Refuge's 'Treatise on the Court', first published in
1616. It was reprinted in French a dozen times or more by 1661,
as well as being translated into Latin, Italian, English and German,
while the English version was retranslated into French. As in the
case of Castiglione, successive editions turned the book more and
more into a work of reference, the marginal annotation, chapter
summaries and full index allowing the treatise to function as a
'manual' serving the reader, according to the advertisement in the
preface, 'promptly' and 'on all occasions'.[16]

The message of Du Refuge was a very different one from
Castiglione's, and close to that of Tacitus and Ducci, both of
whom the author cited in his text. The court was presented as a
place of danger and corruption. All the same, Du Refuge told his
readers how to 'advance yourself at court'. After a brief discussion
of affability and civility (as means to an end rather than as qualities desirable in themselves), he turned to more important matters, such as how to acquire favour and avoid disgrace: 'dexterity'
in avoiding dangerous topics, 'dissimulation' of one's own emotions ('hiding our joy, sadness, hope, desire, fear, anger'), and
knowledge of those of the prince, in order to 'accommodate'
oneself to his humour. Du Refuge did not forget to express moral
scruples, but somehow he always found a way around them.
'There is no help for it, it is sometimes necessary to use flattery to
gain an advantage over these people – but not any kind of
flattery.'[17]

15 Faret (1630), 50–1; Strozzi (1982), 167, 171, 189; cf. Woodhouse (1982);
Accetto (1641).
16 Du Refuge (1616); cf. Anglo (1983).
17 Du Refuge (1616), 1.35, 2.5, 2.7, 2.10.

An even greater success in early modern Europe, as well as a more memorable work of literature, was the 'Oracle' (1647) written by the Spanish Jesuit Baltasar Gracián, and translated, in the course of the seventeenth and eighteenth centuries, into French, Dutch, English (three times), German (five times), Italian (twice), Latin (twice), Russian and Hungarian. Indeed, the success of the book was such as to puzzle the intellectual historian Paul Hazard, whose comment was that 'There are some things that defy explanation.'[18] My own view is that Baltasar was able to replace Baldassare thanks to the help of his fellow-Jesuits, whose many colleges played an important role in the education of noblemen in Catholic Europe between the late sixteenth and the late eighteenth centuries.[19]

The book is Tacitean – not to say oracular – in its brevity. Its 300 short paragraphs dazzle its readers with epigrams and offer them weary and worldly-wise advice for survival in a world in which life is 'a manoeuvre against the malice of men'. How is political survival to be achieved? 'Avoid victories over your superior . . . Conceal your purpose . . . Know how to be all things to all men.'[20]

Gracián was a moralist in the tradition of Seneca, himself a Spaniard at the court of Nero. The ideal presented in his 'Oracle' was that of 'a man without illusions' (*varón desengañado*), 'a wise Christian', as well as 'a courtier-philosopher'. His reference to 'all things to all men' echoed the founder of his order, St Ignatius Loyola, who was in turn echoing St Paul, and his final advice to the reader was to 'be a saint'. However, his book was read, or at any rate presented to its readers, as yet another manual for courtiers. In its French translation, it was entitled *L'homme de cour*, and the title stuck, partly because further translations were made from the French rather than the Spanish. In English, the book was known as *The Courtier's Oracle*; in German, *Kluger Hof- und Weltmann*; in Italian, *L'uomo di corte*; in Latin, *Hominis aulici oraculum*; and in Hungarian, *Udvari Kátó* (the Hungarian word for 'court' is *udvár*). There are signs that the

18 Details in Gracián (1647), introduction, 43–6. Cf. Hazard (1935), 366–7.
19 Brizzi (1976); Dainville (1978).
20 Gracián (1647), nos 7, 13, 98, 100. Cf. Borinski (1894); Jansen (1958).

book was read as the new title suggested. The single reference to 'the famous Gratian' in *The Spectator*, for example, on 5 February 1712, describes his book as maxims 'for a Man's advancing himself at Court'. Like Castiglione's dialogue, Gracián's aphorisms had been reduced to a collection of tips for aspiring courtiers.

The last chapter suggested that Castiglione and his book were rejected by some people because they were regarded as too cynical. The message of this section, however, has been exactly the opposite. It has argued that Castiglione went out of fashion, at least at court, because his book was not cynical enough. The contrast offers yet another illustration of the different ways in which this 'open' dialogue can be, and has been, read.

If the late Renaissance shift from republics to principalities had given Castiglione his opportunity, the rise of absolute monarchs in the seventeenth century had made his book obsolete. It had been an asset in one stage of the taming of a rough and warlike nobility, but it turned into a liability in a later, more political stage of their domestication.

Manuals of Civility

If aspirants to success at court now threw away the *Courtier*, this does not mean that Castiglione's dialogue was entirely obsolete after 1630. It continued to be used, alongside more up-to-date texts, as a guide to what was now called 'civility' in the everyday life of the upper classes. Among these rivals, not only in England but on the Continent as well, were Locke's *Thoughts on Education* and the *Letters* of Lord Chesterfield. At this point, distinguishing Castiglione's influence from the general tradition of courtesy-literature becomes an operation as difficult and as fruitless as tracing the movements of a bottle of ink poured into a stream. Confluence obliterates influence.

Early in the seventeenth century, Castiglione's contribution remains reasonably clear. Du Refuge's brief discussion of 'civility', defined as 'a certain decency, propriety or good grace', whether in words, clothes or facial expression, is close to the *Courtier*.[21] The

21 Du Refuge (1616), 1.2.

same point might be made about Gracián. His 'Oracle' devoted one aphorism to courtesy, which 'costs little and is worth much', and another to 'charm' (*despejo*). His earlier treatise, the 'Hero' (1637), discussed grace and the need to avoid affectation and even quoted Castiglione ('the Count', as he called him) as an authority on courtiers.[22] It is interesting to discover that Gracián's aristocratic patron, the marquis of Lastanosa, had a copy of Castiglione in Boscán's translation in his library.

The *Honnête homme* of Nicolas Faret, which took so much from the *Courtier*, as we have seen (p. 93), also drew on Du Refuge.[23] Faret's treatise, which seems to have launched the phrase *honnête homme* to describe a man who knows 'how to please at court', went through twelve editions between 1630 and 1681, besides being translated into English, German, Spanish and even Italian. In that sense it was the classic account of civility in the age of classicism.

As a writer on styles of behaviour, Faret had a number of successors in the age of Louis XIV. Jacques Du Bosc, for instance, wrote a companion-piece for women, *L'honnête femme* (1632), which included a chapter on *bonne grace*, defined like Castiglione's *sprezzatura* as the art 'of doing everything as if by nature and without effort' (*la bonne grace se remarque à faire tout comme par nature, et sans effort*).[24] The chevalier de Méré wrote on the nature of *honnêteté* and on the art of conversation, and, like Castiglione, he cited Plato and Cicero as models.[25] The duc de La Rochefoucauld published his *Maxims* (1665), a cool, sharp appraisal of the social code of the elite of his age as well as of human frailty in general. 'In every station in life', he remarked, for instance, 'everyone presents a style of behaviour and an exterior (*une mine et un extérieur*) so as to appear what they would like others to think them to be.' Or again: 'Civility is a desire to be treated politely and to be considered polite oneself.'[26] The most popular writer at the time, however, was Antoine de Courtin, whose 'New Treatise on Civility' (1671) had reached its thirteenth edition by 1700.

22 Aubrun (1958); Morreale (1958); Hinz (1991).
23 Faret (1630), xxxviii–xxxix.
24 Du Bosc (1632), 292.
25 Méré (1930), 78.
26 La Rochefoucauld (1665), nos 256, 260.

The French writers on civility gradually developed their own terminology for the precise description of behaviour – *bonne mine, bon air, civilité, galanterie, bonnes manières, politesse*, and so on, and they placed more emphasis than their predecessors on the informal rules of conversation. They did not forget the court – how could they, in the age of Louis XIV's Versailles? – but they wrote for Parisians and doubtless for provincials as well. They were concerned with good behaviour 'in company', and not only in the presence of the prince. As for the terms *grâce, négligence* and *nonchalance*, they survived in French literary theory of the seventeenth century, warning us not to interpret the rules of classicism too rigidly in the France of Racine and La Fontaine any more than in the Rome of Bembo, Raphael and Castiglione.[27]

Like their French counterparts, the English writers who were formulating or reformulating the ideal of the gentleman, notably Locke and Chesterfield, wrote about behaviour in 'society', rather than at court. Locke's *Thoughts on Education* (1693) was, like Gracián's 'Oracle', a book of European appeal. It was translated into French, German, Swedish and Italian, as well as reaching its fourteenth English edition by 1772. Locke's aim was to offer advice not on education in the narrow sense of the term but on the training of a gentleman in 'civility', paying attention to his postures, gestures and 'carriage' as well as to his reading. His condemnation of affectation and praise of 'gracefulness' are reminiscent of Castiglione. So is Locke's emphasis on keeping the child's spirit 'easy'. 'Ease', in the sense of freedom from awkwardness or embarrassment, became something of a keyword in eighteenth-century England, a local equivalent for *sprezzatura*. Indeed, both the eighteenth-century English translations of the *Courtier* define *sprezzatura* in precisely these terms, to refer to people who 'do everything easy' or act 'naturally and easily'.

Locke's reflections were developed by Richard Steele in an article on the qualities of the 'fine gentleman' in *The Guardian* (no. 34, 1713). Writing in the persona of 'Old Ironside', a device which allowed him a necessary measure of ironic distance from the topic (since a true gentleman could hardly tell another how to behave), Richard Steele put forward his version of the British ideal, a man

27 Lapp (1971), 2–3.

'modest without Bashfulness, frank and affable without imperti-
nence, obliging and complaisant without servility'. 'Everything
he says or does', remarked Steele in a passage reminiscent of
Castiglione on grace, 'is accompanied with a Manner, or rather
a Charm, that draws the Admiration and Good-will of every
Beholder.'

Dr Johnson was another writer who praised manners and
conversation which were 'without effort'.[28] However, the most
famous of the eighteenth-century English formulations of the ideal
of the effortless superiority of the gentleman is surely the *Letters* of
Lord Chesterfield, first published posthumously in 1774, and often
reprinted (it had reached its eleventh edition by 1800, besides
adaptations or translations into French and German). Writing to
his son, Chesterfield formulated what he called 'some rules of
politeness and good breeding', emphasizing the need to avoid
'awkwardness', to enter a room 'with gracefulness and a modest
assurance', and to achieve 'a genteel, easy manner and carriage', 'a
graceful address', or 'a graceful noble air'.[29] The presentation of
public advice in the form of private letters gives an attractive
impression of informality, like Locke's 'thoughts'. In both cases
we may reasonably suspect that this informality was studied.

Survivals and Revivals

The impression that both the French tradition of writing about the
honnête homme and the English tradition of writing about the
gentleman (to say nothing about other parts of Europe), still owed
something, at least a *je ne sais quoi*, to Castiglione's example, is
strengthened by an examination of editions of his book between
1662 and 1771, together with records of its presence in private
libraries of the period.

In France, for example, a number of major figures in the cultural
life of the period are known to have owned copies of the *Courtier*.
Nicolas Fouquet, for instance, the financier who preceded Louis
XIV as the patron of the architect Louis Le Vau, the painter

28 Piozzi (1974), 122.
29 Chesterfield (1774), 7, 9, 135, 137; cf. Woodhouse (1991).

Charles Lebrun, and the poet Jean de La Fontaine (not to mention
Corneille and Molière), owned a sixteenth-century Italian edition
of Castiglione which is now in the British Library. Pierre-Daniel
Huet, a former tutor to the Dauphin, owned a bilingual edition.
Louis XIV's minister Jean-Baptiste Colbert, or his son, owned an
Italian edition. Jean Chapelain, the writer who advised Colbert on
the artistic policies of the government, owned no fewer than five
copies, four of them in Italian, appropriately enough for someone
who knew that language well enough to write verse in it. That he
also owned copies of Du Refuge and Faret offers a clue to the way
in which Chapelain read the text.[30]

Given the similarity between the salons of seventeenth-century
Paris and what might be called the 'proto-salon' of Urbino, it
would be fascinating to know whether such bluestockings as the
comtesse de Lafayette, Madeleine de Scudéry, and the marquise de
Sablé had read it. So far as I have been able to discover, however,
the only French lady of the old regime known to have owned the
book was Madame de Pompadour, whose copy, like Fouquet's, is
now in the British Library.

However, the marquise de Sablé's friend the duc de La
Rochefoucauld, whose pitiless analysis of social behaviour was
mentioned above, did own a copy of *Le parfait courtisan*, almost
certainly the new translation of the *Courtier* published in 1690.
The translation was the work of Jean-Baptiste Duhamel, an
Oratorian priest, who was also secretary of the state-supported
Academy of Sciences, and so part of the cultural Establishment. It
is interesting to note that this translation was advertised on the
title-page as a work which will help the reader 'succeed in fine
conversations'. In other words, the *Courtier* was coming to be
read as an example of the treatises on the art of conversation
which proliferated in seventeenth-century France.[31] In similar
style, an anonymous translation of the *Courtier* into German,
published at Dresden in 1685, gave the dialogue the new title of
'Gallant Night Conversations', the term *galante* being used in its
seventeenth-century French sense, as a synonym for 'polished' or
'courteous'.

30 Searles (1912), nos 522–6, 529, 532.
31 Burke (1993), 102–8.

The most interesting regional examples of renewed interest in the *Courtier* are surely those of the Dutch and the British. Of the two, the Dutch example is the more significant as an indicator of social change. The first Dutch translation of the *Courtier* was published in Amsterdam in 1662. One might have expected the population of the Dutch Republic to have had little need or little time for a book about courts, and there is indeed little evidence of such interest before 1650, but significant social changes were taking place in the republic at about this time. The burgomasters and town councillors of major Dutch cities such as Amsterdam, Rotterdam, Leiden, and so on, the so-called 'regents', were changing their style of life and coming to behave more and more like an aristocracy. Some of them were knighted by foreign monarchs, while others began to call themselves by the titles of recently purchased landed estates.[32]

It seems plausible to suggest that new nobles like these felt anxiety about their social behaviour and also that they were attracted by foreign models – not only Castiglione but also Courtin, whose instructions on 'civility' (translated as 'good-manneredness', *welgemanierdheit*), appeared in Dutch a few years later, in 1677.[33] The hypothesis of a link between the publication of 'The Complete Courtier' (*De volmaeckte hovelinck*, as it was known in Dutch) and the process of 'aristocratization', as social historians describe it, becomes more plausible if we look at the paratext. The translation of the *Courtier* was dedicated to Jan Six, a burgomaster of Amsterdam who was also active as a poet and playwright. Six had apparently praised Castiglione's work highly in conversation, while his substantial library contained three copies of the book. Six's portrait was painted by Rembrandt, and it has been suggested that its fluent, spontaneous and 'impressionistic' style was itself a form of *sprezzatura*. After all, Rembrandt himself was sufficiently interested in Castiglione to sketch the famous Raphael portrait (see plate 1), which was located in Amsterdam at the time.[34]

The Dutch scholar Nikolaes Heinsius owned three copies of the *Courtier*, while the Dutch diplomat Abraham de Wicquefort

32 Roorda (1964); Burke (1974), ch. 9; Spierenburg (1981), 19–30.
33 Spierenburg (1981), 16–17.
34 Jongh (1985); Smith (1988).

advised ambassadors to read this 'admirable treatise'. Indeed, his own examination of 'The Ambassador and his Functions' (1681) which portrays the birth, studies, and behaviour of a model ambassador, may reasonably be regarded as a late example of the creative imitation of Castiglione. Wicquefort's ambassador had to be 'not only skilful, but also a gentleman, or at least to appear one', and the way to do this was to follow Castiglione's rules.[35]

In the English case, there was a revival of interest in Castiglione's book in the first half of the eighteenth century, with seven editions altogether, including two new translations of the text. Clerke's Latin translation (the work, it will be remembered, of a Fellow of King's College) was reprinted by Cambridge University Press in 1713. It was followed in 1724 and 1727 by the rival English translations by Robert Samber and A. P. Castiglione, who claimed on his title-page to be 'of the same family' as Baldassare.

Both new-born translations came into the world under the protection of powerful godfathers. Samber dedicated his version to the duke of Montagu, while A. P. Castiglione dedicated his to King George, publishing a list of more than 500 of the great and the good who had subscribed in advance to the work (the bishop of London took ten copies, the Regius professor of history at Oxford took six, and so on).

Why should interest in the *Courtier* have revived in this way? Anxiety about gentility on the part of merchants and lawyers who were trying to join the gentry does not seem a sufficient explanation for this concern, since this trend has lasted for so long as to form a structural feature of English history. Even the redefinition of 'polite society' in terms of manners rather than birth does not seem a sufficient explanation for such a flurry of concern with a book on behaviour first published in 1528.[36] Could there have been a political explanation? Opposition to the dominance of Sir Robert Walpole often took the form of attacks on the court. Indeed, earlier in the century, a Whig intellectual, the third earl of Shaftesbury, had denounced grace as 'theatrical action' and made an effort to 'dissociate politeness from the court'.[37] It would cer-

35 Wicquefort (1681), vol. I, 83.
36 Langford (1989), 59–121; cf. Raven (1992).
37 Klein (1994), 189–90.

tainly be a simplification to see the republication of Castiglione in the 1720s as a Tory version of cultural history – the Whig Lord Chesterfield was among the subscribers. All the same, it may well have been intended as a defence of court values at a time when they seemed to be threatened.

The republication of Castiglione also formed part of a revival of interest in the culture of sixteenth-century Italy which we might describe as a 'renaissance of the Renaissance'. In Italy, the eighteenth century was a time when scholarly editions of a number of Renaissance classics made their appearance, including previously unpublished works by Benvenuto Cellini and by Niccolò Machiavelli (whose gravestone in the church of Santa Croce in Florence dates from this time). The *Courtier* was republished in 1733, 1766 and 1771, alongside other Renaissance 'classics' from Castiglione's circle such as the works of Bembo, Fracastoro, Navagero and Sadoleto. One of the editors involved in this enterprise described Castiglione as 'the most talented [or versatile] Italian of the sixteenth century' (*il più virtuoso uomo italiano del secolo xvi*), praise indeed. One eighteenth-century Italian critic, Gianvicenzo Gravina, compared Castiglione to Cicero, and another, Pierantonio Serassi, to Dante.

This renaissance of the Renaissance affected England too. For example, the treatises of the Renaissance architects Andrea Palladio and Leonbattista Alberti were published in English translation in 1715 and 1726 respectively. New editions of Palladio followed in 1728 and 1738, to inspire the construction of 'Palladian' houses. In the case of painting, English gentlemen on the Grand Tour seem to have found more time than their predecessors to admire the work of Raphael and other Renaissance artists as well as examining classical antiquities.[38] In the case of literature, there were new translations of the epics of both Tasso (1763) and Ariosto (1773–83), both by John Hoole, who moved in the circle of Samuel Johnson.

Since it is often illuminating to decompose movements and trends and to discover the individuals who set them in motion, it is worth drawing attention to some Italians who were living in England at this time, among them the Venetian architect Giacomo

38 Hale (1954).

Leoni, who played an important role in the rise of Palladianism, the Piedmontese writer Giuseppe Baretti, and the Roman poet and librettist Paolo Rolli, who taught Italian to members of the royal family. Baretti was somewhat ambivalent towards Castiglione, writing that the count 'understood how to behave much better than how to write good Italian'.[39] Rolli, on the other hand, compared Bembo and Castiglione to Addison and Steele as examples of 'perfection and taste' fifty years before Dr Johnson's famous comparison of Addison with Castiglione as authors of courtesy-books.[40]

It is in the context of revival rather than survival that we should locate references to the *Courtier* in eighteenth-century England. Daniel Defoe owned two copies of the book, one in Italian and one in English, perhaps as an aid to the composition of his treatise on *The Compleat English Gentleman*. Lord Chesterfield was among the many subscribers to A. P. Castiglione's translation. Samuel Johnson – who was, incidentally, a friend of Baretti's – praised the book. It may be difficult to imagine the bear-like Johnson as an admirer of the count's elegance, but he assured Boswell that the *Courtier* was 'the best book that ever was written upon good breeding', thus managing to praise Castiglione and to damn Chesterfield – whose *Letters* he abominated – in a single breath.[41]

Johnson's friends David Garrick and Sir Joshua Reynolds were also admirers of the book. One might of course have expected an actor and a portrait-painter to have been particularly interested in a dialogue on self-presentation.[42] Finally, a fascinating if ambiguous testimony to late eighteenth-century attitudes comes from a copy of the 1603 edition of the *Courtier* now in the British Library, which is signed 'William Shakespeare' in the hand of the forger William Ireland. Why did he do this? Did he consider Castiglione, like Shakespeare, to be a representative of the Renaissance?

39 Baretti (1763), vol. I, 21.
40 Rolli (1728), 12–13; cf. Dorris (1967), 197ff; Johnson (1779–81), vol. I, 407.
41 Boswell (1791), vol. V, 276; cf. vol. I, 266.
42 Arnott (1975), no. 383.

The Nineteenth and Twentieth Centuries

In a small volume which is primarily concerned with the period
1528–1619 it is clearly impossible to treat the nineteenth and
twentieth centuries in any detail. What I should like to do in this
final section, little more than a coda to a coda, is to return to
the original problem of the distance between modern readings of
the *Courtier* and traditional ones, concentrating on the British
Isles and noting the way in which further changes in attitudes
and values have led to new perceptions of Castiglione and his
dialogue.[43]

In Italy, Castiglione was 'canonized' in the sense of becoming a
literary classic, to be studied in schools. The first time his book
was described as a 'classic', in this sense was, as far as I know, in
the 1770s, by the literary historian Girolamo Tiraboschi. At much
the same time, the poet Giuseppe Parini, who taught in a college in
Milan, declared that the *Courtier* 'deserves to be studied for the
natural and elegant manner in which it is written'.[44]

In 1803, as if in response to these comments, the text was
republished by the 'typographical society of Italian classics'; in
1822, in the 'select library of ancient and modern Italian works';
in 1831, in the 'economical library'. By the late nineteenth century,
it was a set book in the schools of the newly united Italy, as the
editions of 1884, 1889 and 1894 all testify. One of the most
famous Castiglione specialists, Vittorio Cian, originally edited the
Courtier for precisely this purpose, and declared in his introduction that it should take its place alongside Boccaccio's *Decameron*
and Ariosto's *Orlando Furioso* as part of the library of 'every
cultivated and serious college student'. There was of course a
political as well as a cultural programme underlying this canoniz-
ation. In 1842, nearly twenty years before unification, a Venetian
publisher described Castiglione in the preface to his edition as one
of the men who had wished 'to raise Italy to nationhood'.

In Britain, on the other hand, the continuing influence of the
Courtier may best be seen in a new ideal of behaviour for upper-

43 On Germany, cf. Burger (1963).
44 Tiraboschi (1772–82), vol. VII, part 2, 590; Parini (1967), 785.

class males. The ideal was embodied in the 'dandy', a new term coined to describe the man who tried to make his life, not to mention his clothes, into a work of art, defining his identity in terms of artifice, in reaction against the Romantic cult of sincerity, and in terms of leisure, by contrast to that of the hard-working, unaesthetic bourgeoisie.[45] There was therefore an element of protest in this construction of identity, in contrast to Castiglione's more conformist ideal. All the same, elements of the courtly style and of the wider gentlemanly tradition were appropriated, reshaped and polished by the dandies.

The archetypical dandy was George Brummell, an English gentleman whose reputation rested less on his friendship with the Prince Regent or even his gift for repartee than on his ability to tie a perfect cravat. His concern with the minutiae of dress looks very like an example of the affectation denounced in the *Courtier*, but the cravat itself expressed an ideal of apparently effortless perfection which is not very far from *sprezzatura*. Incidentally, the term 'effortless' came into use in English at just this time, early in the nineteenth century, a little later than 'insouciance', according to the OED, but somewhat before 'aplomb'.

'Beau' Brummell quickly became an exemplary figure. His ideal of elegance informs Edward Bulwer Lytton's novel *Pelham: or, Adventures of a Gentleman* (1828) in which the hero tells his valet to 'give an air of graceful negligence' to his appearance. The reader learns that 'the distinguishing trait of people accustomed to good society, is a calm impeturbable quiet', sometimes expressed by a 'nonchalant yawn of ennui'.[46] The novel's eight editions between 1828 and 1840 suggest that this ideal appealed to the imagination of many readers.

The age of Victoria was rather less sympathetic to dandies and other frivolities than the Regency had been. The Victorians also seem to have had little time for Castiglione, though a portrait of his wife Ippolita Torelli, by Charles Eastlake, was exhibited at the Royal Academy in 1851. The aesthetic ideal resurfaced only at the end of the century, embodied in figures such as Oscar Wilde, with his long hair and velvet suits, and the 'delicately dandified'

45 Franci (1977); Stanton (1980).
46 Lytton (1828), vol. I, 5; vol. II, 12, 245.

Max Beerbohm, as Lord David Cecil once called him.[47] In his novel *Zuleika Dobson* (1911), Beerbohm created the figure of the Duke of Dorset as a perfect expression of what he called 'the dandiacal temper'. 'He played polo, cricket, racquets, chess and billiards as well as such things can be played. He was fluent in all modern languages, had a very real talent in water-colour, and was accounted, by those who had had the privilege of hearing him, the best amateur pianist on this side of the Tweed.'[48] How is that for a modern version of Castiglione's universal man?

If Beerbohm's ideal sounds like pure fantasy, let us turn from fiction to Arthur Balfour and his circle. Balfour, a nephew of the marquess of Salisbury, studied at Eton and Trinity before becoming a Member of Parliament at the age of twenty-six and Prime Minister in 1902. Balfour managed to give the impression of 'lounging indolence' and a 'composed exterior' in the Pelham style, combined with wit, fluency and intellectual interests ranging from politics to philosophy (he published a *Defence of Philosophic Doubt*). According to John Maynard Keynes he was 'the most extraordinary *objet d'art* our society has produced'. If any modern Briton would have made a hit at a Renaissance court, it would surely have been Balfour. In fact, in the 1880s he regularly participated in an up-to-date equivalent of the conversations at Urbino, the house-parties of the 'Souls', in which the members of this select society (including Oscar Wilde) discussed poetry and played intellectual parlour-games, while the animating role of Elisabetta Gonzaga was played by Margot Tennant, who married Herbert Asquith in 1894.[49]

If the Souls sound impossibly remote from the world of Castiglione, it should be added that a regular guest at these parties was Sir Walter Raleigh, a professor of English at Liverpool who published an edition of the *Courtier* in 1900. His characterization of Castiglione's ideal as the man who 'trained himself like a racehorse and cultivated himself like a flower' evokes the worlds of both the athlete and the dandy. His edition was dedicated to George Wyndham, a former officer in the Coldstream Guards who

47 DNB, s.v. 'Beerbohm'.
48 Beerbohm (1911), 21.
49 Young (1963), xv, 27, 141–5; Egremont (1980), 28, 115.

became Balfour's private secretary and combined a political career with the study of the Renaissance, especially Shakespeare and Ronsard.

Wyndham was not the last English descendant of the Renaissance courtier – far from it. Sir Ernest Barker, whose reflections on the *Courtier* were quoted at the beginning of this essay, bears witness to the survival of the ideal of *sprezzatura* among Oxford students in the 1890s, and quoted the phrase of an old member about 'the tranquil consciousness of an effortless superiority' characteristic of a Balliol man.[50] Cambridge was no different from Oxford in this respect. 'We have all met them', an émigré scholar wrote with some acerbity in the late 1940s, 'the devotees of *sprezzatura* – the prizemen who never do a stroke of work, the Blues who never do any training.'[51] When I went up to Oxford in the late 1950s, it was still not done to be seen to work too hard. Effortlessness was still the ideal.

Raleigh called the *Courtier* a 'mirror of the complete gentleman', as if the ideal it portrayed was timeless. In similar fashion the historian John Addington Symonds – a Balliol man – wrote that 'The crowning merit of the *Courtier* is an air of good breeding and disengagement from pedantic prejudices', as if it were a work of his own day.[52] On the other hand, the introduction to the Italian edition of 1822 noted that good manners had changed their outward forms since Castiglione's day, even if their 'essence' was eternal. In similar fashion Raleigh's introduction described the text as 'an abstract or epitome of the chief moral ideas of the age'.

This historicist view of the text soon began to gain ground, at a time when the *Courtier* was undergoing yet another revival (a new English translation in 1901, a new German translation in 1907, and so on). For example, a biography of Castiglione published in 1908 called the *Courtier* 'in many ways the most representative book of the Italian Renaissance'. Another biography, published the very same year, described Castiglione as 'the ideal representative of that great age'.[53]

Vittorio Cian had also presented Castiglione, in the preface to his edition of the *Courtier*, as 'a figure eminently representative of

50 Barker (1953), 304, 307.
51 Schenk (1949), 94.
52 Symonds (1875–86), vol. II, 265.
53 Raleigh (1900), viii–ix; Hare (1908), 200; Cartwright (1908), vii.

his times'. Indeed, Castiglione had already begun to play this role
in Jacob Burckhardt's famous essay on the Renaissance, first published in 1860. One of the central concepts in this essay is a
Hegelian one, that of the 'work of art' (*Kunstwerk*) in the sense
of a self-conscious, planned achievement. In his first chapter
Burckhardt discusses the state as a work of art in that sense, while
in his fifth chapter he studies 'sociability' (*Geselligkeit*) in the same
way. Castiglione is of course a key example of a self-conscious
social ideal. His dialogue was perceived by Burckhardt in terms
of a German tradition of self-cultivation associated with Goethe
and Wilhelm von Humboldt. It was viewed as a guide to the
construction of the self as a work of art.[54]

It was for similar reasons that Renaissance Italy so much appealed to such aesthetes as Walter Pater, Oscar Wilde and the
young W. B. Yeats. It was Wilde, after all, who said that 'form is
everything' and that 'the first duty in life is to be as artificial as
possible.' 'Every summer', wrote Yeats in 1908 or thereabouts, 'I
have some book read out to me, and last year I brought into the
country the *Courtier* of Castiglione, in Hoby's translation.' It
seems to have been his friend Lady Gregory who introduced Yeats
to the book, whether in Italy, where they visited Urbino together,
or in her house at Coole Park in Galway. In any case, he came
to identify Urbino with Coole Park. For Yeats, these two great
houses were symbols of aristocratic values which he felt to be
under threat in his day. In his poems 'To a Wealthy Man' (1912)
and 'The People' (1915), Urbino became 'That grammar school of
courtesies/Where wit and wisdom learned their trade', the palace
'where the Duchess and her people talked/The stately midnight
through until they stood/In their great window looking at the
dawn'.

Yeats came to see the *Courtier* as a symbol of an age which
fascinated him not only because of the achievements of
Michelangelo, Veronese, Spenser and Ronsard, but also because of
what he called its 'unity of being'. This idea that Renaissance
selves were united, while modern selves are divided, was a central
part of Yeats's view, or more precisely his personal myth of the
Renaissance. 'The men of the Renaissance', he once wrote, 'sought
at all times the realization of something deliberately chosen, and

54 Burckhardt (1860); Bruford (1975).

they played a part always as if upon a stage before an audience, and gave up their lives rather than their play.' He compared courtesy in daily life to style in the arts, and himself tried to write with *sprezzatura* or as he called it, following Hoby, 'recklessness'. Like Burckhardt, then, Yeats saw the *Courtier* as an illustration of social life as a work of art. On the other hand, he used Castiglione and Urbino, like Coole Park, to articulate his personal protest against modern society.[55]

Coole Park makes an appropriate place at which to end this brief survey of the place of the *Courtier* in the post-Renaissance world.

55 Yeats (*c*.1908); Stein (1949); Salvadori (1965); Carpenter (1969–70); Harris (1974).

8

The Courtier *in European Culture*

‒‒‒‒◈‒‒‒‒

Centred on an imagined Urbino, this essay has moved far away from it in different directions in space and time alike. To conclude, and to attempt to tie at least some of the threads together, it may be useful to summarize responses to the *Courtier* in three dimensions – chronological, geographical and sociological – as well as to reconsider its place in the history of western civilization.

The chronology of the book's editions tells a clear story. In the 1530s, around twenty-two editions (counting translations) made their appearance. In the 1540s, the number rose to a peak of around twenty-eight editions. Between the 1550s and the 1580s, sales seem to have remained more or less steady at a lower level. There were about fourteen editions in the fifties, nineteen in the sixties, twelve in the seventies and thirteen in the eighties. By the 1590s and 1600s, however, editions were down to around six per decade, and by the 1610s, they were down to four.

The rise of interest in the book would appear to be related to the well-known shift from republics to courts in Renaissance Italy, a shift which made Italian cultural models easier to imitate elsewhere. The book's popularity was doubtless encouraged by the fashion for Italian culture in Spain, France, England and elsewhere, though these trends do not of course explain why the *Courtier* was more successful than rival treatises on similar topics. In the case of the decline of interest in the seventeenth century, there would seem to have been opposite reasons for this downward trend. Some religious readers, Catholic and Protestant alike, viewed the book as at least a little immoral. On the other hand, the *Courtier* failed to compete with some rival treatises because it was not sufficiently Machiavellian, or at least Tacitean. The decline of interest in the text also seems to be related to changes in the structure of courts, notably the rise of absolute monarchy.

In order to be better understood, these broad trends need to be broken down by region and by the social groups to which readers belonged.

The Geography of Reception

Let us begin with the geography of the diffusion, especially the European cities in which around 130 editions of the book had been printed by 1699. The leading city by a very long way was Venice, with its forty-eight editions or so in the period. Then came Paris, with about seventeen editions of the French translation; London, with twelve editions (either in English or in Latin); Lyon, with nine (either in French or Italian); Florence, with about seven; and Antwerp, with six (all in Spanish). Printing was a somewhat decentralized industry in Spain and the German-speaking world, so that it is no surprise to find the eight or more Spanish editions scattered over Barcelona, Medina del Campo, Salamanca, Seville and Toledo, or the nine German editions (mostly in Latin) spread over Dillingen, Frankfurt, Munich, Strasbourg and Wittenberg.

To establish the geography of the readership is more interesting as well as more difficult. What follows is based on the 328 sixteenth- and seventeenth-century readers who are listed in appendix 2. With more than a hundred editions, and a probable average print-run of a thousand copies a time (as in the case of the first edition), we might assume that there were more than 100,000 copies of the *Courtier* in circulation in the century following its publication.[1] A conservative estimate of three readers per copy in these three generations produces a total of 300,000 or more readers. In other words, appendix 2 lists only one reader in every

1 Contrast Cavagna (1989), 138, who estimates that only 18,000 to 40,000 copies were in circulation.

thousand. All the same, the geographical and social distribution of these 328 readers may be of interest.

The Italian share of this group amounts to eighty-nine, or more than a quarter of the total, most of them from the north of the peninsula, from Padua, Mantua, Ferrara, Florence and especially from Venice. The fact that Venice was a republican regime without a court seems to have been no obstacle to interest in the book. One Venetian publisher, Curtio Navo, dedicated his 1538 edition of the dialogue to a young patrician, Alvise Giorgi, and attributed to him most of the 'ornaments' of the ideal courtier, while Ludovico Dolce dedicated one of his editions to Giorgio Gradenigo, who was to become a distinguished senator. Readers from the south of Italy, where the manuscript had circulated before publication, included the Neapolitan writer Fabrizio Luna and the Sicilian lawyer Argisto Giuffredi.

The eighty-three English-speaking readers, more than a quarter of the total, may reflect no more than the fact that it has been relatively easy for an English historian to discover references. Only ten or eleven editions of the text had been published in England by 1699. On the other hand, there were twenty-six editions in France in the same period (counting the Italian editions printed in Lyon), but only sixty-eight French-speaking readers, including three from sixteenth-century Besançon, which did not become part of France till the later seventeenth century. As a clue to the book's importance in France, it should be added that out of a sample of 219 inventories from sixteenth-century Paris which mention books, no fewer than eighteen contained copies of the *Courtier*.[2] The total of twenty-seven Iberian readers (including five Catalans and six Portuguese) is also much too low, given the number of editions of the Spanish translation.

The remainder of the readership was scattered over much of Europe, with the largest contingent coming from the German-speaking world, nineteen readers in the list, not counting the thirteen Austrian nobles with the book in their libraries, mentioned but not named by the historian Otto Brunner.[3] It is worth noting that the republican Swiss did not spurn the book. In 1613,

2 Schutz (1955).
3 Brunner (1956).

for instance, a certain Samuel Grunerus of Berne wrote his name in a copy which has survived. In 1668, the *Courtier* was reprinted in Zurich, while in 1764 the public library in Berne had three copies of the dialogue, suggesting that the city may have been witnessing a process of 'aristocratization' like Amsterdam's in the later seventeenth century.[4]

Other regional groupings are rather small. There are twelve readers from Scandinavia (nine Danes and three Swedes), and seven Dutch readers, mostly in the seventeenth century (above, pp. 129–30). In central Europe, readers included four Hungarians, three Poles, one individual Bohemian, Johannes Dernschwam, and one aristocratic family, the Lobkovič, which owned no fewer than five copies. I have found no Norwegian, Finnish, Russian, Bulgarian, Serbian, Moldavian, Wallachian, or Irish readers, although a recent study of sixteenth-century Irish literature drew attention to the possible use of the *Courtier*, in Hoby's translation, in the anonymous poem *Fuar dó féin*.[5]

Readers of the *Courtier* were not confined to Europe. The tradition that members of the Japanese embassy which visited Italy in 1585 took the book back to Japan with them is perhaps less implausible than that of the seventeenth-century Moscow translation. Given Japanese concern with correct behaviour and a tradition of interest in the West which goes back at least as far as Oda Nobunaga (1534–82), the story is at least *ben trovato*, symbolically appropriate.[6] However, all the empirical evidence I have been able to find regarding the *Courtier* outside Europe concerns Europeans in Asia and the Americas. In 1586, for example, a Florentine merchant, Filippo Sassetti wrote home from Cochin, on the coast of south-west India, that he had found a copy of the *Courtier* 'in the shop of someone who sells matches'.[7]

Although Irving Leonard's well-known study of the place of books in the Spanish conquest and settlement of the New World makes no mention of Castiglione, a few Spaniards in Peru can be shown to have owned the *Courtier*. In 1545, a shipment including a copy of the dialogue went to Diego de Narváez, of Cuzco. In 1582, a similar shipment went to Antonio Dávalos, treasurer of

4 Sinner (1764), vol. II, 810.
5 MacGraíth (1990), 64.
6 Donesmondi (1616), vol. II, 151–2.
7 Sassetti (1855), no. 102.

New Castile and a resident of Lima. In the same year, as we have seen (p. 105), Fray Juan de Almaraz, Inquisitor in Lima, tried to censor the *Courtier*. Finally, two copies of a book called the *Cortesano* (either Castiglione in Spanish, or the books by Milán or Palmireno) were found in the library of the Peruvian writer, the Inca Garcilaso de la Vega, in 1616, whether he had bought them in his own country or in Spain, where he was living at the time of his death.

It is no surprise that a book which was so popular in Renaissance Spain should have attracted interest among Spaniards in the New World. It was less to be expected, perhaps, that it would have appealed to colonial Americans in the late seventeenth and early eighteenth centuries. It was owned by John Winthrop Junior, the governor of Connecticut. Again, the inventory made in 1701 of the goods of the Virginia planter Ralph Wormeley II includes the mysterious entry 'courtior of coubaldy', which has been brilliantly decoded as 'Courtier of Count Baldassare', the clerk presumably working to dictation.[8] Indeed, we are told that the book appears 'again and again' in inventories of the property of eighteenth-century Virginia gentlemen.[9] It also turns up in eighteenth-century Philadelphia.[10] Should we interpret this interest as a sign of the 'cultural lag' of a provincial society, remote from any metropolis?

At all events, some of Castiglione's lessons were well learned. Colonel John Pierce, writing in 1784 to his sister in New York, advised her to study 'walking, standing and sitting, all the movements of which though they appear in a polite person natural, are the effects of art'. He stressed the need for 'a natural careless genteel air . . . which totally hides all the art of it'. He might have been translating a passage from the *Courtier*.[11]

The Sociology of Reception

It is difficult to interpret regional variations without raising the question of which social groups were most interested in the

8 Wright (1940), 133, 197n., 210.
9 Fithian (1943), xxiii, without references.
10 Wolf (1974).
11 Bushman (1992), 371–2.

Courtier, and whether different groups read the text in diverse ways. Did it appeal to nobles, for instance, although they were supposed not to need the lessons it imparted? Or to members of the bourgeoisie, although they had little experience of courts? Or to women, despite their minor role in the dialogue itself? Given the minute size of the sample, let alone the overlap between the main forms of social classification (male and female, noble and commoner, lay and clerical, court and country, and so on), there is little point in offering any percentages (readers are welcome to calculate their own from the list in appendix 2). All that can be done, as in the case of the Italians discussed in chapter 3, is to pick out a few 'faces in the crowd' in a number of different social categories.

The majority of readers listed in the appendix were male and legally noble, though the category of 'noble' was far from uniform, as we shall see. The list includes no fewer than eighteen members of ruling families, including Charles V, François I, Erik XIV of Sweden, Mary Queen of Scots, Prince Christian of Denmark and the Emperor Rudolf II. Today, we tend to see the Emperor Rudolf as a withdrawn, scholarly figure and his court at Prague as a centre of occult studies, but a translation of the *Courtier* was dedicated to the emperor and his ennoblement of half-a-dozen artists suggests that Rudolf shared at least some of the values expressed in the dialogue.

Among the higher nobility, we find the Spaniard Lastanosa, the Frenchman La Rochefoucauld, the Swede Brahe, the central Europeans Lobkovič and Pázmány; and such English peers as Thomas Sackville, Lord Buckhurst; John Lord Lumley; and Henry Howard, earl of Northampton. They would of course have learned how to behave as aristocrats when they were children, so it is to be presumed that the appeal of the book for them was that it exemplified fashionable Italian trends.

All these men necessarily knew the world of the court at first hand, like the different kinds of professional courtier, whether they were active in a ruler's household or the administration of a kingdom. Among the administrators, we find Thomas Cromwell, Philip II's minister Cardinal Granvelle, the French financier Nicolas Fouquet and the Danish chancellor Jacob Ulfeldt. Other courtiers include the Spaniard Luis Zapata, a former page of the Empress Isabel; the poet Tasso, at the court of Ferrara; the Hungarian noble Bálint Balassa at the court of King Stefan Batory, of Poland; and Sir Christopher Hatton, who knew very well how to court Queen Elizabeth. Indeed, Hatton was said to have gained the royal favour through 'the graces of his person and dancing', a remark which should perhaps be added to the English criticisms of 'Castilio' discussed in an earlier chapter (above, p. 109).[12]

Despite the dialogue's favourable references to the profession of arms, only a few soldiers are known to have owned or read the *Courtier*, including Odet de Foix, Marshal of France, Alonso Barros, François de La Noue, George Whetstone, and Nicolas d'Herberay, Seigneur des Essarts and *commissaire ordinaire de l'artillerie*. On the other hand, Castiglione, who had been employed as an ambassador himself, seems to have appealed to diplomats, at least eleven of them, including Diego Hurtado de Mendoza, Thomas Hoby, Thomas Sackville, John Dymock, Sir Thomas Killigrew, Erik Rosenkrantz, and Abraham de Wicquefort. Dymock and Killigrew both used the text in a way which the author would have been the first to appreciate, as a diplomatic gift, a means to court the favour of a foreign monarch.

Castiglione's book could also be found in the libraries of country gentlemen who lived on their estates far from any court. Michel de Montaigne, for instance, at Montaigne near Bordeaux; Sir Thomas Knyvett in Norfolk; William More of Loseley, Surrey; Sir Thomas Tresham in Northamptonshire; or William Drummond of Hawthornden in Scotland. It also appealed to urban patricians – not only to Venetians but also to Catalans such as Juan Boscán, Netherlanders such as Jan Six, or central Europeans such as the Fuggers and the Welsers.

In the case of the Fuggers and Welsers, families who entered the nobility after making their money from trade, we are approaching the world of the 'new men' who might be assumed to have needed the *Courtier* most and to have used it as a guide to good behaviour and impression management. English examples include Daniel Defoe and Thomas Cromwell, the son of a blacksmith from Putney who turned to politics and acquired an earldom before he

12 Naunton (1641), 27.

ended his life on the scaffold. French examples include Jean-Baptiste Colbert, an administrator whose family had recently been engaged in trade, and Nicolas Faret, the son of a shoemaker turned expert on courtly behaviour.

Leaving aside the eight booksellers, only a few practising merchants are known to have owned the book, among them the Florentine Filippo Sassetti, the Venetian Giovanni Zanca, Pierre Bablan of Compiègne, and Firmin de Forcheville, *marchand hôtelier* of Amiens (one wonders whether he bought it for the use of his guests). A few doctors took an interest in the book, not only the court physician Benedictus Olai but five others as well. Lawyers (at least fifteen of them), appear to have been avid readers of the *Courtier*, from Sicily, where Argisto Giuffredi recommended it to his sons, to Exeter, where William Martyn did the same thing, as well as adapting the text, in the words of one historian, 'to the tastes of common citizens'.[13] Lawyers were of course on the margins of nobility, some of them being members of what the French called the *noblesse de robe*, magistrates in the parlements. This was the position of Jacques-Auguste de Thou, for instance, or Nicolas Pasquier, both in Paris. Montaigne, another magistrate, was a relatively new noble whose family had made their money in the wine trade and who had himself served as a magistrate in Bordeaux before retiring to his estate.

University teachers were another group of apparently enthusiastic readers, including the Italians Maggi, Riccoboni, Speroni and Varchi, the Spaniard Cristóbal be Villalón, the Dane Peder Scavenius, the German Johann Heinrich Boeckler and the Dutchman Nikolaes Heinsius. At least fourteen Fellows of Oxford and Cambridge colleges owned or referred to the book, among them Robert Burton and John Locke.[14] It is tempting to interpret this interest as a sign of the status problems of members of a new profession. In the case of Gabriel Harvey, at least, there can be little doubt about the anxieties associated with upward social mobility. The son of a ropemaker from Saffron Walden, Harvey became a Fellow of two Cambridge colleges, Pembroke and

13 Wright (1935), 124.
14 Kiessling (1988); Harrison and Laslett (1965); Ovenell (1950); Korsten (1980); Leedham-Green (1987).

Trinity Hall, but was sometimes mocked for his awkward behaviour and humble origin. The annotations in his copies of the *Courtier*, discussed above (pp. 78–9), are very much concerned with good behaviour.

One might not have expected great clerical interest in the *Courtier*, although its author ended his life in minor orders and in papal service. All the same, appendix 2 includes twenty-nine members of the clergy (excluding Fellows of Oxford and Cambridge colleges). Even if we eliminate the two censors, we are left with twenty-seven clerical readers, three Protestants (Edmund Bonner, Thomas Wryght and John Hacket, another 'new man') and twenty-four Catholics, including one pope, three cardinals and ten bishops. In other words the book appealed especially to those clergymen who spent much time at the courts of princes or held court themselves.

Musicians, artists and, above all, writers frequently owned or referred to the *Courtier*. The musicians included Luis Milán, Thomas Whythorne, and (in all probability) Giulio Caccini. Raphael died before his friend's dialogue was published, but Italian readers included Il Rosso (as early as 1531), Giorgio Vasari, and Gianpaolo Lomazzo, while among foreign artists we find the Netherlander Karel van Mander and the Spaniard Velázquez.

In the case of Rembrandt, Rubens, and Joachim von Sandrart, who all copied the Raphael portrait of Castiglione, it is not easy to say whether they were expressing interest in the painter or the sitter. However, it is likely that the choice of the Castiglione portrait was no coincidence in any of these three cases. Like Castiglione, Rubens was employed on diplomatic missions, like him he worked for the Gonzaga family, and his manners as well as his letters were courtly. Rembrandt was concerned to the point of obsession with self-presentation, and it has been suggested that he assimilated Castiglione's face to his own features (see plate 3). Joachim von Sandrart, an artist with a noble lifestyle, was the underbidder when the portrait of Castiglione was put up for auction in Amsterdam. Sandrart, like Vasari, was and is best known not so much for his paintings as for his lives of artists, in which he emphasized the need for good manners (*Höflichkeit*). He praised Rubens because he was 'courteous and friendly to everyone', and Van Dyck for his 'grace and ease' (*Gratia und Annehmlichkeit*).[15]

As for the writers, they include some of the most famous names of the sixteenth and seventeenth centuries. The evidence for interest in the *Courtier* on the part of Cervantes and Shakespeare is indirect, but a list of writers which includes Ariosto, Tasso, Montaigne, Rojas (author of the famous Spanish play the *Celestina*), Garcilaso de la Vega, Gracián, Ben Jonson and Daniel Defoe is impressive enough.

I have left the female readers to the last because the question is, or at any rate was, a controversial one. The German Johannes Ricius, who rendered the first book of the *Courtier* into Latin, ignored book III, he explained in his preface, because he thought the book 'of more interest to men than to women'. Again, as we have seen (p. 91), Łukasz Górnicki's transposition of the *Courtier* made all the speakers male because he considered Polish women not well enough educated to participate in the discussions.

On the other hand, the humanist Bishop Paolo Giovio claimed that Castiglione wrote 'especially for women'. In Spain, France and England alike, women encouraged the translation of Castiglione's book, while the German translation of 1593 was dedicated to a married couple, Christoffer and Maria Fugger. The list in appendix 2 includes twenty-one female readers, despite the fact that inventories are a source biased in favour of males. For example, there is no way of telling whether the copy of the English translation of the *Courtier* in the library of John Lord Lumley bears witness to his concerns or to those of his wife Jane, a translator of Euripides and one of the best-known learned ladies of her time. The evidence for interest in the book on the part of sixteenth-century Italian ladies has been discussed already, but it may be worth adding a few details about other countries.

In Spain, the translator Juan Boscán explained in his preface that the translation had been encouraged, indeed commanded by a woman, Gerónima Palova de Almogáver. Boscán went on to declare that 'a perfect courtier requires a perfect lady', and to reply in advance to possible criticisms that the book deals with 'depths of knowledge' inappropriate for ladies. To his testimony may be

15 Chapman (1990), 73; Sandrart (1675–80).

added that of the musician Luis Milán, who recorded a conversation with 'certain ladies of Valencia who held in their hands the *Courtier* of Count Baldassare Castiglione', inspiring his comment

Más quería ser vos conde	I should prefer to be you, count
Que no don Luis Milán,	Than Don Luis Milán,
Por estar en esas manos	In order to be in those hands
Donde yo quería estar.	Where I should like to be.[16]

In the case of France, the evidence is more indirect. Two manuscripts survive of sixteenth-century French versions of book III alone.[17] It is likely, though impossible to prove, that one of these translations was made at the initiative of Marguerite de Navarre, who owned a copy of the printed text. It is hardly surprising that Marguerite de Navarre knew the book, since she was interested in neoplatonism, corresponded with Vittoria Colonna, had her Italian poems published in Italian anthologies, and was involved in the French *querelle des femmes*.[18]

Another female reader was Catherine de' Medici, a Florentine who married into the French royal family in 1533. She was close to Marguerite de Navarre, and was herself interested in mathematics, painting and literature. When her husband became King Henri II, he regularly held 'a kind of court' in the queen's apartments, a sort of *salon* in which the courtiers tried to shine in conversation.[19] Catherine's daughter Marguerite de Valois also owned a copy of the *Courtier*.

In England, it was Elizabeth, marchioness of Northampton (née Elizabeth Brook, daughter of Lord Cobham), second wife of his patron, William Parr, who originally asked Hoby to translate book III, as the translator confesses in his prefatory 'epistle' to Lord Hastings. In the same letter he quotes the names of five Italian noblewomen who distinguished themselves as writers, as if to encourage Englishwomen to emulate them. The Latin translation was dedicated to Queen Elizabeth, who may well have been familiar with the original, since she learned Italian as a girl and

16 Milán (1561), 4.
17 Klesczewski (1966), 82–97.
18 Jourda (1930), 684; Telle (1937).
19 Solnon (1987), 140.

was tutored by Roger Ascham. It is difficult to believe that Lady Jane Grey, who moved in the circle of Cheke and Hoby, and Mary Sidney, countess of Pembroke, who was compared, as we have seen (p. 77) to the duchess of Urbino, did not also know the book. As for more general testimony, in their play *Westward Ho!* (1605), Dekker and Webster make a character refer to 'the young Gentlewoman' who 'hath read in the Italian *Courtier*, that it is a special ornament to gentlewomen to have skill in painting' (Act I, scene 1). As in the dialogue itself, the female element among the readership of the *Courtier* is more significant than it may appear at first sight.

So much for general social categories. Again and again in the course of this essay, reference has been made to personal links between readers of the *Courtier*, and the importance of these networks deserves a final comment. An Italian edition of the *Courtier* now in the University Library in Cambridge bears the charming if conventional inscription 'I belong to Bernard Hampton and his friends' (*Sum Barnardi Hamptoni eiusque amicorum*). One might have expected people to pass the book on to their friends, but for historians it is satisfying to be able to document the process, at least on occasion.

Pairs of readers turn up again and again. For example, the 1538 edition of the French translation of the *Courtier* includes a letter by Etienne Dolet to Melin de Saint-Gelais, reminding him that they were reading the book together in Lyon. The friendship of Montaigne and La Boétie was and is well known. Johann Heinrich Boeckler was a friend of Georg Philipp Harsdörffer, a fellow-student at the University of Strasbourg; the preacher Secondo Lancellotti, a friend of Gabriel Naudé; the marquis of Lastanosa, the patron of Baltasar Gracián; Everard Guilpin, a cousin of John Marston; Pontus de Tyard II, the great-nephew of Pontus de Tyard I (the bishop who moved in the circle of the Pléiade); and Mary Queen of Scots, the mother of James VI and I.

Groups of three, four or five readers are not difficult to find either. Mario Equicola was the secretary of Margherita Cantelma and Isabella d'Este and the correspondent of Girolamo Cittadini. Matteo Bandello dedicated the story in which he mentions a discussion of the *Courtier* to Enea Pio, the brother of Lady Emilia and of Margherita di San Severino, in whose house the discussion took place. The Spanish translator Juan Boscán was a friend of both Garcilaso de la Vega and Andrea Navagero, a Venetian who was in turn linked to Ramusio and to Bembo, who had both helped see the first edition of the *Courtier* through the press. In France, Marguerite de Navarre was linked not only to her relatives François I and Catherine de' Medici but also to her clients Bourbon, Des Périers and Héroet. In England, Thomas Cromwell knew Edmund Bonner and Sir Thomas Elyot. Elyot's nephew George Puttenham knew Thomas Sackville. Sackville also knew Clerke and Hoby, while his father had been a friend of Roger Ascham's. Ben Jonson was a friend of William Drummond and an acquaintance of Thomas Coryate. Thomas Coryate was in turn an acquaintance of Henry Peacham. Peacham was the tutor to the sons of the earl of Arundel, who also employed Junius. Erik Rosenkrantz was gentleman of the chamber to Prince Christian of Denmark, and he studied at the noble Academy of Sorø at the same time as two other readers, Joachim Gersdorff and Cornelius Lerche, a coincidence which suggests that the *Courtier* might have been on the syllabus in that institution, in which, as in other colleges for the nobility, riding, fencing and dancing were as important as more academic subjects.[20]

Individual copies of the *Courtier* sometimes offer evidence of networks of readers. For example, one copy of the 1571 Latin translation has three names inscribed in it, those of James Dalton, Richard Daulton and Edward Higgins. All three were members of Brasenose College, Oxford in the later sixteenth century, so the names prove unusually explicit evidence of the common process of the circulation of books within a small institution.

The largest network known to me, apart from the many friends and relatives of Castiglione himself, centres on St John's College, Cambridge, where the English translator of the *Courtier*, Sir Thomas Hoby, once studied. Hoby's teachers included Sir John Cheke, a Fellow of St John's, who advised him on the translation, and probably Roger Ascham, another Fellow of the college whose interest in Castiglione has been mentioned several times. Another St John's man, the Italian exile Pietro Bizzarri, also referred to the text. This network did not end at the college gates, for Killigrew,

20 Cf. Conrads (1982), 143–52.

the diplomat who presented the *Courtier* to Mary Queen of Scots, was Hoby's brother-in-law.

Reception and Transformation

What did these different kinds of reader see in the *Courtier*? The work of the editors in turning an open dialogue into a closed manual or recipe-book has already been discussed at some length. What of the reactions of individual readers? From printed comments and manuscript annotations alike, a fairly coherent picture begins to emerge. When, for instance, a sixteenth-century reader marks the passage discussing the art of riding a horse, one can be fairly sure that he views the dialogue as a manual.[21] The same goes for the reader who marked a passage on ball-games, or for the German writer, Hippolytus a Collibus, who was particularly impressed by the remarks on clothes. Vittoria Colonna's praise of the 'maxims' suggests a similar conclusion, while the French translation of 1580 was furnished with an elaborate table of maxims such as 'Qualities which a prince should possess', 'Gestures required for telling a funny story', declaring that 'Honour is the bridle of women', and so on.

Again, contemporaries took considerable interest in the discussion of humour in book II, which modern readers often find rather tedious. Vittoria Colonna, the poet Giangiorgio Trissino and the critics Vincenzo Maggi and Antonio Riccoboni all singled the jokes out for special mention.[22] One reader, Giuffredi, recommended his sons to learn the stories by heart. Another, Sansovino, drew attention to the witty repartees (*motti*). Ben Jonson's reference to the dialogue concerns the anecdotes alone, while anonymous readers not infrequently underlined them.

One group of readers, mainly Italian men of letters, paid particular attention to the debate on language. As we have seen, another group was particularly concerned with the exposition of neoplatonism in book IV. The praises of women were marked by

21 TCC, Grylls 11.412.
22 Colonna (1889), no. 18; Sansovino (1564), cited Hinz (1992), 264; Trissino and Maggi cited Ossola (1980), 34, 35n.; Riccoboni (1579), 457.

the reader of a copy of the Venice 1587 edition (now in Cambridge), while the earl of Oxford drew attention to this aspect of the book in his letter in the Clerke translation.

Castiglione's passage on *sprezzatura* was marked in two copies of the Spanish translation, now in Madrid.[23] Gabriel Harvey and Henry Howard also marked this passage, among others. Other readers marked passages concerned with 'grace' or 'affectation'. There is also indirect evidence that Lodovico da Canossa's remarks were taken very seriously by at least one group of readers – the artists.

Count Lodovico had extended his remarks on gracefully negligent behaviour to painting, praising the effectiveness of a brush stroke executed with such facility 'that it seems that the hand moves to its goal by itself without being guided by any kind of effort or skill' (1.28). Among the artists who were and are famous for such calculated spontaneity, or 'facility', as Vasari called it, we find Giulio Romano, Velázquez and Rembrandt, all three men associated in their different ways, as we have seen, with Castiglione and his book.[24]

Elites and Civilization

It is time to return to the question of the effects of the *Courtier* on western civilization, indeed its effects on the 'civilizing process' itself, to return to the famous formulation of Norbert Elias. Despite the probability that the text had 300,000 readers in the early modern period, the question of its influence remains somewhat elusive. It is elusive not only because of the active process of reception but also because, as we have seen, Castiglione's gift was not for original thought so much as for the vivid, witty and memorable evocation of a tradition of behaviour to which Aristotle, Cicero, rules for monks, and courtesy-books for knights and ladies all made contributions. Hence a later discussion which seems to echo the *Courtier* may be written in complete ignorance of Castiglione's existence.

23 BNM, R.7319, R.7909.
24 Gombrich (1986); Brown (1986), 146–8, 204–5; Chapman (1990), 72.

Take the case of Tolstoy, for example. Count Leo Nikolayevich, describing his youth in the 1840s, confessed his desire to be *comme il faut* in his speech, his dress and his behaviour. 'I did not then know', he ruefully admitted, 'that one of the chief conditions of being *comme il faut* is secrecy as to the efforts by which that *comme il faut* is attained.'[25] This is the paradox of *sprezzatura* in a nutshell. Yet Castiglione's dialogue had not been translated into Russian, while it had ceased to be read in France long before Tolstoy's day. In similar fashion, contemporary western adolescents who value behaviour which is unflustered or 'cool' are formulating a democratic version of *sprezzatura* without being aware of their place in a long tradition. Perhaps one should also include television personalities who rehearse in order to seem more natural – though their deliberately informal style pays homage to the ideal of sincerity rather than to that of elegant performance.

It might even be argued that all groups who believe themselves to be superior to others have behaved in a similar manner for similar reasons all over the world, adopting a style of life which emphasizes their distinction from ordinary mortals. Forty years before Elias published his *The Process of Civilization*, concerned almost exclusively with developments in the West, another sociologist, Thorstein Veblen, had put foward this universalist argument in his *Theory of the Leisure Class*, noting how elites who do not need to work like to show off their leisure.[26] The French sociologist Pierre Bourdieu, who resembles Veblen in his merciless analysis of social ploys, has written of 'the unselfconsciousness that is the mark of so-called "natural" distinction'.[27]

I would rather speak of recurrent social strategies than of universal ones, on the grounds that some non-western cultures offer closer parallels than others to the ideal of the Renaissance courtier. In eighteenth-century Japan, for example, guides to the pleasure quarters of the great cities told their readers that they should show a quality known as *iki*, which has been translated as 'aristocratic nonchalance'.[28] Thanks to the work of the anthropologist Clifford

25 Tolstoy (1857), 269.
26 Veblen (1899); Elias (1939).
27 Bourdieu (1982), 11.
28 Buruma (1984), 81.

Geertz, we know that in traditional Java, for instance, the court was an 'exemplary centre', a model for behaviour.[29] Although the court was apparently less exemplary in traditional China, its culture is worth examining in a little more detail.

One of Veblen's most memorable examples came from China, the long fingernails of the mandarins being interpreted as conspicuous signs that they did not need to use their hands. The culture of the Chinese mandarins also offers parallels for two famous propositions discussed in Castiglione's dialogue, *sprezzatura* and the need for members of an elite to know how to practise the arts, notably poetry, painting and music. Even before the age of the mandarins, Confucius (551–479 BC) had already formulated an ideal of the 'princely man' or gentleman (*ch'ün tzu*) in which ostentation was condemned but the cultivation of the self recommended. The parallel between the princely man of Confucius and the magnanimous man of Aristotle is a striking one. One of the sayings of Confucius was that 'a gentleman is not an implement', and this was interpreted to mean that specialists were inferior, while the superior man did not get his hands dirty.[30]

The mandarins who entered the imperial administration after excelling in examinations based on the Confucian classics exemplified the ideal of the amateur who can turn his hand to anything and do it well but not too well. Writing poetry had long been an occupation of the scholar-officials, but by the twelfth and thirteenth centuries, if not before, their interests had extended to painting. The effect of spontaneity so much appreciated in Chinese painting, as in its sister art of calligraphy, has been interpreted as another manifestation of the amateur ideal. 'Scholar-painting' was distinguished from professional painting, which showed more technical skill but less spirit. The execution of scholar-painting should be rapid, and there was nothing wrong in its being inspired by wine. Literary men ought to paint well, but not too well.[31]

It would be fascinating to know how Castiglione would have reacted to the Chinese scholar-painters or scholar-officials if he could have been taken to Peking, like his fellow-countryman

29 Geertz (1977).
30 Dawson (1981), ch. 5; Hamburger (1959).
31 Levenson (1958), part 1, ch. 2; Cahill (1960); Bush (1971).

Matteo Ricci later in the sixteenth century. The point of the Chinese example, however, is to remind readers that the West has no monopoly of either amateurs or gentlemen. From the perspective of world history, the *Courtier* may be seen as a classic formulation of a style of behaviour which can also be found in other cultural traditions.

All the same, in Europe this style of behaviour has a special 'tincture', as Sir Ernest Barker called it. At the beginning of this essay, the suggestion was made that the *Courtier* could be used as a kind of litmus paper, to test the 'Europeanization of Europe', in other words the extent to which the continent was culturally unified.[32] What conclusions follow from this experiment?

From this point of view, Europe can be divided into three areas. In one, essentially Italy, Spain and France, the *Courtier* was welcomed very quickly indeed. In a second, mainly northern, area – Britain, central Europe, and Scandinavia – the dialogue spread (with individual exceptions) after some delay, from the middle of the sixteenth century onwards. Further east the dialogue seems to have been completely unknown, in Muscovy and in the Christian parts of the Ottoman empire (Serbia, Moldavia, Wallachia, Bulgaria, etc.).

This distribution recalls the discussion of the 'three historical regions of Europe' by the Hungarian historian Jenö Szücs. Szücs argued that for the last 1,000 years or so, Europe has been divided – economically, politically, socially and culturally – into East and West, with an 'east-central' region (Hungary, for instance), mediating between the two and so acquiring a dual heritage. The fortunes of the *Courtier* would appear to confirm the 'Three Europes' hypothesis, as well as qualifying it, since the 'central' region was considerably larger in this particular case while the periphery, which Castiglione did not reach, included the Celtic world, and the northern parts of Scandinavia.[33]

Why should eastern Europeans, as opposed to east-central Europeans, have ignored or rejected Castiglione's book? As we have seen, it was possible to break through the language barrier, but other obstacles were more effective, three in particular. In the

32 Bartlett (1993), 269–91.
33 Szücs (1983).

first place, rulers had long been accustomed to autocracy. It is difficult to imagine that Ivan IV, 'the Terrible', would have liked his boyars to speak out as freely as Ottaviano Fregoso had recommended. In the second place, literacy was relatively low in this part of early modern Europe, and printing presses were extremely rare. In the third place, high culture was virtually controlled by the Orthodox clergy, at least until the later seventeenth century. By the time that Peter the Great had determined to westernize his nobles, the dominant cultural model was no longer Italian but French.

In this third Europe, east of Poland and the Habsburg empire, the Renaissance never arrived, so that the Middle Ages may be said to have lasted until 1700 or thereabouts. The first major cultural movement in which the elites all over Europe participated was the Enlightenment.

Appendix 1
Editions of the Courtier,
1528–1850

━━━━━━◆◆◆◆◆◆◆◆◆◆◆◆◆◆━━━━━━

This list is a revision of the one provided by Leonard Opdycke in his translation of the *Courtier* (1901), 419–22, with the help (in the case of editions of the French translations), of Klesczewski (1966), 177–81. Where possible, I have mentioned libraries where copies are to be found; where no library is mentioned, the existence of the edition remains in doubt. It should be noted that Opdycke himself owned copies of French and Spanish editions which have now vanished. Editions marked with an asterisk are those I have examined.

 1* Italian, Venice (Aldus), 1528, folio [BL (5 copies), BNP (2 copies); Queens' College, Cambridge, TCC, UL]
 2   Italian, Florence (Giunta), 1528, octavo
 3   Italian, Florence (Giunta), 1529, octavo [BNP]
 4   Italian, Tusculano (Paganino), *c.*1529, 12mo
 5* Italian, Parma (Viotti), 1530, octavo [BL]
 6* Italian, Florence (Giunta), 1531, octavo [BL, BNP]
 7* Italian, Florence (Giunta), 1531, octavo
 8   Italian, Parma (Viotti), 1531, octavo
 9   Italian, Parma (Viotti), 1532, octavo
10* Italian, Venice (Aldus), 1533, octavo [BL, BNP; King's College, Cambridge]
11* Italian, Venice (no publisher), 1533, octavo [BNP]
12* Spanish, Barcelona (Montpezat), 1534, folio [BNM]
13* Italian, Florence (Giunta), 1537, octavo [BL]
14   Italian, Lyon, 1537, octavo

15* French, Paris (Longis & Sertenas), 1537, octavo [BNP; Bibliothèque Mazarine, Paris]

16 French, Paris (Longis & Sertenas), 1537, octavo [not in Opdycke: Herzog August Bibliothek, Wolfenbüttel]

17* French, Lyon (Harsy), 1537, octavo [BNP; Staatsbibliothek, Munich]

18 French, no place, 1537, 12mo

19* Italian, Venice (Curtio Navo), 1538, octavo [BLO]

20* Italian, Venice (Federico Torresano), 1538, octavo [BLO, BNP]

21 Italian, Venice (Vettor de' Robani), 1538, octavo

22* French, Lyon (Juste), 1538, octavo [BL, BNP, Wolfenbüttel]

23* French, no place, 1538, octavo [BLO, Munich]

24 Italian, Venice (Tortis), 1539, octavo

25 Italian, no place, 1539, octavo, abbreviated

26* Spanish, Toledo, no printer, 1539, quarto [BNM]

27 French, Paris, no printer, 1540, octavo [BL, Mazarine]

26 Spanish, Salamanca (Touans), 1540, quarto [BNM]

28* Italian, Venice (Aldus), 1541, octavo [BL, BLO, BNP, TCC]

29* Italian, Venice (Giolito), 1541, 12mo [TCC, Juel Jensen]

30* Italian, Venice (Tortis), 1541, octavo [BL: not in Opdycke]

31 Spanish, no place, 1541

32 Spanish, Medina del Campo, 1542 [Opdycke cited BL]

33 Spanish, no place, 1542 [Opdycke cited BNM, perhaps a mistaken reference to the 1549 edition]

34* Spanish, Seville (Cromberger), 1542, quarto [BL, BNM]

35 Italian, Venice (Giolito), 1543, octavo

36* Italian, Venice (Giolito), 1544, octavo [BL, TCC; St Catharine's College, Cambridge]

37 Italian, Venice (Tortis), 1544, octavo [Rome, Biblioteca Chigiana]

38 Italian, no place, 1544, octavo

39* Spanish, Antwerp (Nucio), 1544, octavo [BNM]

40* Italian, Venice (Aldus), 1545, folio [BL, BNP, TCC, UL]

41* French, Paris (Nicolas du Chemin), 1545, 16mo [BL, BLO]

42* Italian, Venice (Giolito), 1546 [BNP]

43 French, Paris (Corrozet), 1546 [not in Opdycke: Munich]

44 French, Paris (L'Angelier), 1546, 12mo [Opdycke's library]

45* Italian, Venice (Aldo), 1547, octavo [BL, BNP, TCC, UL]

46 Italian, Venice (Giolito), 1547, octavo

47 Italian, Venice (Giolito), 1549, 12mo

48 Italian, Venice (Tortis), 1549, octavo [Rome, Biblioteca Vittorio Emmanuele]

49 French, Paris (Ruelle), 1549, 16mo [Erlangen, University Library]

50* French, Paris (Grouleau), 1549, 16mo [London Library; Landes-
bibliothek, Stuttgart]

51 French, Paris (Corrozet), 1549 [not in Opdycke but cited by
François de La Croix du Maine, *Bibliothèque françoise*, Paris
1584]

52 French, Paris (Lor) 1549, 160 [Vittorio Emmanuele]

53* Spanish, no place, 1549, quarto [BNM]

54* Italian, Lyon (Rouille), 1550, 16mo [UL]

55* Italian, Venice (Giolito), 1551, 12mo [BL, BNP, UL]

56* Italian, Venice (Giglio), 1552, 12mo [BNP]

57 Italian, Venice, no printer, 1552 [not in Opdycke: cited by
Klesczewski]

58* Italian, Venice (Giolito), 1552, octavo [BL, BNP]

59 Spanish, Saragossa (Capilla), 1553

60* Italian, Lyon (Rouille), 1553, 12mo [BL, Emmanuel College]

61 Italian, Florence (Giunta), 1554, 16mo [Biblioteca Marciana,
Venice]

59* Italian, Venice (Giolito), 1556, octavo [BL, Emmanuel College,
TCC]

62 Italian, Venice (Scoto), 1556 [Biblioteca Cavriani, Mantua]

63 French, Paris (L'Angelier), 1557, 160 [City Library, Lübeck]

64* Italian, Venice (Giolito), 1559, octavo [TCC]

65* Italian, Venice (Fagiani), 1559, octavo [BL]

66 Spanish, Toledo, 1559, quarto

67* Italian, Venice, Giolito, 1560, octavo [BL]

68* Italian, Lyon (Rouille), 1561, 16mo [BNP]

69* Spanish, Antwerp (Nucio), 1561, octavo [BNM]

70 Latin, Wittenberg (Crato), 1561 [University Library, Jena]

71* English, London (Seres), 1561, octavo [UL]

72* Italian, Lyon (Rouille), 1562, 16mo [BL, TCC]

73* Italian, Venice (Giolito), 1562, 12mo [Rome, Biblioteca Angelica]

74* Italian, Venice, no printer, 1562, octavo [BNP]

75 Italian, Venice (Giolito), 1563, 12mo

76* Italian, Venice (Giolito), 1564 [TCC]

77 Italian, no place, 1564, octavo

78* Italian, Venice (Cavalcalovo), 1565, 12mo [BL]

74* German, Munich (Berg), 1565, octavo [Wolfenbüttel]

79 Italian, Venice (Domenico), 1568, 12mo [BL, according to
Opdycke]

80 Italian, Venice (Giolito), 1569, 12mo [Vittorio Emmanuele]

81* Latin, Wittenberg (Schwertel), 1569, octavo [not in Opdycke:
Antwerp, University Library]

82 Latin, Wittenberg (Crato), 1569, octavo [probably identical with last entry]

83 French, Paris, 1569, 12mo [not in Opdycke or Klesczewski: Holkham; Hassall (1950), no. 1095]

84* Spanish, Valladolid (Fernandez), 1569, octavo [BL, BNM]

85* Latin, London (Day) 1571, octavo [UL]

86* Italian, Venice (Comin da Trino), 1573, octavo [BL]

87 Italian, Venice (Comin da Trino), 1574, octavo

88 Italian, Venice (Giolito), 1574, octavo

89* Italian, Venice (Farri), 1574, octavo [BL, BNP]

90* Spanish, Antwerp (Nucio), 1574, octavo [BNM, BNP, UL; St Catharine's College, Cambridge]

91 French, Paris (Gaultier), c.1577 [Opdycke's library]

92 English, London (Denham), 1577 [BL]

93* Latin, Strasbourg (Jobinus), 1577, octavo [BLO]

94* Latin, London (Bynneman), 1577, octavo [BLO, BNP; King's College, Cambridge]

95 Spanish, Antwerp, 1577, octavo

96* French and Italian, Lyon (Cloquemin), 1579 or 1580, octavo [BL]

97* Spanish, Salamanca (Lasso), 1581 octavo [BNM]

98* Italian, Venice (Basa), 1584, octavo [BL]

99 Latin, Frankfurt (Jobinus), 1584 [Rome, Biblioteca Alessandrina]

100 Latin, London, 1584, octavo

101* Latin, London (Dawson), 1585, octavo [BL, UL]

102 French, Lyon (Huguetan), 1585, octavo [Vittorio Emmanuele]

103* French and Italian, Paris (Bonfons), 1585, octavo [BNP]

104* French, Paris (Micard), 1585, octavo [BNP]

105 c.1586, Urbino [not in Opdycke: mentioned by Giglio, next entry]

106* Italian, Venice (Giglio), 1587, 12mo [BNP; Jesus College, Cambridge]

107* Latin, Strasbourg (Iobinus), 1587, octavo [BLO]

108* French, English and Italian, London (Wolfe), 1588, octavo [BL, BLO]

109* Italian, Venice (Tortis), 1589, octavo [BL]

110* French, Paris (L'Angelier), 1592, octavo [BNP]

111 Italian, Venice (Mimima), 1593, octavo [Marciana]

112* German, Dillingen (Mayer), 1593, octavo [Wolfenbüttel; Rome, Angelica]

113* Latin, London (Bishop), 1593, octavo [BL, BNP, UL]

114* Italian, Venice (Ugolino), 1599, octavo [BLO, University Library Oslo]

115 Spanish, Antwerp (Nucio), 1599

116   Italian, Florence (Giunta), 1600, quarto
117   Italian, Venice (Alberti), 1601
118*   English, London (Creede), 1603 [BL]
119*   Latin, London (Bishop), 1603, octavo [BL, UL]
120   Italian, Venice (Alberti), 1606, octavo
121*   Latin, Frankfurt (Zetzner), 1606 [BL, BNP]
122*   Latin, London (Adams), 1612, octavo [BL, Emmanuel College, Cambridge UL]
123*   Latin, Strasbourg (Zetzner), 1619 [BL, UL]
124   Latin, Strasbourg (Jobinus), 1619 [Rome, Biblioteca Casanatense]
125   Latin, London, 1619, octavo
126   Latin, Strasbourg, 1639 [not in Opdycke: preface to 1713 edn]
127   Dutch, Amsterdam (Wolfganck), 1662 [not in Opdycke: de Jongh, 1985]
128   Latin, Strasbourg (Paulli), 1663, octavo [BNP]
129   Latin, Strasbourg (Jobinus), 1667, octavo
130   Latin, Zurich, 1668, octavo
131*   Dutch, Amsterdam, 1675 [not in Opdycke: Amsterdam, University Library]
132   German, Frankfurt (Schäffer), 1684 [introduction to Wesselski's German translation, 1909]
133   German, Dresden (Günther), 1685 [not in Opdycke: Wesselski]
134*   French, Paris (Loyson), 1690, 12mo [BNP]
135*   Latin, Cambridge (University Press), 1713, octavo [BL, BNP, UL]
136*   English, London (Bettesworth), 1724, octavo [BL, UL]
137*   Italian and English, London (Bowyer), 1727, quarto [BL, UL]
138*   English, London (Curll), 1729 [BL]
139*   Italian, Padua (Comino), 1733, quarto [BL]
140   English, London (Payne), 1737, quarto
141*   English London (Nourse), 1737, quarto [BNP]
142*   Italian and English, London (Slater), 1742 [BL]
143   Italian, Padua (Comino), 1755 [cited in 1803 edn]
144*   Italian, Padua, 1766, quarto [BL]
145*   Italian, Vicenza (Vendramin Mosca), 1771, octavo [BL, BNP]
146   Italian, no place, 1772, octavo
147*   Italian, Milan (Società tipografica de' classici), 1803, octavo [BNP, UL]
148*   Italian, Milan (Silvestri), 1822, 16mo [BL, BNP]
149   Italian, Bergamo (Mazzolini), 12mo [Milan, Brera]
150*   Italian, Milan (Bettoni), 1831, 2 vols [BL]
151*   Italian, Venice (Tasso), 1842, octavo [BL]
152   Italian, Parma (Fiaccadori), 1842, 16mo [Milan, Ambrosiana]
153   French, Copenhagen (Schultz), 1848, quarto [BL, BNP, UL]

Appendix 2
Readers of the Courtier before 1700

This list includes individuals, or occasionally families, who owned the book, whether the evidence comes from inventories, dedications, names or bookplates (208 cases); or referred to the book or its author (85 cases); or used the book without naming it (35 cases). In the case of the last category one has to use one's judgement and I have omitted Shakespeare, Sidney, Spenser and Wyatt for lack of evidence. I have also omitted owners about whom I could find no further information (Angelo del Bufalo, Johannes Botrevicus, Barnard Hampton, Matheus Karadasius, Marsili Lippi, Lodovico Usper, Robert Uvedale, Jacopo Zonia, etc.).

1 Pfalzgraf Albrecht of Bavaria, dedicatee of 1565 Munich edition.
2 Huijch van Alckemade of Leiden owned copy in French (inventory 1568: information from Frieda Heijkoop).
3 Fray Juan de Almaraz, inquisitor at Lima, tried to censor, 1582 (Guibovich Pérez 1989).
4 Gerónima Palova de Almogáver, Catalan noblewoman, dedicatee (Darst 1978, 27).
5 Alfonso Ariosto, nobleman of Ferrara, dedicatee.
6 Ludovico Ariosto (1474–1533), nobleman of Ferrara, referred to text (1516, Canto 3).
7 Roger Ascham (c.1515–68), mentioned author in his *Schoolmaster* (1568).
8 Jean Aubry, Frenchman, bookseller of Vienna, sold a copy in 1577 (Keserű 1983, 421).
9 Pierre Bablan, merchant, from Compiègne, wrote name in copy of

1592 edn now in BNP (Res E*3487).

10 Francis Bacon (1561–1626), Viscount St Albans, English statesman and writer, used text without naming (Martin 1993, 64–6).

11 Thomas Baker (1656–1740), of Durham gentry family, Fellow of St John's, Cambridge, owned five copies (Korsten 1990, nos 493, 699, 985, 3544, 3966).

12 Bálint Balassa (1554–94), Hungarian nobleman, borrowed from the text without naming (Di Francesco 1994, 240, 243).

13 Matteo Bandello (1485–1561), Lombard friar, mentioned MS of text (1554, book II, no. 57).

14 Scipione Bargagli (1540–1612), Sienese nobleman, referred to text (1572, 35; 1587, 118).

15 Alonso Barros (c.1552–1604), Spanish soldier, two copies of the 'Cortesano' (Castiglione, Luis Milán, or Palmireno: Dadson 1987, nos 98, 130).

16 Cornelius Baseminius, 'medicus', wrote name in copy of 1565 Venice edn now in British Library.

17 Boldizsár Batthyány (c.1535–90), Hungarian nobleman, bought copy in 1577 (Keserű 1983, 421).

18 Philippe Baudesson, *procureur au Châtelet*, Paris, 1556, owned text in Italian (Schutz 1955, no. 13).

19 Nicolas de Bauffremont, Seigneur de Senessey, dedicatee of Lyon 1579 edn.

20 Remi Belleau (1528?–77), poet, owned text in French (Boucher 1986, 54).

21 Pietro Bembo (1470–1547), Venetian patrician, cardinal, read manuscript.

22 Francis Bernard (1627–98) London physician, owned copy in Italian (Lievsay 1969, 59).

23 François Billon (c.1522–79), French writer, used text without naming (Telle 1937, 59).

24 Pietro Bizzarri (1525–c.1586), Italian, Fellow of St John's, Cambridge, referred to text (Firpo 1971, 39).

25 Traiano Boccalini (1556–1613), Italian writer, referred to author (1612–14, vol. III, 27).

26 Johann Heinrich Boeckler (1611–72), professor of rhetoric at Strasbourg, referred to text (Bonfatti 1979, 67).

27 Jean-Baptiste Boisot (1638–94), abbé of Besançon, owned Granvelle's copy (Jolly 1988–92, 469).

28 Edmund Bonner (c.1500–69), diplomat and bishop, asked Thomas Cromwell for loan of text (Hogrefe 1929–30).

29 Giulio Borgarucci, physician at Padua and Cambridge, wrote poem

prefixed to Clerke translation.

30 Vincenzo Borghini (1515–80), Florentine patrician and Benedictine, referred to text (Woodhouse 1978, 360).

31 Lambert van den Bos, seventeenth-century Dutch writer, translated text.

32 Juan Boscán Almogáver (c.1487–1542), patrician of Barcelona, translated text.

33 Cardinal Charles de Bourbon (1523–90), 'Charles X' for the opponents of Henri IV, owned copy in Italian (*Revue des bibliothèques* 1912, 426).

34 Nicolas Bourbon (c.1503–c.1550), French poet, wrote Latin poem prefixed to 1538 Lyon edn.

35 Per Brahe (1520–90), Swedish noble, recommended text (Brahe 1581, 34).

36 Richard Brathwaite (c.1588–1673), English poet, used without naming in *English Gentleman* (1630).

37 Nicholas Breton (c.1545–c.1626), English writer, referred to text (Breton 1618).

38 Reynold Bridge, bookseller, Cambridge, 1590, owned three copies of Latin edition (Leedham-Green 1987).

39 Sir George Buc, English gentleman, referred to author in 1615 (Hale 1976, 231).

40 Robert Burton (1577–1640), 'Student' (i.e. Fellow) of Christ Church, Oxford, owned Latin edition (Kiessling 1988, no. 310).

41 Thomas Byng, Master of Clare College, Cambridge, wrote poem prefixed to Clerke translation.

42 Pierre Cabat, *marchand libraire*, owned text in French (Schutz 1955, no. 42).

43 Giulio Caccini (c.1545–1618), Florentine musician, used without naming (1600, preface).

44 John Caius (1510–73), physician and academic, praises style of author in preface to Clerke translation.

45 Pietro Andrea Canonhiero, Italian writer, refers in 1609 (Hinz 1992, 269).

46 Count Lodovico da Canossa (1475–1532), Italian nobleman, diplomat and bishop, received two presentation copies (Cartwright 1908, vol. II, 368).

47 Margherita Cantelma, née Maloselli, received presentation copy (Cartwright 1908, vol. II, 368).

48 Arthur Capel, student of Trinity College, Cambridge 1571, recommended to read by Harvey.

49 Mme de Carvenonay (Anne Hurault, wife of François, *conseiller de*

la chambre du roi), owned text in French (Schutz 1955, no. 45).

50 Giovanni Della Casa (1503–56), Florentine bishop, used without naming (in *Galateo*, 1558; ed. D. Provenzal 1950, Milan).

51 Castell family, German nobles, owned copy (Pleticha 1983, 113).

52 Camillo Castiglione (1520–98), soldier, son of author, concerned with censorship of text (Cian 1887).

53 Count Nicola di Castiglione received presentation copy (Cartwright 1908, vol. II, 368).

54 Sabba di Castiglione (1485–1554), knight of the Order of Rhodes, used text without naming (Scarpati 1982, 49–50, 57).

55 Catherine de' Medici (1519–89), Florentine noblewoman, queen of France, owned text (Mariéjol 1920, 35).

56 Filippo Cavriani (1536–1606), Mantuan nobleman and physician, owned copy in Italian (Opdycke 1901, 420).

57 Miguel Cervantes (1547–1616), Spanish writer, used text without naming (Lopez Estrada 1948; Fucilla 1950).

58 Jean Chapelain (1595–1674), French writer, owned five copies, four in Italian and one in Spanish (Searles 1912, nos 522–6).

59 Jean Chaperon, translated book I into French, 1537 (Klesczewski 1966).

60 Gabriel Chappuys (*c.*1546–*c.*1613), French writer, translated text (1585).

61 Charles V (1500–58), emperor, received presentation copy.

62 Sir John Cheke (1514–57), professor at Cambridge, letter prefixed to Hoby translation.

63 Francesco Agostino della Chiesa, Italian writer, referred to text (1620, s.v. H. Torella).

64 Christian (1602–47), son of Christian IV, owned German edition (inventory, 1647, information from Harald Ilsøe).

65 Antonio Ciccarelli of Foligno (died 1599), doctor of theology, expurgated the text (Cian 1887).

66 Vincenzo Cimarelli, friar, inquisitor, referred to text (1642, 126).

67 Girolamo Cittadini, Milanese nobleman, wrote asking to see it in 1519 (Danzi 1989, 293, 301).

68 Scipio Claudio, noble of Abruzzi, published summary of text in 1539 (Volpe 1733, 416).

69 James Cleland, English writer, recommended text (1607, 153, 266).

70 Clement VII (1478–1534), formerly Giulio de' Medici, received presentation copy.

71 Bartholomew Clerke (1537?–90), professor of rhetoric at Cambridge, translated text into Latin.

72 Edward Coke (1552–1634), owned copy in French (Hassall 1950,

no. 1095).

73 Colbert family owned copy in Italian (1728, no. 3180).

74 Jacques Colin (died 1547), cleric and diplomat, probable translator of text into French (Klesczewski 1966, 24f).

75 Richard Collet, Fellow of Caius College, Cambridge, late sixteenth century, owned Latin translation (Leedham-Green 1987).

76 Hippolytus a Collibus (1561–1612), German writer, referred to text (Collibus 1599, 310, 345, 346).

77 Vittoria Colonna (1490–1547), Italian noblewoman, referred to text (Colonna 1889, nos 19, 34).

78 Thomas Coryate (c.1577–1617) English traveller, referred to text (Coryate 1611, vol. I, 268).

79 João de Costa, Portuguese, confessed ownership to Inquisition, 1550 (Brandão 1944).

80 Thomas Cromwell (c.1485–1540), statesman, earl of Essex, asked for copy by Bonner, 1530 (Hogrefe 1929–30).

81 James Dalton, student of Brasenose College, Oxford, wrote name in copy of Latin translation, now in UL (Syn. 8.57.24).

82 Richard Daulton, student of Brasenose College Oxford, wrote name in copy of Latin translation, now in UL (Syn. 8.57.24).

83 Antonio Dávalos, of Lima, treasurer, imported text, 1582 (information from Teodoro Hampe).

84 Jean de Boyssières (1555–after 1580), at court of dukes of Alençon and Mercoeur, translator of Ariosto, prefixed poem to French translation (Cioranescu 1938, vol. I, 99–100).

85 Daniel Defoe (1660–1731), English writer, owned copies in Italian and English (Heidenreich 1970, nos 494, 1268).

86 Thomas Dekker (c.1570–c.1641), English writer, reference in *Westward Ho!*, 1605.

87 John Denys, Cambridge bookseller, owned Latin translation (Leedham-Green 1987).

88 Hans Dernschwam (1494–1568), Bohemian patrician humanist, owned Italian edition (Dernschwam 1984, 198).

89 Henry Dethick, lawyer (died 1613), contributed poem to Latin translation.

90 Michel de Vaulx, *avocat* at Parlement of Paris, owned Italian edition (Quilliet 1975, 148).

91 Ludovico Dolce (1510–68), Venetian citizen and professional writer, edited text.

92 Etienne Dolet (1509–46), French humanist and printer, revised Colin translation.

93 Ludovico Domenichi (1515–64), Italian professional writer,

referred to text (1549, 242b, 257a).

94 Anton Francesco Doni (1513–74), Italian professional writer, referred to text (1550, 29–30).

95 Caspar Dornau (1577–1632), German humanist, cited text in 1617 (Bonfatti 1979, 156).

96 Jean Doultremepuys (died 1545), of Boulogne, *procureur général du roi*, owned French translation (Schutz 1955, no. 158; Labarre 1971, 385).

97 Samuel Drake (*c.*1686–1753), Fellow of St John's College, Cambridge, edited 1713 edn.

98 Laurens Drouet, *marchand bourgeois* in sixteenth-century Paris, owned copy in French (Schutz 1955, no. 67).

99 William Drummond of Hawthornden (1585–1649), Scottish gentleman and poet, owned three copies, in Italian, Spanish and English (Macdonald 1971, nos 719, 1212; Lievsay 1969, 41n.).

100 Noël Du Fail, Breton gentleman, criticized without naming (Smith 1966, 134–6).

101 Jean-Baptiste Duhamel (1624–1706), Oratorian priest, translated text (1690).

102 John Dymock, gentleman extraordinary to Henry VIII, gave copy to Erik XIV (Andersson 1948, 167).

103 Echter family, German nobles, owned copy (Pleticha 1983, 45).

104 Queen Elizabeth (1533–1603), dedicatee of Latin translation.

105 Sir Thomas Elyot (*c.*1490–1546), English gentleman, used without naming (Hogrefe 1967, 118, 129, 138–9, 149–50, 152).

106 Mario Equicola (*c.*1470–1525), secretary to Isabella d'Este, was asked for the manuscript in 1519 (Danzi 1989, 293, 301).

107 Erik XIV of Sweden, given French translation in 1561 (Andersson 1948, 167).

108 Isabella d'Este (1474–1539), Italian noblewoman, received presentation copy (Cartwright 1908, vol. II, 368).

109 Robert Estienne (1503–59), French printer, criticized text without naming it (Smith 1966).

110 Nicolas Faret (*c.*1600–46), French secretary and administrator, borrowed from text without acknowledgement (1630).

111 André Félibien (1619–95), historian to Louis XIV, bookplate in copy in Italian now in BNP (Res. E*3490).

112 Sir Geoffrey Fenton (*c.*1539–1608), English translator, dedication to Lady Hoby, 1572.

113 Apollonio Filareto, secretary to Paul III (fl. 1540s), owned copy now in University Library, Prague (Hobson 1975, 92).

114 Ippolita Fioramonda, marchesa di Scaldasole, Pavia, received

presentation copy (Cartwright 1908, vol. II, 368).

115 John Florio (*c.*1553–1625), son of Italian exile, translator, referred to text (1591, dedication).

116 Odet de Foix-Lautrec (*c.*1481–1528), Marshal of France, asked for copy of MS in 1520 (Kolsky 1991, 184n.).

117 Charles Fontaine (1514–*c.*1564), French writer, used without naming in his *Contr'amie*.

118 Firmin de Forcheville, *marchand hôtelier*, Amiens, 1576, owned copy in French (Schutz 1955, no. 82; Labarre 1971, 226).

119 Nicolas Fouquet (died 1680), French financier, owned 1562 Italian edition, now in BL (C. 46.a.22).

120 François I (1494–1547), king of France from 1515, received presentation copy (BNP Res. E*52).

121 M. della Fratta, Italian nobleman, cited author, 1548 (Donati 1988, 71, 75).

122 Niels Friis of Favrskov (1584–1651), Danish nobleman, bought copy at Orléans, 1604 (Heiberg 1988, no. 1436).

123 Christoffer Fugger (1566–1615), Freyherr zu Kirchberg, dedicatee, 1593.

124 Maria Fugger, wife of Christoffer, dedicatee, 1593.

125 Ulrich Fugger (1526–84), German patrician, owned copy in French (Lehmann 1960, 239).

126 Mario Galeota, Italian gentleman, praised text (Cian 1887, 663n.).

127 Galiot du Pré, Paris bookseller, owned sixty-five copies in French, 1561 (Schutz 1955, no. 88).

128 Veronica Gambara (1485–1550), Lombard noblewoman and poet, received presentation copy (Cartwright 1908, vol. II, 368).

129 Garcilaso de la Vega (*c.*1501–36), Spanish noble, recommended text to Boscán.

130 Garcilaso the Inca (1539–1612), noble from Peru, owned two books called 'cortesano' (Castiglione, Luis Milán, or Palmireno: Durand 1948, nos 167, 176).

131 Tommaso Garzoni (1549–89), Italian cleric, used text without naming (1585).

132 Fernand Gauthiot of Besançon (late sixteenth century), owned copy (Febvre 1911, 360).

133 René Gentil, *conseiller*, Paris, 1537, owned copy in Italian (Schutz 1955, no. 93).

134 Joachim Gersdorff (1611–61), Danish diplomat, *Rigshofmester*, bought Latin copy in Leipzig in 1631 (Walde 1932, 23).

135 Giovanni Andrea Gilio da Fabriano, Italian priest, refers to text, 1564 (Ossola 1980, 75f; Hinz 1992, 249–55).

136 Alvigi Giorgio, Venetian patrician, dedicatee, 1538.

137 Paolo Giovio (1483–1552), Italian bishop, referred to text (1546, 47–8ff.).

138 Argisto Giuffredi, Sicilian lawyer, referred to text *c.*1585 (1896, 83).

139 John Glover (died 1578), Fellow of St John's, Oxford, owned copies in Italian and French (Curtis 1959, 140).

140 Aloysia Gonzaga, mother of author, received presentation copy (Cartwright 1908, vol. II, 368).

141 Eleonora Gonzaga, duchess of Urbino, received presentation copy (Cartwright 1908, vol. II, 368).

142 Federico Gonzaga (1500–40), marquis of Mantua, received presentation copy (Cartwright 1908, vol. II, 368).

143 Cardinal Scipione Gonzaga helped avoid strict censorship of text in 1575 (Cian 1887).

144 Łukasz Górnicki (1527–1603), Polish courtier, adapted text, 1566.

145 Wawrzyniec Goślicki (*c.*1533–1607), used text without naming (1568).

146 Baltasar Gracián (1601–58), Spanish Jesuit, cited text.

147 Giorgio Gradenigo (1522–*c.*1599), Venetian patrician, dedicatee.

148 Jean Granger, Seigneur de Lyverdis, *conseiller-et maître d'hôtel du roi*, Paris 1597, owned copy in French (Schutz 1955, no. 100).

149 Cardinal Granvelle (1517–86), from Franche-Comté, owned Italian edition (Picquard 1951, 206).

150 Robert Greville, Lord Brooke, owned copy in Spanish (1678, 74, no. 13).

151 Pellegro Grimaldi (Robio), referred to text 1543 (Prosperi 1980, 73; cf. Hinz 1992, 229ff.).

152 Pietro Gritio, referred to text (1586, 103).

153 Jean Grolier (*c.*1486–1565), French treasurer in Lombardy, owned twelve copies (Schutz 1955, no. 102; Austin 1971).

154 Sigvard Grubbe, (1566–1636), Dane, *Rigsraad*, owned Italian edition (Walde 1932, 49n.).

155 Samuel Grunerus of Berne, wrote his name in 1613 in copy in French and Italian now in BNP (Res. R.2050).

156 Joan Guardiola, bookseller of Barcelona, had twenty-four copies in Italian at his death in 1561 (Kamen 1993, 412).

157 Stefano Guazzo (1530–93), Piedmontese gentleman, referred to text (1574, f.252b).

158 Antonio de Guevara (*c.*1480–1545), Spanish bishop, discussed without naming (Redondo 1976).

159 Everard Guilpin (*c.*1572–after 1598), English poet, referred to author (Guilpin 1598).

160 Georg Gumpelzhaimer, German jurist, cited text in 1621 (Bonfatti 1979, 161).

161 Louis Guyon, Sieur de La Nauche, referred to author (Guyon 1604, 202).

162 John Hacket (1592–1670), English bishop, wrote name in copy in Latin now in UL (L*15.10).

163 Jan Hanneman, *rentmeester* of north Holland, tried to censor text *c*.1570 (information from Frieda Heijkoop).

164 John Harington (1561–1612), English poet, praised Clerke as translator (1591, preface).

165 Georg Philipp Harsdörffer (1607–58), German noble, cited text (1641–9, vol. III, 101).

166 Gabriel Harvey (*c*.1550–1631), Fellow of Trinity Hall, Cambridge, owned copies in Italian, Latin and English (Stern, 1979). His annotated English copy is now in the Newberry Library, Chicago. His Italian copy, now lost, was in 1904 'in the possession of the late Rev. Walter Bagley' of Hampstead (Moore Smith 1913, 81).

167 Lord Henry Hastings (1535–95) dedicatee of Hoby translation.

168 Sir Christopher Hatton (1540–91), English courtier, probable owner of copy in French (Hassall 1950, no. 1095).

169 Nikolaes Heinsius (1620–81), Dutch scholar, owned three copies (Heinsius 1682, p. 203).

170 Nicolas d'Herberay, Seigneur des Essarts, *commissaire ordinaire de l'artillerie*, 1552, owned text in Italian (Schutz 1955, no. 107).

171 Antoine Héroet, (*c*.1492–1568) French bishop, used without naming (Screech 1959, 113, 116).

172 Edward Higgins (died 1588), Fellow of Brasenose College, Oxford, owned copies in English, French, Italian, Latin (Curtis 1959, 141; UL Syn. 8.57.24).

173 Sir Thomas Hoby (1530–66), English gentleman, translated text.

174 Gilbert de Hodia, notary, Paris, 1549, owned copy in French (Schutz 1955, no. 109).

175 Francisco de Holanda (*c*.1517–84), Portuguese humanist, used text without naming (Deswarte 1989, 16).

176 John Hoskyns (1566–1638), English lawyer, referred to text (Osborn 1937, 121, 157).

177 Jean Hovard, notary, Paris, 1564, owned copy in French (Schutz 1955, no. 111).

178 Henry Howard, earl of Northampton (1540–1614), owned copy in Italian and referred to text in 1569 (Barker 1990; Peck 1991, 150).

179 Pierre-Daniel Huet (1630–1721), French bishop, bookplate in copy in French now in BNP (R.2050).

180 Don Diego Hurtado de Mendoza (1503–75), Spanish nobleman and diplomat, owned three copies of 'libro del cortesano' (González Palencia and Mele 1941–3, appendix 119, nos 255–7).

181 Francisco Idiáquez, Spanish administrator, owned two copies of text, one in Italian (Le Flem 1973, nos 424–5).

182 Giuseppe Renato Imperiali, Genoese patrician, owned two copies (*Catalogus*, Rome 1711).

183 James VI and I (1566–1625), owned copy in Latin (*Library* 1840, 17; cf. Warner 1893).

184 Ben Jonson (1572–1637), English dramatist and poet referred to text (1953, 100).

185 Franciscus Junius (1589–1677), Dutchman, librarian to earl of Arundel, referred to text (Taylor 1948, 225).

186 Sir Henry Killigrew (died 1603), English diplomat, gave English translation to Mary Queen of Scots (Warner 1893, lvii).

187 Sir Thomas Knyvett (*c.*1539–1618), Norfolk gentleman, owned copies in Italian and Latin (McKitterick 1978, nos 748, 1123).

188 Laurentz Kratzer, German customs official, translated text.

189 Etienne de La Boétie (1530–63), French nobleman, referred to text (1892, 275).

190 Bertrand de La Borderie (1507–after 1541), French nobleman, criticized text without naming (1541).

191 Pierre Lallemant, notary, *secretaire du roi*, Paris 1562, owned copy in French (Schutz 1955, no. 120).

192 Secondo Lancellotti (1583–1643), Italian preacher, referred to author (Raimondi 1960, 288).

193 François de La Noue (1531–91), French nobleman and soldier, used without naming (1587, 235).

194 François de La Rochefoucauld (1613–80), French duke, owned copy in French (Gérard 1984, no. 35).

195 Vincencio Juan de Lastanosa (1607–84), Spanish nobleman, owned copy in Spanish (Selig 1960, no. 131).

196 Jean de La Taille (1533–1608), French Protestant gentleman, translated Ariosto, mentioned 'Chastillon' (1878–82, vol. III, xxvii, xci).

197 Louis Le Caron (1534–1613), French lawyer, criticized text without naming (Smith 1966, 148–50).

198 A. Legrain, *conseiller au Châtelet*, Paris 1567, owned copy in French (Schutz 1955).

199 Carlo Lenzoni (1501–51), Florentine man of letters, referred to text (Pozzi 1988, 366).

200 Cornelius Lerche (1615–81), Danish diplomat, owned copy in Italian (1682, 140, no. 473).

201 Zdenek Lobkovič (1568–1628), Bohemian nobleman, owned five copies (Kasparová 1990, nos 133–7).

202 John Locke (1632–1704), English philosopher and physician, student, (i.e. Fellow) of Christ Church, Oxford, owned three copies in Italian and Latin (Harrison and Laslett 1965, nos 626–627a).

203 John Logan (1674–1751), of Philadelphia, owned two copies in Italian and Spanish (Wolf 1974, nos 430–1).

204 Giovanni Paolo Lomazzo (1538–1600), Italian artist, referred to text (Lomazzo 1590, ch. 7).

205 John Lord Lumley (fl. 1560), owned a copy in English now in British Library (Jayne and Johnson 1956, no. 1643).

206 Fabrizio Luna (died 1559), Neapolitan, mentioned text in 1536 (Sabbatini 1986, 39).

207 John Lyon, Lord Glamis (died 1578), Lord High Chancellor of Scotland, gave Mary Queen of Scots a copy in Italian (Warner 1893, lii).

208 Vincenzo Maggi (died c.1564), professor at Ferrara, referred to text (Ossola 1980, 35n.).

209 A. Massario Malatesta, Italian riding-master, referred to text (1573, f.128).

210 Jehan de Malerippe, *greffier des eaux et forêts*, Paris 1557, owned copy in Italian (Schutz 1955, no. 136).

211 Karel van Mander (1548–1606), artist from Netherlands, referred to text (1604, 124–5).

212 Francisco Manuel de Mello (1608–66), Portuguese nobleman, referred to text in his *Hospital de Letras* (Rodrigues Lôbo 1619, x).

213 Paolo Manuzio, Italian printer, gave manuscript to Grolier.

214 Marguerite de Navarre (1492–1549) owned a copy in Italian (Jourda 1930, 684).

215 Marguerite de Valois, French princess, owned a copy in French (Mariéjol 1928, 321–2; Boucher 1986, 54).

216 Bernardino Marliani, Italian nobleman, referred to the text (1583).

217 John Marston (1576–1634), English dramatist, referred to author (1961, 30).

218 Jacques Martin, noble, *avocat* at the Parlement of Paris, 1555, owned copy in French (Schutz 1955, no. 142).

219 Robert Martin, London bookseller, offered Italian edition for sale in 1633 (Lievsay 1969, 43–4).

220 William Martyn (1562–1617), lawyer, recorder of Exeter, referred to text (1612).

221 Mary Queen of Scots (1542–87), owned copies in Italian and English (Warner 1893, lii, lvii).

222 Charles Merbury, used text in his *Royal Monarchy* (1581: Lievsay

1964, 124).

223 Francesco Melchiori, sixteenth-century Italian nobleman, wrote in copy now in BL (G.2457 (1)).

224 Luis Milán (c.1500–61), Spanish musician, referred to text (1561).

225 Charles Montagu (1661–1715), earl of Halifax, owned copy in Italian, later property of Garrick (Arnott 1975, no. 383).

226 Michel de Montaigne (1533–92), French nobleman, used without naming (Villey 1908, vol. I, 95–6).

227 Hipòlit Montaner, lawyer of Barcelona, owned copy in Spanish (inventory 1626, information from Jim Amelang).

228 William More of Loseley, Surrey, gentleman, owned copies in French and Italian (inventory 1556, in Evans 1855, 290–1).

229 John Morris (c.1580–1658), English gentleman, owned copies in Italian and Latin (Birrell 1976, nos 331–2).

230 William Mount (died 1602), chaplain to William Cecil, wrote poem prefixed to Latin translation.

231 Diego de Narváez, of Cuzco, received copy in 1545 (information from Teodoro Hampe).

232 Thomas Nashe (1567–1601), English writer, referred to text (1589, dedication).

233 Gabriel Naudé (1600–53), French scholar, referred to text (1641, 114).

234 Andrea Navagero (1483–1529), Italian humanist and diplomat, helped see text through press.

235 Antonio Beffa Negrini, secretary to Camillo Castiglione, referred to text (1606, no. 70).

236 Agostino Nifo (1473–1546), Italian philosopher and physician, used without naming (Prandi 1990, 37n.).

237 Johann Engelbert Noyse translated text.

238 Benedictus Olai (1523–82), Swede, physician to Erik XIV, owned copy (Kock 1920).

239 Lorenzo Palmireno (c.1514–c.1580), Spanish humanist, referred to text (1573, preface).

240 Elizabeth Parr, marchioness of Northampton asked Hoby to translate text.

241 William Parr (1513–71), marquess of Northampton, patron of Hoby.

242 Nicolas Pasquier, French lawyer, used text without naming (1611).

243 William Patten (fl. 1548–80), referred to text (1548, sig. H vii recto).

244 Miklós Pázmány, Hungarian nobleman, owned copy in Italian, inventory 1667 (Ötvös, 1994, no. 167).

245 Henry Peacham (*c*.1576–*c*.1643), English schoolmaster and writer, used text without naming (1622).

246 Piero Peri, Florentine patrician, owned copy in 1571 (Florence, Archivio di Stato, Pupilli dopo il Principato, busta 2709, 99; information from Dora Thornton).

247 Bonaventure Des Périers (*c*.1510–44), French writer, used without naming (Hassell 1953, 566).

248 Philibert de Vienne, probably an *avocat*, criticized without naming (1547).

249 Emilia Pia, Italian noblewoman, received presentation copy (Cartwright 1908, vol. II, 368).

250 Alessandro Piccolomini (1508–78), Sienese nobleman, used without naming (1539, 58).

251 Bernardino Pino (*c*.1530–1601), Italian cleric and writer, referred to text (1604, 5b).

252 Heitor Pinto, Portuguese friar, used without naming (1563–72).

253 Jeanne Popière, printer's wife, sixteenth-century Paris, owned copy in Italian (Schutz 1955, no. 168, misdated 1523).

254 Antoine III du Prat (*c*.1500–67), *prévôt de Paris*, owned copy in French (Connat and Mégret 1943, no. 402).

255 Johannes Purcell MD, wrote name in copy of 1573 edition, now in BL (1484.e.22).

256 George Puttenham (died 1590), English gentleman and writer, used text without naming (1589, cf. Javitch 1972).

257 John Rainolds (1549–1607), Fellow of Corpus Christi, Oxford, referred to text (1986, 336).

258 Gianbattista Ramusio (1485–1557), secretary to the government of Venice, received two presentation copies (Cartwright 1908, vol. II, 368).

259 Antonio Riccoboni (1541–99), professor at Padua, referred to text (Ossola 1980, 35).

260 Johannes Ricius (fl. *c*.1580), professor at Marburg, translated book I into Latin.

261 Francisco Rodrigues Lôbo (*c*.1573–1621), Portuguese nobleman, imitated text without naming.

262 Fernando de Rojas (*c*.1465–1541), Spanish writer, owned copy in Spanish (Lersundi 1929, 382).

263 Rutgero Rolando, his praise of the author noted on the title-page of the German translation of 1684.

264 Annibale Romei (died 1590) nobleman of Ferrara, used without naming (Prandi 1990, 193n.).

265 Girolamo Rosati, 'Reviser to Inquisition in Florence', MS revisions

to 1531 edn (BL catalogue).

266 Erik Rosenkrantz (1612–81), Danish diplomat, owned copies in Italian and French (1688, no. 668).

267 Janus Rosenkrantz, owned seven copies, one Latin, five Italian, one French (1696, octavo, Latin, no. 55; octavo, vernacular, nos 9, 32, 45, 65, 69; 16mo, vernacular, no. 53).

268 Il Rosso (1495–1540), Florentine painter, owned a copy (inventory 1531, in Hirst, 1964).

269 Francesco Maria II della Rovere, duke of Urbino, dedicatee 1584.

270 Rudolf II (1552–1612), emperor, ruled from 1576, dedicatee 1587.

271 Nicholas Rücker (fl. 1599), German jurist, mentioned author (Bonfatti 1979, 136).

272 Girolamo Ruscelli (c.1504–66), Italian writer, referred to text (Collenuccio 1552, f. 207).

273 Francisco de Sá de Miranda (c.1481–c.1558), Portuguese nobleman and poet, used without naming (Earle 1980, 29–30).

274 Thomas Sackville (1536–1608), Lord Buckhurst, later earl of Dorset, praised work in prefaces to English and Latin translations.

275 Jacopo Sadoleto (1477–1547), Italian bishop, asked by author in letter of 1514 to read manuscript.

276 Melin de Saint-Gelais (1491–1558), poet and courtier, revised French translation.

277 Alonso Jerónimo de Salas Barbadillo (1581–1635), Spanish writer, imitated without naming (1620).

278 Joachim von Sandrart (1606–88), German artist, quoted author (1675–80, vol. I, 125).

279 Margherita di San Severino, Italian noblewoman, received presentation copy (Cartwright 1908, vol. II, 368).

280 Francesco Sansovino (1521–83), Italian writer, referred to text (1582, 70 verso, 169 verso).

281 Filippo Sassetti (1540–88), Florentine merchant, referred to text (1855, 358).

282 Peder Scavenius (1623–85), Danish professor, owned copy in Italian (1665, 164, no. 166).

283 Baron Sennecey, member of privy council, spokesman of nobles in Estates, 1576, dedicatee of French translation.

284 Joaquim Setantí, 'honoured citizen' of Barcelona, owned copy in Spanish (inventory 1617, information from Jim Amelang).

285 Miguel da Silva (c.1480–1556), Portuguese nobleman, bishop of Viseu, dedicatee.

286 Jan Six (1618–1700), burgomaster of Amsterdam, owned three copies of text (Möller 1984, 70).

287 Antonio Solís (1610–86), Spanish writer, owned copies in Spanish and Italian (information from Jim Amelang).

288 Sperone Speroni (1500–88), Italian academic, annotated a copy now in Biblioteca Marciana, Venice.

289 Irene di Spilimbergo (died 1561), noblewoman from Friuli, one of her favourite books (Atanagi 1561; Schutte 1991).

290 Francis Sterling (1652–92), Fellow of Jesus College, Cambridge, name in Italian copy now in Jesus (0.12.66).

291 Jacques Tahureau (1527–55), French gentleman, criticized without naming (Smith 1966, 29, 136, 149).

292 Torquato Tasso (1544–95), Italian poet, referred to text (1583).

293 Alessandro Tassoni (1565–1635), Italian nobleman and writer, owned copy now in Biblioteca Marciana, Venice.

294 William Thomas (*c.*1507–1554), clerk to privy council, referred to text (1549, 127).

295 Jacques-Auguste de Thou (1553–1617), French lawyer, owned two copies in Italian, one now in BLO (Thou 1679, 400; cf. Coron 1988).

296 Abraham Tilman (died 1589), Fellow of Corpus Christi, Cambridge, owned copies in Italian and Latin (Jayne 1956, 187–8; Leedham-Green 1987).

297 Claudio Tolomei (1492–1555), Sienese nobleman and writer, referred to author in 1529 (Pozzi 1988, 200).

298 Sir Roger Townsend, East Anglian gentleman, owned two copies in English (Fehrenbach and Leedham-Green 1992, 3.41, 3.53).

299 Sir Thomas Tresham (*c.*1543–1605), Northamptonshire gentleman, owned copies in Italian and Latin, (BL, Add. MSS 39, 830, ff. 178b, 187b).

300 Giangiorgio Trissino (1478–1550), nobleman of Vicenza, poet, referred to text (Ossola 1980, 34; Hinz 1992, 191n.).

301 Margherita Trivulzio, countess of Somaglia, Lombard noblewoman, given presentation copy (Cartwright 1908, vol. II, 368).

302 Johannes Turler (fl. *c.*1560), German scholar, made Latin translation.

303 Robert Turquan, *bourgeois de Paris*, owned copy in French (Schutz 1955, no. 207, misdated 1519).

304 Brian Twyne (*c.*1580–1644), English academic, owned copy in Latin (Ovenell 1950, 17).

305 Sir Roger Twysden (1597–1672), English gentleman, quoted text (Jessup 1965, 203–4).

306 Pontus I de Tyard (1521–1605), French bishop and poet, owned copy in French (Boucher 1986).

307 Pontus II de Tyard (1582–1634), great-nephew of Pontus I, owned copy in French (Baridon 1950, no. 713).

308 Jakob Ulfeldt (1567–1630), Danish nobleman, diplomat and *Rigskansler*, owned copies in French and Spanish (Ulfeldt 1923).

309 Giovanni Francesco Valier (died 1542), illegitimate son of Venetian patrician, received two presentation copies (Cartwright 1908, vol. II, 368).

310 Benedetto Varchi (1503–65), Florentine writer, referred to text.

311 Giorgio Vasari (1511–74), Tuscan artist and writer, used without naming (1550, 1568).

312 Diego de Silva y Velázquez (1599–1660), Spanish painter and courtier, owned copy in Italian (Rodríguez Marín 1923, 55).

313 Edward Vere (1550–1604), 17th earl of Oxford, wrote letter prefixed to Latin translation.

314 Cristóbal Villalón (*c.*1500–58), Spanish humanist, referred to text (1911, preface).

315 John Webster (*c.*1580–*c.*1625), English dramatist, referred to text in *Westward Ho!*, 1605.

316 Marcus Welser (1558–1614), Augsburg patrician, owned copy in Italian (Roeck 1990, 126).

317 Thomas Wentworth, English gentleman, dedicatee, 1713.

318 George Whetstone (1544–87), soldier and writer, used without naming (Izard 1942, 94–8).

319 Thomas Whythorne (1528–96), English musician, referred to text (Whythorne 1961, 68).

320 Abraham de Wicquefort (1598–1682), Dutch diplomat, recommended (1680–1, vol. I, 83).

321 John Winthrop Junior (1606–76), governor of Connecticut, owned copy (Stewart 1946, 322).

322 Ralph Wormeley II (1650–1701), Virginia planter, owned copy (Wright 1940, 197n.).

323 Benjamin Worsley, owned two copies in Latin (1678, 27, nos 92–3).

324 Thomas Wryght, chaplain of Trinity College, Cambridge, wrote name in copy of 1562 Italian edn (TCC, T.22.24).

325 Giovanni Zanca, Venetian merchant, owned copy, 1582 (Rossato 1987, 234).

326 Luis Zapata (*c.*1532–*c.*1595), Spanish noble, page of Empress Isabel, referred to author (1935, no. 85).

327 Antonio Zara, bishop of Aquileia, borrowed without naming (1615, 207–17).

328 Zygmunt II August (1520–72), king of Poland, asked for text to be translated (Górnicki 1566).

Bibliography

━━━━━━━━━━━◆━━━━━━━━━━━

The following list includes the books and articles cited in the notes and appendices, with the exception of editions of the *Courtier* before 1850, for which see appendix 1.

Accetto, Torquato (1641) *Della dissimulatione onesta*, rpr. Bari 1928

Ambrose (1984) *De officiis clericorum*, ed. and trans. M. Testard, Paris

Andersson, Ingvar (1948) *Erik XIV*, 3rd edn, Stockholm

Andrieu, Jean (1954) *Le dialogue antique: structure et présentation*, Paris

Aneau, Bartolomé (1552) *Les singeries des italiens*, Paris

Anglo, Sydney (1977) 'The Courtier: the Renaissance and Changing Ideals', in A. G. Dickens, ed. (1977) *The Courts of Europe*, London, 33–53

Anglo, Sydney (1983) *The Courtier's Art: Systematic Immorality in the Renaissance*, Swansea

Arbizzoni, Guido (1983) *L'ordine e la persuasione: Pietro Bembo personaggio nel Cortegiano*, Urbino

Aretino, Pietro (1534–6) *Ragionamenti*, ed. Giovanni Aquilecchia, Bari 1969

Ariosto, Ludovico (1516) *Orlando Furioso*, ed. Dino Provenzal, Milan 1955

Aristotle (1926) *Nicomachean Ethics*, ed. and trans. H. Rackham, London and Cambridge, Mass.

Arnott, J. F., ed. (1975) *Sale Catalogues of the Libraries of Eminent Persons*, vol. XII, *Actors*, London

Ascham, Roger (1568) *The Schoolmaster*, facsimile edn, Menston 1967

Atanagi, Dionigi, ed. (1561) *Rime in morte della Signora Irene di Spilimbergo*, Venice, prefaced by an unpaginated 'Vita della Signora Irene'

Aubrun, Charles V. (1958) 'Gracián contre Faret', *Homenaje a Gracián*, Zaragoza, 7–26

Austin, G. (1971) *The Library of Jean Grolier*, New York

Bakhtin, Mikhail M. (1929) *Problems of Dostoyevsky's Poetics*, English trans. Manchester 1984

Bakhtin, Mikhail M. (1981) *The Dialogic Imagination*, Austin

Bałtuk-Ulewiczowa, Teresa (1988) 'The *Senator* of Wawrzyniec Goślicki and the Elizabethan Councillor', in *The Polish Renaissance in its European Context*, ed. Samuel Fiszman, Bloomington and Indianapolis, 258–77

Bandello, Matteo (1554) *Novelle*, ed. G. G. Ferrero, Turin 1974

Bareggi, Claudia Di Filippo (1988) *Il mestiere di scrivere: lavoro intellettuale e mercato libraio a Venezia nel '500*, Rome

Baretti, Giuseppe (1763) *La frusta letteraria*, ed. Luigi Piccioni, 2 vols, Bari 1932

Bargagli, Scipione (1572) *Dialogo de' giuochi*, Siena

Bargagli, Scipione (1587) *I trattenimenti*, ed. L. Riccò, Rome 1989

Baridon, Silvio F. (1950) *Inventaire de la bibliothèque de Pontus de Tyard*, Geneva and Lille

Barker, Ernest (1948) *Traditions of Civility*, Cambridge

Barker, Ernest (1953) *Age and Youth*, Oxford

Barker, Nicolas (1990) 'The Books of Henry Howard Earl of Northampton', *Bodleian Library Record* 13, 375–81

Barnett, George, L. (1945) 'Gabriel Harvey's *Castilio sive aulicus* and *de aulica*', *Studies in Philology* 42, 146–63

Baron, Hans (1955) *The Crisis of the Early Italian Renaissance*, 2 vols, Princeton

Barros, Alonso de (1587), *Filosofia cortesana*, Madrid

Bartlett, Robert (1993) *The Making of Europe: Conquest, Colonization and Cultural Change, 950–1350*, London

Barycz, Henryk (1967) 'Italofilia e Italofobia nella Polonia del Cinque- e Seicento', in *Italia, Venezia e Polonia tra umanesimo e rinascimento*, ed. M. Brahmer, Wroclaw, 142–8

Bataillon, Marcel (1939) *Erasme en Espagne*, Paris, revised and enlarged Spanish edn, 2 vols, Mexico City 1950

Bates, Catherine (1992) *The Rhetoric of Courtship in Elizabethan Language and Literature*, Cambridge

Battisti, Saccaro G. (1980) 'La donna, le donne nel *Cortegiano*', in Ossola, 219–50

Baxandall, Michael (1980) *The Limewood Sculptors of Renaissance Germany*, New Haven

Beerbohm, Max (1911) *Zuleika Dobson*, rpr. London 1967

Bembo, Pietro (1960) *Prose e rime*, ed. Carlo Dionisotti, Turin

Benini, Gian Vincenzo (1778) *Elogio del più virtuoso uomo italiano del secolo sedicesimo*, third edn Venice 1788

Benson, Pamela J. (1992) *The Invention of the Renaissance Woman*, Philadelphia

Bergalli, Luisa, ed. (1726) *Componimenti poetici delle più illustri rimatrici d'ogni secolo*, 2 vols, Venice

Bhattacherje, M. M. (1940) *Courtesy in Shakespeare*, Calcutta

Binns, James W. (1990) *Intellectual Culture in Elizabethan and Jacobean England*, Leeds

Birrell, T. A. (1976) *The Library of John Morris*, London

Bleznick, D. W. (1958) 'The Spanish Reaction to Machiavelli in the Sixteenth and Seventeenth Centuries', *Journal of the History of Ideas* 19, 542–50

Blunt, Anthony (1940) *Artistic Theory in Italy*, Oxford

Boas, George (1940) 'The Mona Lisa in the History of Taste', *Journal of the History of Ideas* 1, rpr. in *Ideas in Cultural Perspective*, ed. P. Wiener and A. Noland, New Brunswick 1962, 127–44

Boccalini, Traiano (1612–14) *Ragguagli di Parnasso*, ed. Luigi Firpo, Bari 1948

Bonfatti, Emilio (1979) *La civil conversazione in Germania*, Udine

Bonner, Stanley F. (1977) *Education in Ancient Rome*, London

Borghini, Raffaele (1584) *Il riposo*, new edn, 3 vols, Milan 1807

Borinski, Karl (1894) *Baltasar Gracián und die Hofliteratur in Deutschland*, Halle

Bornstein, Diane (1983) *The Lady in the Tower: Medieval Courtesy Literature for Women*, Hamden, Conn.

Boswell, James (1791) *Life of Johnson*, ed. G. B. Hill, revised edn, 6 vols, Oxford 1934

Boucher, Jacqueline (1986) *La cour de Henri III*, La Guerche-de-Bretagne

Bourdieu, Pierre (1972) *Outlines of a Theory of Practice*, English trans. Cambridge 1977

Bourdieu, Pierre (1982) *In Other Words*, English trans. Cambridge 1990

Bracciolini, Poggio (c.1440) 'De nobilitate', in his *Opera*, Basle 1538, rpr. Turin 1964, 64–83

Brahe, Per (1581) *Oeconomia*, ed. J. Granlund and G. Holm, Lund 1971

Breton, Nicolas (1592) *Pilgrimage to Paradise*, London

Breton, Nicolas (1618) *Court and Country*, London

Brewer, Derek S. (1966) 'Courtesy and the Gawain-Poet', in *Patterns of Love and Courtesy: Essays in Memory of C. S. Lewis*, ed. J. Lawlor, London, 54–85

Brizzi, Gian Paolo (1976) *La formazione della classe dirigente nel '600–'700*, Bologna

Brown, Jonathan (1986) *Velazquez, Painter and Courtier*, New Haven and London

Brown, Peter M. (1967) 'Aims and Methods of the Second *Rassettatura* of the Decameron', *Studi Secenteschi* 8, 3–40

Brownstein, Leonard (1974) *Salas Barbadillo and the New Novel of Rogues and Courtiers*, Madrid

Bruford, W. H. (1975) *The German Tradition of Self-Cultivation from Humboldt to Thomas Mann*, Cambridge

Brunner, Otto (1956) 'Österreichische Adelsbibliotheken des 15. bis 18. Jht', in *Neue Wege der Sozialgeschichte*, second edn Göttingen 1968, 281–93

Brunner, Otto, Werner Conze and Reinhart Koselleck, eds (1972–90) *Geschichtliche Grundbegriffe*, 6 vols, Stuttgart

Bryskett, Ludovick (1606) *A Discourse of Civil Life*, London

Burckhardt, Jacob (1860) *Civilization of the Renaissance in Italy*, English trans. 1878, revised edn Harmondsworth 1990

Burger, Heinz Otto (1963) 'Europäischer Adelsideal und deutsche Klassik', in his *'Dasein heisst eine Rolle spielen': Studien zur deutschen Literaturgeschichte*, Munich, 211–32

Burke, Peter (1969) 'Tacitism', in *Tacitus*, ed. T. A. Dorey, London, 149–71

Burke, Peter (1972) *Culture and Society in Renaissance Italy*, 3rd edn as *The Italian Renaissance*, Cambridge 1986

Burke, Peter (1974) *Venice and Amsterdam*, revised edn Cambridge 1994.

Burke, Peter (1987) *The Renaissance*, London

Burke, Peter (1993) *The Art of Conversation*, Cambridge

Buruma, Ian (1984) *A Japanese Mirror*, London

Bush, Susan (1971) *The Chinese Literati on Painting*, Cambridge, Mass.

Bushman, Richard L. (1992) *The Refinement of America*, New York

Buxton, John (1954) *Sir Philip Sidney and the English Renaissance*, London

Caccini, Giulio (1600) *L'Euridice*, Florence, rpr. Bologna 1968

Caccini, Giulio (1601) *Le nuove musiche*, Florence, rpr. New York 1973

Cacho Blecua, Juan Manuel (1979) *Amadís: heroísmo mítico cortesano*, Madrid

Cahill, James F. (1960) 'Confucian Elements in the Theory of Painting', in *The Confucian Persuasion*, ed. Arthur F. Wright, Stanford, 115–40

Carpenter, William M. (1969–70), 'The *Green Helmet* Poems and Yeats's Myth of the Renaissance', *Modern Philology* 67, 50–9

Cartwright, Julia (1908) *Baldassare Castiglione*, 2 vols, London

Castiglione, Sabba da (1549), *Ricordi*, new edn Venice 1554

Castori, Bernardino (1622) *Institutione civile*, Rome

Cavagna, Anna Giulia (1989) 'Editori e lettori del *Cortegiano* fra Cinque e Settecento', *Schifanoia* 7, 5–40

Certeau, Michel de (1980) *The Practice of Everyday Life*, English trans. Berkeley 1984

Chapman, H. Perry (1990) *Rembrandt's Self-Portraits: a Study in Seventeenth-Century Identity*, Princeton

Chartier, Roger (1987) *The Cultural Uses of Print in Early Modern France*, Princeton

Chesterfield, Philip Dormer Stanhope, earl of (1774) *Letters*, ed. R. K. Root, London 1929

Chevalier, Maxime (1966) *L'Arioste en Espagne*, Bordeaux

Chevalier, Maxime (1976) *Lectura y lectores en la España de los siglos xvi y xvii*, Madrid

Chiesa, Francesco Agostino della (1620) *Theatro delle donne letterate*, Mondovi

Cian, Vittorio (1887) 'Un episodio della storia della censura in italia nel secolo xvi: l'edizione spurgata del *Cortegiano*', *Archivio Storico Lombardo* 14, 661–727

Cian, Vittorio (1951) *Un illustre nunzio pontificio del Rinascimento: Baldassare Castiglione*, Vatican City

Cicero, Marcus Tullius (1913) *De officiis*, ed. and trans. Walter Miller, London and Cambridge, Mass.

Cicero, Marcus Tullius (1939) *Orator*, ed. and trans. H. M. Hubbell, London and Cambridge, Mass.

Cimarelli, Vincenzo (1642) *Istorie dello stato di Urbino*, Brescia

Cioranescu, A. (1938) *L'Arioste en France*, 2 vols, Paris

Cleland, James (1607) *Heropaideia, or the Institution of a Young Nobleman*, London

Clough, Cecil (1978) 'Francis I and the Courtiers of Castiglione's *Courtier*', *European Studies Review* 8, 23–70

Clubb, Louise G. (1983) 'Castiglione's Humanistic Art and Renaissance Drama', in Hanning and Rosand, 191–208

Colbert, Jean-Baptiste (1728) *Bibliotheca*, 3 vols, Paris

Collenuccio, Pandolfo (1552) *Compendio dell'historia del regno di Napoli*, ed. Girolamo Ruscelli, Venice

Collibus, Hippolytus a (1599) *Princeps, consiliarius, palatinus sive aulicus*, Hanau

Colonna, Vittoria (1889) *Carteggio*, ed. E. Ferrero and G. Müller, Florence

Connat, M. and J. Mégret (1943) 'Inventaire de la bibliothèque des du Prat', *Bibliothèque d'Humanisme et Renaissance* 3, 72–122

Conrads, Norbert (1982) *Ritterakademien der frühen Neuzeit*, Göttingen

Corominas, J. M. (1980) *Castiglione y la Araucana*, Madrid

Coron, Antoine (1988) 'Jacques-Auguste de Thou et sa bibliothèque', in Jolly, vol. II, 101–25

Coryate, Thomas (1611) *Crudities*, rpr. 2 vols, Glasgow 1905

Coseriu, Annamaria (1987) 'Zensur und Literatur in der italienischen Renaissance des xvi Jhts. Baldassar Castigliones *Libro del Cortegiano* als Paradigma', in *Literatur zwischen immanenten Bedingtheit und äusserem Zwang*, ed. A. Noyes-Weidner, Tübingen, 1–121

Cox, Virginia (1992) *The Renaissance Dialogue: Literary Dialogue in its Social and Political Contexts, Castiglione to Galileo*, Cambridge

Curtis, M. H. (1959) *Oxford and Cambridge in Transition*, Oxford

Dadson, Trevor J. (1987) 'La biblioteca de Alonso de Barros', *Bulletin Hispanique* 89, 27–53

Dainville, François de (1978) *L'éducation des jésuites (16e–18e siècles)*, Paris

Daley, Tatham A. (1934) *Jean de La Taille*, Paris

Damiani, Enrico (1929) reviews Pollak's edition of Górnicki, *Giornale Storico della Letteratura Italiana* 93, 156–64

Danzi, Massimo (1989) 'Girolamo Cittadini poeta milanese di primo '500', in Cesare Bozzetti, Pietro Ghibellini and Ennio Sandel, eds (1989) *Veronica Gambara e la poesia del suo tempo*, Florence, 293–315

Darnton, Robert (1986) 'History of Reading', reprinted in *New Perspectives on Historical Writing*, ed. Peter Burke, Cambridge 1991, 140–67

Darst, David H. (1978) *Juan Boscán*, Boston

Dawson, Raymond (1981) *Confucius*, Oxford

Dernschwam, Hans (1984) *Könyvtár*, Szeged

Deswarte, Sylvie (1989) *Il 'perfetto cortegiano' D. Miguel da Silva*, Rome

Deswarte, Sylvie (1991) 'Idea et Image dans les dialogues de Frei Heitor Pinto', *Estudos Portugueses a L. Stegagno Picchio*, Lisbon, 929–56

Di Benedetto, Arnaldo (1971) 'Alcuni aspetti della fortuna del *Cortegiano* nel '500', rpr. in *Stile e linguaggio*, Rome 1974, 101–15

Dickens, Arthur G. (1959) *Thomas Cromwell and the English Reformation*, London

Dickinson, G. Lowes (1931) *Plato and his Dialogues*, London

Di Francesco, Amadeo (1994) 'Castelletti e Balassi', in Klaniczay, 233–49

Dionisotti, Carlo (1952) review of Cian, *Giornale Storico della Letteratura Italiana* 129, 31–57

Dionisotti, Carlo (1965) 'La letteratura italiana nell'età del concilio di Trento', rpr. in his *Geografia e storia della letteratura italiana*, Turin 1967, 183–204

Dolce, Ludovico (1545) *Dialogo della institutione delle donne*, revised edn Venice 1547

Dolce, Ludovico (1557) *Aretino*, ed. Mark W. Roskill, New York 1968

Domenichi, Ludovico (1549) *La nobiltà delle donne*, Venice

Domenichi, Ludovico (1564) *La donna di corte*, Lucca

Donati, Claudio (1988) *L'idea di nobiltà in Italia: secoli xiv–xvii*, Rome and Bari

Donesmondi, Ippolito (1616), *Istoria ecclesiastica di Mantova*, 2 vols, Mantua

Doni, Antonfrancesco (1550) *La libreria*, Venice

Dorris, George E. (1967) *Paolo Rolli and the Italian Circle in London, 1715–44*, The Hague

Du Bosc, Jacques (1632) *L'honnête femme*, Paris

Duby, Georges (1968) 'The Diffusion of Cultural Patterns in Feudal Society', *Past & Present* 38, 1–10

Duby, Georges (1972) 'The History of Systems of Values', rpr. in his *Chivalrous Society*, London, 216–25

Duby, Georges (1978) *The Three Orders*, English trans. Chicago 1980

Ducci, Lorenzo (1601) *Arte aulica*, Ferrara

Durand, J. (1948) 'La biblioteca del Inca', *Nueva revista de filología hispánica* 2, 239–64

Du Refuge, Etienne (1616) *Traité de la cour ou instruction des courtisans*, revised and enlarged edn Rouen 1631

Earle, T. F. (1980) *Theme and Image in the Poetry of Sá de Miranda*, Oxford

Eco, Umberto (1981) *The Role of the Reader*, London

Egremont, Max (1980) *Balfour*, London

Elias, Norbert (1939) *The Process of Civilization*, English trans., 2 vols, Oxford 1978–82

Elias, Norbert (1969) *The Court Society*, English trans. Oxford 1983

Elyot, Thomas (1531) *The Book Named the Governor*, ed. Stanford Lehmberg, London 1962

Erasmus, Desiderius (1530) 'De civilitate morum puerilium', trans. Brian McGregor in *Collected Works*, vol. XXV, Toronto 1985, 273–89

Estienne, Henri (1578) *Deux dialogues*, ed. Pauline M. Smith, Geneva 1980

Etter, Else-Lilly (1966) *Tacitus in der Geistesgeschichte des 16. und 17. Jahrhunderts*, Basle and Stuttgart

Evans, John, ed. (1855) 'Extracts from the Private Account Book of Sir William More of Losely in Surrey', *Archaeologia* 36, 284–310

Fahy, Conor (1956) 'Three Early Renaissance Treatises on Women', *Italian Studies* 11, 30–47

Faret, Nicolas (1630) *L'honeste homme ou l'art de plaire à la cour*, ed. M. Magendie, Paris 1925

Febvre, Lucien (1911) *Philippe II et le Franche-Comté*, Paris

Fehrenbach, R. J. and Elizabeth S. Leedham-Green, eds (1992) *Private Libraries in Renaissance England*, vol. I, Binghamton

Finucci, Valeria (1989) 'La donna di corte: discorso istituzionale e realtà nel *Libro del Cortegiano*', *Annali d'Italianistica* 7, 88–103

Firpo, Massimiliano (1971) *Pietro Bizzarri: esule italiano del '500*, Turin

Fish, Stanley (1980) *Is there a Text in this Class? The Authority of Interpretive Communities*, Cambridge, Mass.

Fithian, Philip (1943) *Journal*, ed. H. D. Farish, Williamsburg

Floriani, Piero (1976) *Bembo e Castiglione*, Rome

Florio, John (1591) *Second Fruits*, London

Fontaine, Charles (1541) *Contr'amie*, rpr. in Screech 1970, 148–200

Foucault Michel (1969) *The Archaeology of Knowledge*, English trans. London 1972

Foucault, Michel (1971) *L'ordre du discours*, Paris

Franci, Giovanni (1977) *Il sistema del Dandy*, Bologna

Fucilla, Joseph G. (1950) 'The Role of the *Cortegiano* in the Second Part of Don Quixote', *Hispania* 33, 291–6

Furnivall, F. J., ed. (1868) *The Babees Book*, London

Gabrieli, C. (1978) 'La fortuna de "Il Cortegiano" in Inghilterra', *La Cultura* 16, 218–52

Gadamer, Hans-Georg (1960) *Truth and Method*, English trans. London 1975

Gagliano, Marco da (1608) *La Dafne*, Florence, rpr. Bologna 1970

Ganz, Peter (1986) 'curialis/hövesch', in *Höfische Literatur, Hofgesellschaft, Höfische Lebensformen um 1200*, ed. G. Kaiser and J. D. Müller, Düsseldorf, 39–56

Garrett, Christina H. (1938) *The Marian Exiles*, Cambridge

Garzoni, Tommaso (1585) *La piazza universale*, Venice

Gay, Peter (1966) *The Enlightenment: the Rise of Paganism*, London

Geertz, Clifford (1977) 'Centers, Kings and Charisma', rpr. in his *Local Knowledge*, New York 1983, 121–46

Genette, Gérard (1981) *Palimpsestes*, Paris

Genette, Gérard (1987) *Seuils*, Paris

Gérard, Mireille (1984) 'Le catalogue de la bibliothèque de La Rochefoucauld à Verteuil', in *Images de La Rochefoucauld*, Paris, 239–80

Gerber, Adolph (1913) *Niccolò Machiavelli: die Übersetzungen*, Gotha

Ghinassi, Ghino (1967) 'Fasi dell'elaborazione del *Cortegiano*', *Studi di Filologia Italiana* 25, 155–96

Ghinassi, Ghino (1971) 'Postille sull'elaborazione del *Cortegiano*', *Studi e Problemi di Critica Testuale* 3, 171–8

Giovio, Paolo (1546) *Elogia*, Venice

Giovio, Paolo (1555) *Dialogo dell'imprese*, rpr. New York 1979 from the 1574 edn

Giraldi Cinzio, Gianbattista (1565) *Discorsi intorno a quello che si conviene a giovane nobile nel servire un gran principe*, rpr. Pavia 1569

Giuffredi, Argisto (1896) *Avvertimenti christiani*, ed. L. Natali, Palermo

Goffman, Erving (1956) *The Presentation of Self in Everyday Life*, 2nd edn New York 1959

Gombrich, Ernst H. (1960) *Art and Illusion*, London

Gombrich, Ernst H. (1986), 'Architecture and Rhetoric in Giulio Romano's Palazzo del Te', in *New Light on Old Masters*, Oxford

González Palencia, A. and E. Mele (1941–3) *Vida y obras de Don Diego Hurtado de Mendoza*, 3 vols, Madrid

Górnicki, Łukasz (1566) *Dworzanin polski*, ed. Roman Pollak, 2nd edn Wroclaw 1954

Goślicki, Wawrzyniec (1568) *De optimo senatore*, Venice

Gouge, William (1622) *Domestical Duties*, London

Gracián, Baltasar (1647) *Oráculo manual*, bilingual edn, ed. L. B. Walton, London 1962

Greenblatt, Stephen (1980) *Renaissance Self-Fashioning from More to Shakespeare*, Chicago

Greene, Robert (1592) *A Quip for an Upstart Courtier*, London

Greene, Thomas (1982) *The Light in Troy: Imitation and Discovery in Renaissance Poetry*, New Haven

Greene, Thomas (1983) 'Il Cortegiano and the Choice of a Game', in Hanning and Rosand, 1–16

Greville, Fulke (1907) *Life of Sir Philip Sidney*, Oxford

[Greville, Robert] (1678), *Catalogue*, London

Gritio, Pietro (1586), *Il Castiglione*, Mantua

Guazzo, Stefano (1574) *La civil conversatione*, ed. Amedeo Quondam, 2 vols, Modena 1993

Guevara, Antonio de (1539a) *Aviso de privados y doctrina de cortesanos*, rpr. Pamplona 1579

Guevara, Antonio de (1539b) *Menosprecio de corte y alabanza de aldea*, ed. Matías Martínez, Burgos and Madrid 1967

Guibovich Perez, Pedro (1989) 'Fray Juan de Alamaraz', *Cuadernos para la historia de la evangelización en América Latina* 4, 31–42

Guidi, José (1977) 'Thyrsis ou la cour transfiguré', *Centre de Recherches sur la Renaissance Italienne* 6, Paris, 141–78

Guidi, José (1978) 'L'Espagne dans la vie et dans l'oeuvre de B. Castiglione', *Centre de Recherches sur la Renaissance Italienne* 7, 113–202

Guidi, José (1980) 'De l'amour courtois à l'amour sacré: la condition de la femme dans l'oeuvre de Baldassare Castiglione', *Centre de Recherches sur la Renaissance Italienne* 8, 9–80

Guidi, José (1982) 'Le jeu de cour et sa codification dans les différentes rédactions du *Courtisan*', *Centre de Recherches sur la Renaissance Italienne* 10, 97–115

Guidi, José (1983) 'Reformulations de l'idéologie aristocratique au 16e siècle: les différentes rédactions et la fortune du *Courtisan*', *Centre de Recherches sur la Renaissance Italienne* 11, 121–84

Guidi, José (1985) 'Visages de la vie de cour selon Castiglione et l'Arétin: du *Cortegiano* à la *Cortegiana*', *Centre de Recherches sur la Renaissance Italienne* 13, 219–28

Guidi, José (1989) 'Une artificieuse présentation: le jeu des dédicaces et des prologues du *Courtisan*', in *L'écrivain face à son public*, ed. C. A. Fiorato and J.-C. Margolin, Paris, 127–44

Guilpin, Everard (1598) *Skialetheia*, ed. D. Allen Carroll, Chapel Hill 1974

Guthrie, William K. C. (1975) *A History of Greek Philosophy*, vol. IV, Cambridge

Guyon, Louis (1604) *Les divers leçons*, Lyon

Hale, John R. (1954) *England and the Italian Renaissance*, revised edn London 1963

Hale, John R. (1976) 'The Military Education of the Officer Class in Early Modern Europe', rpr. in his *Renaissance War Studies*, London 1983, 225–46

Hale, John R. (1983) 'Castiglione's Military Career', in Hanning and Rosand, 143–64

Hamburger, Michael (1959) 'Aristotle and Confucius', *Journal of the History of Ideas* 20, 236–49

Hampe Martínez, Teodoro (1993) 'The Diffusion of Books and Ideas in Colonial Peru', *Hispanic American Historical Review* 73, 211–33

Hanning, R. W. and David Rosand, eds (1983) *Castiglione: the Ideal and the Real in Renaissance Culture*, New Haven

Hare, Christopher (1908) *Courts and Camps of the Italian Renaissance*, London

Harington, John (1591) *Orlando Furioso in English Heroical Verse*, ed. R. McNulty, Oxford 1972

Harris, Daniel A. (1974) *Yeats: Coole Park and Ballylee*, Baltimore

Harrison, John and Peter Laslett (1965) *The Library of John Locke*, Oxford

Harsdörffer, Georg Philipp (1641–9) *Frauenzimmers Gesprächspiele*, Nuremberg

Harvey, Gabriel (1578) *Gratulationum Valdinensium libri IV*, London

Harvey, Gabriel (1884) *Letter-Book*, ed. Edward J. L. Scott, London

Hassall, W. O., ed. (1950) *A Catalogue of the Library of Sir Edward Coke*, New Haven

Hassell, J. W. (1953) 'Des Périers' Indebtedness to Castiglione', *Studies in Phiology* 50, 566–72

Hawkins, Richmond L. (1916) *Maistre Charles Fontaine, Parisien*, Cambridge, Mass.

Hazard, Paul (1935) *The European Mind 1680–1715*, English trans., 2nd edn Harmondsworth 1964

Heiberg, Steffen, ed. (1988) *Christian IV and Europe*, Copenhagen

Heidenreich, Helmut (1970) *The Libraries of D. Defoe and P. Farewell*, Berlin

Heinsius, Nikolaes (1655) *Catalogus librorum*, Leiden

[Heinsius, Nikolaes] (1682) *Catalogus*, Leiden

Heltzel, Virgil B. (1942) *A Check List of Courtesy Books in the Newberry Library*, Chicago

Hempfer, Klaus W. (1987) *Diskrepante Lektüren: Die Orlando-Furioso-Rezeption im '500*, Wiesbaden

Héroet, Antoine (1542) *La parfaite amie*, rpr. in Screech 1970, 3–68

Héroet, Antoine (1909) *Oeuvres poétiques*, ed. Ferdinand Gohin, Paris

Hinz, Manfred (1991) 'Castiglione und Gracián', in *El mundo de Gracián*, ed. Sebastian Neumeister and Dietrich Briesemeister, Berlin, 127–48

Hinz, Manfred (1992) *Rhetorische Strategien des Hofmannes: Studien zu den italienischen Hofmannstraktaten des 16. und 17. Jhts*, Stuttgart

Hinz, Manfred (1993) 'Il Cortegiano e il Tacitismo', in Montandon, 191–8

Hirst, Michael (1964) 'Rosso: a document and a drawing', *Burlington Magazine* 106, 120–6

Hobson, Anthony (1975) *Apollo and Pegasus: an Enquiry into the Formation and Disposal of a Renaissance Library*, Amsterdam

Hoby, Thomas (1902) *A Booke of the Travaile and Life of Me Thomas Hoby*, ed. E. Powell, London, Camden Miscellany, vol. X

Hogrefe, Pearl (1929–30) 'Elyot and "the boke called Cortigiano in Ytalian"', *Modern Philology* 27, 303–9

Hogrefe, Pearl (1967) *The Life and Times of Sir Thomas Elyot, Englishman*, Ames, Ia.

Hudson, Winthrop S. (1980) *The Cambridge Connexion and the Elizabethan Settlement of 1559*, Durham, NC

Huizinga, Johan (1915) 'Historical Ideals of Life', trans. in his *Men and Ideas*, New York 1959, 77–96

Insulanus, Gulielmus (1539) *Aula*, rpr. London 1612

Isaia the Abbot (1851), 'Regula', in Migne, vol. CIII, 427–34

Izard, Thomas C. (1942) *George Whetstone*, New York

Jackson, Heather J. (1992–3) 'Writing in Books and Other Marginal Activities', *University of Toronto Quarterly* 62, 217–31

Jaeger, Stephen C. (1985) *The Origins of Courtliness*, Philadelphia

Jaeger, Werner (1933–45) *Paideia*, 3 vols, English trans. Oxford 1939–45

Jansen, Hellmut (1958) *Die Grundbegriffe des Baltasar Gracián*, Geneva and Paris

Jardine, Lisa and Anthony Grafton (1990) 'How Gabriel Harvey Read his Livy', *Past & Present* 129, 30–78

Jauss, Hans-Robert (1974) *Toward an Aesthetic of Reception*, English trans. Manchester 1982

Javitch, Daniel (1971) 'The Philosopher of the Court', *Comparative Literature* 23, 97–124

Javitch, David (1972) 'Poetry and Court Conduct', *Modern Language Notes* 87, 865–82

Javitch, David (1978) *Poetry and Courtliness in Renaissance England*, Princeton

Jayne, Sears (1956) *Library Catalogues of the English Renaissance*, London

Jayne, Sears and F. R. Johnson, eds (1956) *The Library of John Lord Lumley*, London

Jessup, F. W. (1965) *Sir Roger Twysden*, London

Johnson, Samuel (1779–81) *Lives of the Poets*, 2 vols, Oxford 1952

Jolly, Claude, ed. (1988–92) *Histoire des bibliothèques françaises*, 4 vols, Paris

Jones, Joseph R. (1975) *Antonio de Guevara*, Boston

Jongh, Eddie de (1985) review in *Simiolus* 15, 65–8

Jonson, Ben (1925–52) *Works*, ed. C. H. Herford and Percy and Evelyn Simpson, 11 vols, Oxford

Jonson, Ben (1953) *Timber*, ed. R. S. Walker, New York

Jordan, Constance (1990) *Renaissance Feminism*, Ithaca

Jourda, Pierre (1930) *Marguerite d'Angoulême*, 2 vols, Paris

Juel-Jensen, Bent (1956) letter in *Book Collector* 5, 172

Kamen, Henry (1993) *The Phoenix and the Flame: Catalonia and the Counter-Reformation*, New Haven and London

Kasparová, Jaroslava, ed. (1990) *Roudnická Knihovna*, vol. Il, Prague

Keen, Maurice (1984) *Chivalry*, New Haven and London

Kelso, Ruth (1929) *The Doctrine of the English Gentleman*, revised edn Urbana 1964

Kelso, Ruth (1956) *Doctrine for the Lady of the Renaissance*, Urbana

Kemp, Walter H. (1976) 'Some Notes on Music in Castiglione's *Il Libro del Cortegiano*', in *Cultural Aspects of the Italian Renaissance*, ed. Cecil Clough, Manchester, 354–76

Kerr, Richard J. A. (1955) 'Prolegomena to an edition of Villalón's *Scholastico*', *Bulletin of Hispanic Studies* 32, 130–9, 203–13

Keserű, Bálint, ed. (1983) *A magyar könyvkultúra multjából*, Szeged

Kiesel, Helmuth (1979) *Bei Hof, bei Höll*, Tübingen

Kiessling, Nicolas K. (1988) *The Library of Robert Burton*, Oxford

Kincaid, J. J. (1973) *Cristóbal de Villalón*, New York

Klaniczay, Gábor (1990) 'Daily Life and Elites in the Later Middle Ages', in *Environment and Society in Hungary*, ed. Ferenc Glatz, Budapest, 75–90

[Klaniczay, Tibor] (1994) *Emlekkönyv* (memorial volume), Budapest

Klein, Lawrence E. (1994) *Shaftesbury and the Culture of Politeness: Moral Discourse and Cultural Politics in Early Eighteenth-century England*, Cambridge and Cambridge, Mass.

Klesczewski, Reinhard (1966) *Die französischen Übersetzungen des Cortegiano*, Heidelberg

Knox, Dilwyn (1991) 'Disciplina', in *Renaissance Society and Culture*, ed. John Monfasani and Ronald G. Musto, New York, 107–35

Kock, Ebbe (1920) 'En Svensk Bokkatalog fran 1500-Talet', *Nordisk Tidskrift för Bok och Biblioteksväsen* 7, 146–53

Kolsky, Stephen (1991) *Mario Equicola: the Real Courtier*, Geneva

Korsten, Frans (1980) *A Catalogue of the Library of Thomas Baker*, Cambridge

Koselleck, Reinhart (1972) 'Begriffsgeschichte and Social History', English trans. in his *Futures Past*, Cambridge, Mass., 1985, 73–91

Krebs, Ernest (1940–2) '*El Cortesano* de Castiglione en España', *Boletín de la Academia Argentina de Letras* 8, 93–146, 423–35; 9, 125–42, 517–43; 10, 53–118, 689–748

Kuhn, S. E. and J. Reidy, eds (1954) *Middle English Dictionary*, Ann Arbor

Labarre, Albert (1971) *Le livre dans la vie amiénois du 16e siècle*, Paris and Louvain

La Boétie, Etienne (1892) *Oeuvres*, Bordeaux and Paris

La Borderie, Bertrand de (1541) *L'Amie de cour*, rpr. in Screech 1970, 111–45

Langford, Paul (1989) *A Polite and Commercial People: England 1727–1783*, Oxford

La Noue, François de (1587) *Discours politiques et militaires*, ed. Frank E. Sutcliffe, Geneva and Paris 1967

Lanzi, Luigi (1795–6) *Storia pittorica d'Italia*, fourth edn, 6 vols, Pisa 1815

Lapp, John C. (1971) *The Esthetics of Negligence: La Fontaine's Contes*, Cambridge

Larivaille, Paul (1980) *Pietro Aretino fra Rinascimento e Manierismo*, Rome

La Rocca, Guido, ed. (1978) *Baldassare Castiglione, Lettere*, vol. I, Verona

La Rochefoucauld, François, duc de (1665) *Maximes*, ed. F. C. Green, Cambridge 1946

La Taille, Jean de (1878–82) *Oeuvres*, ed. René de Maulde, 4 vols, Paris

Latham, R. E., ed. (1965) *Revised Medieval Latin Word-List*, London

Leedham-Green, Elizabeth (1987) *Books in Cambridge Inventories*, 2 vols, Cambridge

Le Flem, Jean-Pierre (1973) 'Une bibliothèque ségovienne au siècle d'or', in *Mélanges Tapié*, Paris, 403–10

Le Gentil, Pierre (1955) *La Chanson de Roland*, Paris

Lehmann, Paul (1960) *Eine Geschichte der alten Fuggerbibliotheken*, Tübingen

Leonard, Irving A. (1949) *Books of the Brave*, Cambridge, Mass.

Lerche, Cornelius (1682) *Catalogus librorum*, Copenhagen

Lersundi, Fernando del Valle (1929) 'Testamento de Fernando de Rojas', *Revista de filología española* 16, 366–88

Levenson, Joseph R. (1958) *Confucian China and its Modern Fate*, 2nd edn as *Modern China and its Confucian Past*, New York 1964

Library (1840) 'The Library of Mary Queen of Scots, and of King James VI', *Miscellany, Maitland Club* 1, 1–23

Lievsay, John L. (1964) *The Elizabethan Image of Italy*, Ithaca

Lievsay, John L. (1969) *The Englishman's Italian Books, 1550–1700*, Philadelphia

Lippe, Rudolf zur (1974) *Naturbeherrschung am Menschen*, 2 vols, Frankfurt

Lloyd, David (1665) *State-Worthies*, second edn London 1670

Lloyd, Geoffrey (1967) *Aristotle*, Cambridge

Lo Brun, Garin (1889) 'L'enseignement', ed. Carl Appel, *Revue des langues romans* 33, 404–32

Lomazzo, Giovanni Paolo (1590) *Idea del tempio di pittura*, ed. R. P. Ciardi, Florence 1975

Loos, Erich (1955) *Baldassare Castigliones Libro del Cortegiano*, Frankfurt

Lopez Estrada, Francisco (1948) *Estudio critico de la Galatea de Miguel de Cervantes*, Tenerife

Löwenfeld, Rafael (1884) *Łukasz Górnicki*, Breslau

Lytton, Edward Bulwer (1828) *Pelham: or, Adventures of a Gentleman*, 3 vols, London

Macdonald, Robert H. (1971) *The Library of Drummond of Hawthornden*, Edinburgh

MacGraíth, Mícheál (1990) 'Gaelic Ireland and the Renaissance', in *The Celts and the Renaissance*, ed. Glanmore Williams and Robert O. Jones, Cardiff, 57–89

McKenzie, Don (1986) *Bibliography and the Sociology of Texts*, London

McKitterick, David J. (1978) *The Library of Sir Thomas Knyvett*, Cambridge

Magendie, Maurice (1925) *La politesse mondaine en France de 1600 à 1660*, Paris

Major, John M. (1964) *Sir Thomas Elyot and Renaissance Humanism*, Lincoln, Nebr.

Malarczyk, Jan (1962) *La fortuna di Niccolò Machiavelli in Polonia*, Wroclaw

Malatesta, Massario A. (1573) *Il cavallerizzo*, Venice

Malory, Thomas (1954) *Morte d'Arthur*, ed. Eugene Vinaver, Oxford

Mander, Karel van (1604) *Den Grondt der Edel Vry Schilder-Const*, ed. Hessel Miedema, Utrecht 1973

Mariéjol, J. H. (1920) *Catherine de' Medici*, Paris

Mariéjol, J. H. (1928) *Daughter of the Medici*, English trans. New York 1929

Marliani, Bernardo (1583) *Vita di Baldassare Castiglione*, prefixed, unpaginated, to Venice 1584 edition of *Il Cortegiano*

Marrou, Henri-Irenée (1948) *A History of Education in Antiquity*, tr. G. Lamb, London 1956

Marston, John (1934–9) *Plays*, ed. H. Harvey Ward, 3 vols, Edinburgh and London

Marston, John (1961) *Poems*, ed. A. Davenport, Liverpool

Martin, Julian (1993) *Francis Bacon, the State and the Reform of Natural Philosophy*, Cambridge

Martyn, William (1612) *Youths Instruction*, London

Mattei, Rodolfo de (1967) 'Un cinquecentista confutatore del Machiavelli: Antonio Ciccarelli', *Archivio Storico Italiano* 125, 69–91

Maxwell Lyte, H. C. (1909) *A History of Dunster*, 2 vols, London

Mayer, C. A. (1951) 'L'honnête homme: Molière and Philibert de Vienne's *Philosophe de cour*', *Modern Language Review* 46, 196–217

Meinecke, Friedrich (1924) *Machiavellism*, English trans. London 1957

Méré, chevalier de (1930) *Oeuvres posthumes*, Paris.

Migne, J.-P. (1844–55) *Patrologia Latina*, 217 vols, Paris

Milán, Luis (1561) *El cortesano*, rpr. Madrid 1874

Miller, Amos C. (1963) *Sir Henry Killigrew*, Leicester

Möller, George J. (1984) 'Het album Pandora van Jan Six', *Jaarboek Amstelodanum* 77, 69–101

Monk, S. H. (1944) 'A Grace Beyond the Reach of Art', *Journal of the History of Ideas* 5, 131–50

Montaigne, Michel de (1580–8) *Essais*, variorum edn Paris 1962

Montalvo, Garci Rodríguez de (1991) *Amadís de Gaula*, ed. V. Cirlot and J. E. Ruiz Doménec, Barcelona

Montandon, Alain, ed. (1993) *Traités de savoir-vivre italiens*, Clermont-Ferrand

Moore Smith, G. C. (1913) *Gabriel Harvey's Marginalia*, Stratford

Mornet, Daniel (1910) 'Les enseignements des bibliothèques privées', *Revue d'histoire littéraire de la France* 17, 449–96

Morreale, Margherita (1958) 'Castiglione y *El Héroe*', in *Homenaje a Gracián*, Zaragoza, 137–44

Morreale, Margherita (1959) *Castiglione y Boscán: el ideal cortesano en el Rinacimiento español*, 2 vols, Madrid

Myrick, Kenneth O. (1935) *Sir Philip Sidney as a Literary Craftsman*, Cambridge, Mass.

Nashe, Thomas (1589) *The Anatomy of Absurdity*, London, rpr. London 1866

Naudé, Gabriel (1641) *Avis pour dresser une bibliothèque*, Paris

Naunton, Robert (1641) *Fragmenta regalia*, London

Negrini, Antonio Beffa (1606) *Elogi*, Mantua

Nicholls, Jonathan (1985) *The Matter of Courtesy*, Woodbridge

Nocera Avila, Carmela (1992) *Tradurre il Cortegiano: The Courtyer of Sir Thomas Hoby*, Bari

Opdycke, Leonard E., ed. (1901) *The Courtier*, New York

Osborn, Louise B. (1937) *The Life, Letters and Writings of John Hoskyns*, New Haven

Ossola, Carlo, ed. (1980) *La corte e il cortegiano*, Rome

Ossola, Carlo (1987) *Dal cortegiano al uomo del mondo*, Turin

Ötvös, Péter (1994) 'Pázmány Miklós gróf könyvei', in Klaniczay, 344–64

Ovenell, R. F. (1950) 'Brian Twyne's Library', *Oxford Bibliographical Society* 4, 3–42

Ovid (Publius Ovidius Naso) (1929) *Ars amoris*, ed. J. H. Mozley, 2nd edn, Cambridge, Mass. 1979

Pachomius (1845) 'Regula', in Migne, XXIII, 65–86

Palau y Dulcet, Antonio (1923–7) *Manual del librero hispano-americano*, 7 vols, Barcelona, second edn 1948–

Palmireno, Lorencio (1573) *El estudioso cortesano*, 2nd edn Alcalà 1587

Parini, Giuseppe (1967) *Opere*, ed. Ettore Bonora, Milan

Passano, G. B. (1878) *I novellieri italiani*, Turin

Paternoster, Annick (1993) 'Le *Sei giornate* di Pietro Aretino: l'*urbanitas* parodiata', in Montandon, 225–36

Patrizi, Giorgio (1984) '*Il libro del Cortegiano* e la trattatistica sul comportamento', *Letteratura italiana*, ed. Alberto Asor Rosa, Turin, vol. III, part 2, 855–90

Patten, William (1548) *The Expedition into Scotland*, London

Peacham, Henry (1622) *The Complete Gentleman*, ed. Virgil B. Heltzel from the 1634 edn, Ithaca 1962

Peck, Linda L. (1982) *Northampton: Patronage and Policy at the Court of James I*, London

Peck, Linda L. (1991) 'The Mentality of a Jacobean Grandee', in *The Mental World of the Jacobean Court*, ed. Peck, Cambridge, 148–68

Pelletier, Thomas (1594) *La nourriture de la noblesse*, Paris

Petreus Herdesianus, Henricus, ed. (1578) *Aulica vita/Vita privata*, 2 vols, Frankfurt

Pettie, George (1576) *A Petite Palace*, London

Philibert de Vienne (1547) *Le philosophe de cour*, ed. Pauline M. Smith, Geneva 1990, English trans. *The Philosopher of the Court*, London 1575

Piccolomini, Alessandro (1539) *La Raffaella*, rpr. Milan 1969

Picquard, Maurice (1951) 'Les livres du cardinal de Granvelle à la bibliothèque de Besançon', *Libri* 1, 301–23

Piéjus, Marie-Françoise (1980) 'Venus bifrons: le double idéal féminin dans *La Raffaella* d'Alessandro Piccolomini', *Centre de Recherches sur la Renaissance Italienne* 8, 81–165

Piéjus, Marie-Françoise (1982) 'La première anthologie de poèmes féminins', *Centre de Recherches sur la Renaissance Italienne* 10, 193–214

Pino, Bernardo (1604) *Del galant'uomo*, Venice

Pinto, Heitor (1563–72) *Imagem de vida cristã*, ed. M. Alves Correia, 4 vols, Lisbon 1940

Piozzi, Hester T. (1974) *Anecdotes of the Late Samuel Johnson*, London

Pleticha, Eva (1983) *Adel und Buch*, Neustadt

Possevino, Antonio (1593) *Bibliotheca selecta*, Rome

Pozzi, Mario, ed. (1988) *Discussioni linguistiche del '500*, Turin

Prandi, Stefano (1990) *Il cortegiano ferrarese: i discorsi di Annibale Romeo e la cultura nobiliare nel '500*, Florence

Praz, Mario (1943) 'Shakespeare, il Castiglione e le facezie', in his *Machiavelli in Inghilterra*, Rome, 193–217

Preto-Rodas, Richard A. (1971) *Francisco Rodrigues Lôbo: Dialogue and Courtly Love in Renaissance Portugal*, Chapel Hill

Procacci, Giuliano (1965) *Studi sulla fortuna del Machiavelli*, Rome

Prosperi, Adriano, ed. (1980) *La corte e il Cortegiano*, vol. II, *Un modello europeo*, Rome

Puttenham, George (1589) *The Arte of English Poesie*, repr. Menston 1968

Quilliet, Bernard (1975) 'Situation sociale des avocats du Parlement de Paris, 1480–1560', in *Espace, idéologie et société au 16e siècle*, Grenoble, 121–52

Quintilian (1921–2) *Institutio Oratoria*, ed. H. E. Butler, 4 vols, London

Quondam, Amadeo (1980) 'La "forma del vivere". Schede per l'analisi del discorso cortigiano', in Prosperi, 15–68

Quondam, Amadeo (1982) 'L'accademia', in *Letteratura italiana*, ed. Alberto Asor Rosa, Turin, vol. I, 823–98

Quondam, Amadeo (1983) 'La letteratura in tipografia', in *Letteratura italiana*, ed. Alberto Asor Rosa, Turin, vol. II, 555–686

Raab, Felix (1964) *The English Face of Machiavelli: a Changing Interpretation, 1500–1700*, London

Raimondi, Ezio, ed. (1960) *Trattatisti del '600*, Milan and Naples

Rainolds, John (1986) *Oxford Lectures on Aristotle's Rhetoric*, ed. and trans. Lawrence D. Green, Newark, Del.

Raleigh, Walter, ed. (1900) *The Courtier*, London

Ramage, Edwin S. (1973) *Urbanitas*, Norman, Okla.

Rankins, William (1588) *The English Ape*, London

Raven, James (1992) *Judging New Wealth: Popular Publishing and Responses to Commerce in England, 1750–1800*, Oxford

Rebhorn, Wayne A. (1978) *Courtly Performances*, Detroit

Redondo, Augustin (1976) *Antonio de Guevara*, Geneva

Reusch, F. Heinrich (1883–5) *Der Index der verbotenen Bücher*, 2 vols, Bonn

Reusch, F. Heinrich, ed. (1886) *Die indices librorum prohibitorum des sechzehnten Jahrhunderts*, Tübingen

Riccoboni, Antonio (1579) *De re comica*, Venice

Richardson, Brian (1994) *Print Culture in Renaissance Italy: the Editor and the Vernacular Text, 1470–1600*, Cambridge

Ricoeur, Paul (1981) 'Appropriation', in his *Hermeneutics and the Human Sciences*, Cambridge, 182–93

Ringhieri, Innocenzio (1551) *Cento giuochi liberali*, Bologna

Rodrigues Lôbo, Francisco (1619) *Côrte na aldeia e noites de inverno*, ed. Alfonso Lopes Vieira, Lisbon 1972

Rodríguez Marín, Francisco (1923) *Francisco Pacheco maestro de Velazquez*, Madrid

Roeck, Bernhard (1990) 'Geschichte, Finsternis und Unkultur', *Archiv für Kulturgeschichte* 72, 115–41

Rolli, Paolo Antonio (1728) *Remarks upon M. Voltaire's Essay on the Epic Poetry of the European Nations*, London

Roorda, Daniel J. (1964) 'The Ruling Class in Holland in the Seventeenth Century', in *Britain and the Netherlands*, ed. John S. Bromley and Ernst H. Kossmann, Groningen, vol. II, 109–32

Rosenkrantz, Eric (1688) *Bibliotheca*, Copenhagen

Rosenkrantz, Janus (1696) *Bibliotheca*, Copenhagen

Rotondò, Antonio (1973) 'La censura ecclesiastica e la cultura', *Storia d'Italia*, Turin, vol. V, 1397–1492

Rotondò, Antonio (1982) 'Cultura umanistica e difficoltà dei censori', *Centre de Recherches sur la Renaissance Italienne* 10, 15–50

Rushdie, Salman (1983) *Shame*, London

Ruutz-Rees, Caroline (1910) 'Some Notes of Gabriel Harvey in Hoby's Translation of Castiglione's *Courtier*', *Publications of the Modern Language Association* 25, 608–39

Ryan, Lawrence V. (1963) *Roger Ascham*, Stanford

Ryan, Lawrence V. (1972) 'Book IV of Castiglione's Courtier: Climax or Afterthought?', *Studies in the Renaissance* 19, 156–79

Sabbatini, Pasquale (1986) *Il modello bembiano a Napoli nel '500*, Naples

Saccone, E. (1979) 'Grazia, sprezzatura and affettazione in Castiglione's *Book of the Courtier*', rpr. in Hanning and Rosand, 45–68

Sadoleto, Jacopo (1737) *Opera omnia*, 2 vols, Verona

Salas Barbadillo, Alonso Jerónimo de (1620) *El caballero perfecto*, ed. Pauline Marshall, Boulder 1949

Salvadori, Corinna (1965) *Yeats and Castiglione*, Dublin

Sandrart, Joachim von (1675–80) *Teutsche Akademie*, 5 vols, Nuremberg

Sansovino, Francesco (1567) *Il simolacro di Carlo Quinto Imperadore*, Venice

Sansovino, Francesco (1582) *Cronologia del mondo*, Venice

Santangelo, G., ed. (1954) *Le epistole de imitatione di Gianfrancesco Pico della Mirandola e di Pietro Bembo*, Florence

Sassetti, Filippo (1855) *Lettere*, ed. Ettore Marcucci, Florence

Sastrow, Bartolomeus (1823) *Leben*, ed. G. C. F. Mohnike, 3 vols, Greifswald

Scarpati, Claudio (1982) *Studi sul '500 italiano*, Milan

Scavenius, Peder (1665) *Designatio librorum*, Copenhagen

Schenk, Wilhelm (1949) 'The *Cortegiano* and the Civilization of the Renaissance', *Scrutiny* 16, 93–103

Schmitt, Jean-Claude (1990) *La raison des gestes dans l'occident médiéval*, Paris

Schnerr, Walter J. (1961) 'Two Courtiers: Castiglione and Rodrigues Lôbo', *Comparative Literature* 13, 138–53

Schrinner, Walter (1939) *Castiglione und die Englische Renaissance*, Berlin

Schutte, Anne J. (1991) 'Irene di Spilimbergo', *Renaissance Quarterly* 44, 42–61

Schutz, Alexander H. (1955) *Vernacular Books in Parisian Private Libraries of the Sixteenth Century*, Chapel Hill

Scott, Mary Augusta (1901) '*The Book of the Courtier*: a Possible Source of Benedick and Beatrice', *Publications of the Modern Language Association* 16, 475–502

Screech, Michael A. (1959) 'An Interpretation of the *Querelle des amyes*', *Bibliothèque d'Humanisme et Renaissance* 21, 103–30

Screech, Michael A., ed. (1970) *Opuscules d'amour*, Geneva

Searles, Colbert, ed. (1912) *Catalogue de tous les livres de feu M. Chapelain*, Stanford

Selig, Karl (1960) *The Library of V. J. de Lastanosa*, Geneva

Seneca, Lucius Annaeus (1917–25) *Epistulae morales*, ed. Richard M. Gummere, 3 vols, London

Serassi, Pier Antonio (1769–71) *Lettere del conte Baldassare Castiglione*, 2 vols, Padua

Seznec, Jean (1940) *The Survival of the Pagan Gods*, English trans. New York 1953

Sidney, Philip (1973) *Miscellaneous Prose*, ed. Katharine Duncan-Jones and Jan van Dorsten, Oxford

Sigismondi, Sigismondo (1604) *Prattica cortegiana morale e economica*, Ferrara

Sinner, Jean R. (1764) *Bibliothecae Bernensis catalogus*, 2 vols,

Berne 1764

Skinner, Quentin (1969) 'Meaning and Understanding in the History of Ideas', rpr. in *Meaning and Context*, ed. James Tully, Cambridge, 1988, 29–67

Smith, David R. (1988) 'I Janus: Privacy and the Gentlemanly Ideal in Rembrandt's Portraits of Jan Six', *Art History* 11, 42–63

Smith, Pauline M. (1966) *The Anti-Courtier Trend in 16th-Century French Literature*, Geneva

Solnon, Jean-François (1987) *La cour de France*, Paris

Sørensen, Villy (1977) *Seneca: humanisten ved Neros hof*, Copenhagen

Sorrentino, Andrea (1935) *La letteratura italiana e il Sant'Ufficio*, Naples

Sozzi, Lionello (1972) 'La polémique anti-italienne en France au 16e siècle', *Atti della Accademia delle Scienze di Torino* 106, ii, 99–190

Spierenburg, Pieter (1981) *Elites and Etiquette: Mentality and Social Structure in the Early Modern Northern Netherlands*, Rotterdam

Stackelberg, Jürgen von (1960) *Tacitus in der Romania*, Tübingen

Stanton, Domna C. (1980) *The Aristocrat as Art*, New York

Starkey, David (1982) 'The Court: Castiglione's Ideal and Tudor Reality', *Journal of the Warburg and Courtauld Institutes* 45, 232–9

Stein, Arnold (1949) 'Yeats: a Study in Recklessness', *Sewanee Review* 57, 603–26

Stern, Virginia (1979) *Gabriel Harvey: His Life, Marginalia and Library*, Oxford

Stevenson, J. ed. (1867) *Calendar of State Papers Foreign, 1562*, London

Stewart, Randall (1946) 'Puritan Literature and the Flowering of New England', *William and Mary Quarterly* 3, 319–42

Stock, Brian (1983) *The Implications of Literacy*, Princeton

Stokes, Michael C. (1986) *Plato's Socratic Conversations: Drama and Dialectic in Three Dialogues*, Baltimore

Stone, Lawrence (1965) *The Crisis of the Aristocracy, 1558–1641*, Oxford

Stöttner, Reinhard (1888) 'Die erste Übersetzung von B. Castigliones *Cortegiano*', *Jahrbuch für Münchener Geschichte* 2, 494–9

Strozzi, Niccolò (1982) 'Avvertimenti necessari per i cortigiani', *Studi Secenteschi* 23, 165–93

Symonds, John A. (1875–86) *The Renaissance in Italy*, 7 vols, London

Szűcs, Jenö (1983) 'The Three Historical Regions of Europe', *Acta Historica Academiae Scientiarum Hungariae* 29, 131–84

Tasso, Torquato (1583) 'Il Malpiglio, o vero de la corte', in *Dialoghi*, ed. Cesare Guasti, 3 vols, Florence 1859, vol. III, 3–21

Tasso, Torquato (1958) 'Il forno, o vero de la nobiltà', in *Dialoghi*, ed.

Ezio Raimondi, 3 vols, Florence, vol. II, 3–113

Taylor, Francis H. (1948) *The Taste of Angels: a History of Art Collecting from Rameses to Napoleon*, London

Telle, Emile V. (1937) *L'oeuvre de Marguerite d'Angoulême e la querelle des femmes*, Toulouse

Thomas, William (1549) *History of Italy*, ed. George B. Parks, Ithaca 1963

Thou, Jacques-Auguste de (1679) *Catalogus bibliothecae Thuanae*, Paris

Thou, Jacques-Auguste de (1713) *Mémoires*, Amsterdam

Thuau, Etienne (1966) *Raison d'état et pensée politique à l'époque de Richelieu*, Paris

Timotei, Michele (1614) *Il cortegiano*, Rome

Tiraboschi, Girolamo (1772–82) *Storia della letteratura italiana*, revised edn, 8 vols, Modena 1787–93

Toffanin, Giuseppe (1921) *Machiavelli e il tacitismo*, Padua

Toldo, Pietro (1900) 'Le courtisan dans la littérature française et ses rapports avec l'oeuvre de Castiglione', *Archiv für das Studium der neueren Sprachen und Literaturen*, 60–85, 75–121, 104, 105, 313–30

Tolstoy, Leo (1857) *Youth*, English trans. Harmondsworth 1964

Trend, J. B. (1925) *Luis Milán and the Vihuelistas*, Oxford

Tresham, Thomas, scrapbook, British Library, Additional MSS 39, 830

Trilling, Lionel (1972) *Sincerity and Authenticity*, London

Uhlig, Claus (1973) *Hofkritik im England des Mittelalters und der Renaissance*, Berlin

Uhlig, Claus (1975) 'Moral und Politik in der europäischen Hoferziehung', *Festschrift L. Borinski*, Heidelberg, 27–51

Ulfeldt, Jakob (1923) 'Catalogus librorum', *Danske Magazin* 6, 177–82

Vallone, Aldo (1955) 'Nobiltà e cortesia dal Boiardo al Tasso', rpr. in his *Dal Rinascimento al Romanticismo*, Naples, 1983, 40–70

Vasari, Giorgio (1550) *Vite*, ed. L. Bellosi and A. Rossi, Turin 1986

Vasari, Giorgio (1564) *Vite*, ed. R. Bettarini, 6 vols, Florence 1966–87

Veblen, Thorstein (1899) *Theory of the Leisure Class*, New York

Vespasiano da Bisticci (1970–6) *Vite*, ed. A. Greco, 2 vols, Florence

Villalón, Cristóbal de (1911), *El scholástico*, ed. Marcelino Menéndez Pelayo, Madrid

Villalón, Cristóbal de (1967), *El scholástico*, ed. Richard J. A. Kerr, Madrid

Villey, Pierre (1908) *Les sources et l'évolution des essais de Montaigne*, 2 vols, Paris

Vincent, E. R. (1964) '*Il Cortegiano* in Inghilterra', in *Rinascimento europeo e rinascimento veneziano*, ed. Vittore Branca, Florence, 97–107

Vives, Juan Luis (1524) *Institutio feminae christianae*, revised edn Basle 1538

Walde, O. (1932) 'Studier i Äldre Dansk Bibliotheks-Historia', *Nordisk Tidskrift för Bok och Biblioteksväsen* 19, 21–51

Waller, Gary F. (1979) *Mary Sidney, Countess of Pembroke*, Salzburg

Warburg, Aby (1932) *Gesammelte Schriften*, Leipzig and Berlin

Warner, G. F. (1893) 'The Library of James VI', *Publications of the Scottish History Society* 15, xi–lxxv

Warnicke, Retha M. (1988) 'Women and Humanism in the Renaissance', in *Renaissance Humanism*, ed. Albert Rabil Junior, Philadelphia, vol. II, 39–54

Weise, Georg (1936) 'Vom Menschenideal und von den Modewörtern der Gotik und der Renaissance', *Deutsche Vierteljahrschrift für Literatur- und Geistesgeschichte* 14, 171–222

Welsh, David J. (1963) 'Il Cortigiano polacco', *Italica* 40, 22–6

White, Lynn (1962) *Medieval Technology and Social Change*, Oxford

Whythorne, Thomas (1961) *Autobiography*, ed. James Osborn, Oxford

Wicquefort, Abraham de (1681) *L'ambassadeur et ses fonctions*, 2 vols, 'Cologne' 1689–90

Williams, Raymond (1976) *Keywords*, revised edn, London 1983

Williamson, Edward (1947) 'The Concept of Grace in the Work of Raphael and Castiglione', *Italica* 24, 316–24

Wilson, Edward M. (1964–8) 'A Cervantes Item from Emmanuel College Library', *Transactions of the Cambridge Bibliographical Society* 4, 363–71

Wilson, Frank P., rev. (1970) *Oxford Dictionary of English Proverbs*, Oxford

Wolf II, Edwin (1974) *The Library of James Logan of Philadelphia, 1674–1751*, Philadelphia

Wolfram von Eschenbach (1927) *Parzival*, ed. Karl Bartsch, 4th edn, 3 vols, Leipzig 1927, English trans. New York 1961

Woodhouse, John R. (1978) *Baldassare Castiglione: a Reassessment of the Courtier*, Edinburgh

Woodhouse, John R. (1979) 'Book 4 of Castiglione's *Cortegiano*: a Pragmatic Approach', *Modern Languages Review* 74, 62–8

Woodhouse, John R. (1982) 'La cortegianía di Niccolò Strozzi', *Studi Secenteschi* 23, 141–61

Woodhouse, John R. (1991) *From Castiglione to Chesterfield: the Decline in the Courtier's Manual*, Oxford

Woodward, W. H. (1906) *Studies in Education during the Age of the Renaissance*, Cambridge

Worsley, Benjamin (1678) *Catalogue*, London

Wright, Louis B. (1935) *Middle-Class Culture in Elizabethan England*, rpr. London 1964

Wright, Louis B. (1940) *The First Gentlemen of Virginia: Intellectual Qualities of the Early Colonial Ruling Class*, San Marino

Wyatt, Thomas (1975) *Collected Poems*, ed. Joost Daalder, Oxford

Xenophon (1914) *Cyropaedia*, ed. Walter Miller, 2 vols, London

Yeats, W. B. (*c.*1908) 'Discoveries: Second Series', *Massachusetts Review* 5 (1963–4), 297–306

Young, Kenneth (1963) *A. J. Balfour*, London

Zancan, Marina (1983) 'La donna nel *Cortegiano* del B. Castiglione', in *Nel cerchio della luna*, ed. Zancan, Venice, 13–56

Zapata, Luis (1935) *Varia Historia*, ed. C. W. Vollgraf, Amsterdam

Zara, Antonio (1615) *Anatomia Ingeniorum et Scientiarum*, Venice

Index